EARLY CHILDHOOD EDUCATIONAL RESEARCH

Sara Miller McCune founded SAGE Publishing in 1965 to support the dissemination of usable knowledge and educate a global community. SAGE publishes more than 1000 journals and over 800 new books each year, spanning a wide range of subject areas. Our growing selection of library products includes archives, data, case studies and video. SAGE remains majority owned by our founder and after her lifetime will become owned by a charitable trust that secures the company's continued independence.

Los Angeles | London | New Delhi | Singapore | Washington DC | Melbourne

CATHY NUTBROWN

EARLY CHILDHOOD EDUCATIONAL RESEARCH

INTERNATIONAL PERSPECTIVES

Los Angeles | London | New Delhi
Singapore | Washington DC | Melbourne

Los Angeles | London | New Delhi
Singapore | Washington DC | Melbourne

SAGE Publications Ltd
1 Oliver's Yard
55 City Road
London EC1Y 1SP

SAGE Publications Inc.
2455 Teller Road
Thousand Oaks, California 91320

SAGE Publications India Pvt Ltd
B 1/I 1 Mohan Cooperative Industrial Area
Mathura Road
New Delhi 110 044

SAGE Publications Asia-Pacific Pte Ltd
3 Church Street
#10-04 Samsung Hub
Singapore 049483

Editor: Jude Bowen
Editorial assistant: Catriona McMullen
Production editor: Nicola Carrier
Copyeditor: Gemma Marren
Proofreader: Audrey Scriven
Indexer: Cathy Heath
Marketing manager: Dilhara Attygalle
Cover design: Wendy Scott
Typeset by: C&M Digitals (P) Ltd, Chennai, India
Printed in the UK

Library of Congress Control Number: 2018931191

British Library Cataloguing in Publication data

A catalogue record for this book is available from the
British Library

ISBN 978-1-5264-3496-8
ISBN 978-1-5264-3497-5 (pbk)

At SAGE we take sustainability seriously. Most of our products are printed in the UK using responsibly sourced
papers and boards. When we print overseas we ensure sustainable papers are used as measured by the PREPS
grading system. We undertake an annual audit to monitor our sustainability.

CONTENTS

LIST OF FIGURES AND TABLES

FIGURES

TABLES

ABOUT THE AUTHOR

Cathy Nutbrown is a Professor of Education at the University of Sheffield. She began her career as a nursery teacher in the 1980s and has since worked with children, parents, teachers and other early childhood educators, in a range of settings and roles.

One of Cathy´s key research areas is early literacy work with parents. This has formed a major part of her research over the past 20 years and collaboration with several children and families' charities has led to successful development of early literacy work with families, including work with imprisoned parents.

Maintaining a focus on early childhood education, and the centrality of children's rights, Cathy's research has sought to highlight the importance of high quality experiences for young children. She chaired a year-long Nutbrown Review – providing independent advice for government on early years and childcare qualifications in 2012. Her work has been recognised by the Economic and Social Research Council, with the prize, in 2013, for Research with Outstanding Impact on Society. In the same year, her commitment to the early years was recognised by the Nursery World Lifetime Achievement Award. In January 2018, Cathy became President of Early Education.

She is Editor in Chief of the *Journal of Early Childhood Research*, and author of over 50 publications on aspects of early childhood education; her ten books include *Threads of Thinking* (2011), *Inclusion in the Early Years* (2013) and *Early Childhood Education: History, Philosophy and Experience* (2014).

PREFACE

Throughout the writing of this book, the international climate has been volatile. The news has been full of political and economic uncertainties, and accounts of war, persecution, suffering, extremism, and in the UK the leaving of the European Union has been the ever-present theme.

Against this international backdrop, some families' lives have been changed forever following the horrors of attacks in Manchester and Borough Market and the Grenfell Tower fire, to name just three closer to home. Yet the education of young children continues; day to day practices continue, and the need persists, to continue to understand all we can about young children's learning and how their world is affected by so many different circumstances and events. So the architecture and furnishings of this book were assembled during a year when the media daily reported difficulty and challenge, and these events have inevitably influenced the way in which I read the many research studies published since the year 2000, and how I have interpreted them. Living through these times inevitably makes us question what is right, what we might do, and how we might respond to the terrors that seem to surround us. Bubbling to the surface throughout this book are the things that I have come to believe *matter*, more and more, and are important research contributions to improving the lives and learning experiences of young children.

Though this book has no explicit political purpose *per se*, its conception and design cannot but reflect something of my own politics (as I set out in Chapter 1); and indeed, I had from the outset of planning a conviction that I could only start with children's rights, and this seems still to be the proper place to start, not least when around the world children's rights are being abused and disregarded. Political sluggishness (if not inertia) is found in many countries in relation to properly understanding and meeting the needs of young children and their families, who are suffering from hunger and famine, from the effects of war, from seriously flawed educational policies and from over assessment. Internationally, we see many instances where young children's rights are still appallingly neglected – en masse and individually. And this is why children's rights research has to be an important and fundamental starting point, and overarching theme of this book.

This book takes an international perspective on the many themes it discusses and as such, does not seek to offer a comprehensive discussion of UK research; however, whilst I was writing this book the *BERA-TACTYC Early Childhood Research Review 2003–2017* (Payler and Wood, 2017) was published, and this provides an excellent position statement on British research, which covers a similar period to this book, on a number of themes, highlighting strengths and areas where work is still needed. Throughout the book, I make reference to this document to identify similarities and differences in the research position in the UK and internationally.

The themes discussed in the chapters of this book have been identified by searches of educational databases and key peer-reviewed early education journals. Priority has been given to papers published, in English, in peer-reviewed journals between 2000 and 2017. These criteria, and the space available, have inevitably limited what could be included, as decisions about the focus and extent of each chapter were made.

The chapters of this book can be read individually, they stand alone. However, the overarching themes of the book remain the collective contribution that as researchers we can make when we seek to address the big issues of children's lives which impact on their learning. The research discussed in these pages highlights the effect of social injustice on children's lives and the importance of tackling and eradicating inequalities if children are to benefit from high quality early childhood education.

REFERENCE

Payler, J. and Wood, E. (eds) (2017) *BERA-TACTYC Early Childhood Research Review 2003–2017*. London: British Educational Research Association. www.bera.ac.uk/wp-content/uploads/2017/05/BERA-TACTYC-Full-Report.pdf?noredirect=1 (accessed 29 January 2018).

ACKNOWLEDGEMENTS

I would like to express my sincere and grateful thanks to the University of Sheffield Library Services, the authors whose work features here, and my doctoral students for the many stimulating conversations. The team at Sage has, as ever, given their professional support and insight into the production of the book and particular thanks go to Marianne Lagrange, Jude Bowen, Catriona McMullen and Gemma Marren. Finally, my thanks to Peter Clough, Richard Kerry and Beth Nutbrown whose support in the writing of this book was invaluable.

Cathy Nutbrown, Sheffield

PUBLISHER'S ACKNOWLEDGEMENTS

The author and the publisher are grateful for permission to reproduce the following material in this book:

Chapter 1, excerpts from Nutbrown, C. (2011) *Threads of Thinking: Schemas and Young Children's Learning*, 4th Edition. Sage London: Reprinted by permission of SAGE publications.

Chapter 1, excerpt from Sheffield LEA (1986) *Nursery Education: Guidelines for Curriculum, Organisation and Assessment*. Sheffield: City of Sheffield Education Department. Reprinted with permission of Sheffield City Council.

Chapter 2, excerpt from 'How we protect children's rights with the UN Convention on the Rights of the Child', UNICEF www.unicef.org.uk/what-we-do/un-converntion-childrights/ Reprinted with permission of UNICEF.

Chapter 2, excerpt from Hazareesingh, S. et al. (1989) *Educating the Whole child: A Holistic Approach to Education in Early Years,* Building Blocks/Save the Children. Reprinted with permission of Save the Children.

Chapter 2, excerpt from *Understanding Schematic Learning at Two* © Brierley, J. & Nutbrown,C. (2017) Bloomsbury Academic, and imprint of Bloomsbury Publishing Plc. Reprinted with permission Bloomsbury Publishing Plc.

Chapter 2, excerpt from Quennerstedt, A. & Quennerstedt, M. (2014) Researching children's rights in education: sociology of childhood encountering education theory. *British Journal of Sociology of Education*. Reprinted by permission of the authors, and Taylor & Francis Ltd, www.tandfonline.com

Chapter 6, excerpts from Morabito,C. & Vandenbroeck, M. (2015) Equality of opportunities, divergent conceptualisations and their implications for early childhood care and education policies. *Journal of Philosophy of Education*, 49(3). Republished with permission of John Wiley & Sons, Inc. and permission conveyed through Copyright Clearance Centre, Inc.

Chapter 6, excerpt from Payler, J. & Wood,L. (2014) *Early Years, Policy Advice and Future Research Agendas,* A BERA Early Childhood Special Interest Group/TACTYC: Association for the Professional Development of Early Years Educators Collaboration. London: BERA and TACTYC. Republished with permission of BERA and TACTYC.

Chapter 7, excerpt from Andereson,S. et al. (2015) 'Helping us find our own selves': exploring father-role construction and early childhood programme engagement. *Early Child Development and Care*, 185(3). Reprinted by permission of Taylor& Francis Ltd, www.tandfonline.com.

Chapter 9, excerpt from Payler, J. & Davies, G. (2017) 'Professionalism: Early years as a career', in Payler, J. and Wood, E. (eds), *BERA-TACTYC Early Childhood Research Review*. London: British Educational Research Association. Reprinted with permission of BERA and TACTYC.

Chapter 9, excerpt from Intepe-Tinger, S.(2017) Multidisciplinary perspectives towards the education of young low-income immigrant children. *Early Child Development and Care,* 187(9). Reprinted by permission of Taylor& Francis Ltd, www.trandfonline.com

Chapter 12, excerpt from Ghirotto, L. & Mazzoni, V. (2013) Being part, being involved: the adult's role and child participation in an early childhood learning context. *Internataional Journal of Early Year,* 21(4). Reprinted by permission of Taylor & Francis Ltd, www.tandfonline.com.

Chapter 12, excerpt from Maier-Hofer, C. (2015) Attitude and passion: becoming a teacher in early childhood education and care. *Early Years,* 35(4), copyright © TACTYC. Reprinted by permission of Taylor & Francis Ltd, www.tandfonline.com on behalf of TACTYC.

Chapter 12, excerpt from Taggart, G. (2016) Compassionate pedagogy: the ethics of care in early childhood professionalism. *European Early childhood Education Research Journal* 24(2), copyright © EECERA. Reprinted by permission of Taylor & Francis Ltd, www.tandfonline.com on behalf of EECERA.

Chapter 13, excerpt from Wood, E. & Hedges, H. (2016) Curriculum in early childhood education: critical questions about content, coherence, and control. *The Curriculum Journal,* (23)(7), © The British Educational Research Association. Reprinted by permission of Taylor & Francis Ltd, www. tandfonline.com on behalf of The British Educational Research Association.

Chapter 13, excerpt from Wood, E., Payler, J. & Georgeson (2017) 'Conclusion: Key messages', in Payler, J. & Wood, E. (eds), *Early Childhood Research Review 2003–2017,* British Educational Research Association Early childhood Special Interest Group and TACTYC: Association for Professional Development in Early Years. London: BERA. Reprinted with permission of BERA and TACTYC.

Chapter 13, excerpt from Wood, E. & Chesworth, L. (2017) 'Play and pedagogy', in Payler, J. & Wood, E. (eds), *Early Childhood Research Review 2003-2017,* British Educational Research Association Early Childhood Special Interest Group and TACTYC: Association for Professional Development in Early Years. London: BERA. Reprinted by permission of BERA and TACTYC.

Chapter 13, excerpt from Williams, P., Sheridan, S. & Sandberg, A. (2014) Preschool – an arena for children's learning of social and cognitive knowledge. *Early Years* 34(3), © TACTYC. Reprinted by permission of Taylor & Francis Ltd, www.tandfonline.com on behalf of TACTYC.

Chapter 13, excerpt from Payler, J. (2007) Opening and closing interactive spaces: shaping four-year-old children's participation in two English setting. *Early Years* 27(3), © TACTYC. Reprinted by permission of Taylor & Francis Ltd, www.tandfonline.com on behalf of TACTYC.

Chapter 16, excerpt from Eckhoff, A. (2015) Ethical considerations of children's digital image-making and image-audiancing in early childhood environments, *Early Child Development and Care,* 185(10). Reprinted by permission of Taylor & Francis Ltd, www.tandfonline.com.

Chapter 18, excerpt from Payler, J. & Wood , E. (2017) *BERA-TACTYC Early Childhood Research Review.* London: British Educational Research Association. Reprinted with permission of BERA and TACTYC.

1

RESEARCH THREADS: WEAVING UNDERSTANDINGS OF EARLY CHILDHOOD EDUCATION FROM THE 20TH CENTURY

In this first chapter I want to trace some of the threads of research interests which have run through my career and to share some thoughts about how they have been woven together – in a variety of ways. Unlike the rest of the book, this chapter is somewhat autobiographical and brings into the picture the foci that have had an important impact on me. Looking back over several decades of research in the late 20th, and the early 21st century, I have chosen eight 'threads' which have influenced me, as a nursery teacher, as a mother and as an academic in higher education, and together they form a sort of platform for the rest of the book. These threads are:

- young children's learning
- parents' roles
- children's rights
- assessment
- early literacy
- inclusion
- the arts
- history.

The discoveries of research in each of these areas opened new windows of thinking for me, and stimulated much of my own work. Some threads are stronger than others, and each has its imperfections, but they each illustrate important factors in early childhood education (ECE) policy, practice and research. These research themes form important starting points for some of the research discussed in later chapters in the book.

YOUNG CHILDREN'S LEARNING

> Young children are imaginative and capable learners; curricula should match their developmental needs and their patterns of learning.

I want to illustrate this with two of my own accounts that reflect young children's thinking.

> A three year old sits on the edge of a river bank. Her toes just touching the gently flowing water. She watches the insects skimming the surface, stares intently at a tiny fish which swims near to her feet. For some twenty minutes this little girl observes patiently. No one knows what she is thinking, but there is no doubt that her diligent study of the environment around her is something which takes up the whole of her being. No one tells her to study the water and the wildlife around her, no one asks her to sits still, to be quiet and to watch. Her interest is fuelled by a natural and instinctive curiosity about the world around her. (Nutbrown, 2011: 3).
>
> John was walking to school with his father. 'If there's woodwork today ... if there's the woodwork things ... if there is I'm gonna, I'm gonna do my plane. I'm gonna finish the nailing and put on the wings – then I think I can paint it.'
> John's father asked, 'Have you got much to do to it?'
> John replied, 'Could be a morning's work there.'
> At four years old John was able to think about what he had done yesterday and plan what he wanted to do in his early years centre that morning. It depended, he knew, on what provision was available that day – on whether the adults made the woodworking bench and tools available as they had done the day before. John's plan was to follow through on something he began the day before, he had plans for how to complete his model plane and was thinking about how long it might take him. He was being consistent, planning his progress through a self-chosen task. What he needed was the right provision – the available equipment and space to enable him to see his plans through. (Nutbrown, 2011: 28)

As a nursery teacher in Sheffield in the mid-1980s, I was privileged to work with two women who are responsible for my discovery of this very first thread, and for it being woven into my own learning and research. Ann Hedley was an amazing and inspiring head teacher of a small nursery-infant school, and Ann Sharp was the forward-looking General Adviser for Early Childhood Education in the local authority in Sheffield. They both introduced me to the work of Chris Athey (2007) and so I was able to set up a nursery environment which was effectively a workshop – full of opportunities for children to do, and explore and create. They asked questions and tested out their theories. And it is such a privilege to be with young children learning; as Einstein said: 'Teaching should be such that what is offered is perceived as a valuable gift and not as a hard duty' (Stachel, 1987: 17).

And so, this first research thread is about children as capable and tenacious learners who play with, and puzzle over, the stuff of the world. Searching for children's schematic patterns of learning and creating curricula to support their forms of thought took me on a research journey – where, for a year in the nursery, I worked with note books by my side – watching the children, thinking about how to extend their learning and writing many accounts of their learning. At a time in the UK when there was no state prescribed curriculum for children under five, play was central to the work and so, for that year, I worked with three- and four-year-old builders, architects, authors, pilots, bus drivers, mothers, cooks, artists and the occasional superman. The ideas that relate to this particular thread of research are picked up again in other chapters, including those that consider play, participation, curricula and pedagogy.

PARENTS' ROLES IN THEIR CHILDREN'S LEARNING

> For all our efforts and professionalism, it is parents and families that are the primary and major educators.

It was whilst working as a nursery teacher that I learned – really learned – about the importance of working closely with young children's parents: the people who put them to bed at night, brought them to school each day, fed them, clothed them, the people who really knew them and loved them in ways that teachers could never hope to match.

Sharing professional knowledge with parents, about child development, and how even very ordinary everyday experiences could be turned into valuable and essential learning opportunities for young children, brought dividends to the children's experience. And there's nothing very new about this idea. In 1885, Charlotte Mason was asked by her vicar to make a donation towards St Mark's Anglican Church in Manningham, Bradford. She did not offer money but suggested that she might give a series of lectures for parents on the education of young children, later published as

Home Education (Mason, 2008). She pioneered the training of teachers of young children, had strong and innovative views about pedagogy, and of the role of mothers in their children's learning. Charlotte Mason remains for many a pioneer of home education, particularly in the USA.

The nursery where I worked in the early 1980s, was rarely without parents in it and I recall an occasion where a father used our woodwork bench to repair some furniture; a mother borrowed our sewing machine to hem some curtains; and through these and many other small events the children saw the nursery staff and their parents cooperating together and sharing their learning and working space. The nursery for much of the time was one large workshop, with different zones of activity and play. The roles of parents are visited in this book with a reprise of some recent research in chapters on parents, early literacy, languages and digital technologies.

It wasn't always easy work in that little school; this was a poor community where families experienced struggle and difficulty and poverty and desperation: when a baby died tragically, many of the staff tried to support the family. Each day brought its challenges, but at the heart of it was Ann Hedley who brought calm and love to us all. It was in this place that as a young teacher I really learned something about what poverty was, and how circumstances of little money, poor housing, inferior educational opportunity and lack of support, all disadvantage families and limit choices. It was in these circumstances of extreme disadvantage that I came to know that all parents wanted the best for their children, and would do what they could, when they could, to help make that happen. The shocking issues of poverty today are considered in Chapter 6, which reflects on the impact of poverty on children's early education.

During the 1980s, and in no small way due to the work of Ann Sharp, innovative work with parents was well established in Sheffield, including the Manor Home Teaching Project, the Mosborough Townships Under Fives Service, home visiting by most nursery teachers in 62 nursery classes around the city, a Bilingual Home Teaching Project in five Sheffield communities, and several parental learning and involvement initiatives (including a course for parents at the local Teachers' Centre). Recent research into some of these themes is considered in chapters focusing on research with parents (Chapter 7), inclusion and diversity (Chapter 8), multi-professional and inter-disciplinary working (Chapter 9), early literacy (Chapter 14), and languages (Chapter 15). For my part, the Sheffield Early Literacy Development Project (Hannon et al., 1990) was the biggest event in my own early professional learning: it began one rainy February day in 1989 when Ann Sharp introduced me to Peter Hannon, who was about to embark on a pilot study involving work with parents to promote their children's early literacy. Together with Jo Weinberger we worked with families in one school in Sheffield, trying out different ways of sharing our ideas of early literacy development. This second thread, of home visiting, sharing professional knowledge with parents, and working from the premise that parents really are their child's first and most enduring teachers was to take me further into the world of research, into working with families around early learning, and to mark the beginning of my academic career at the University of Sheffield.

CHILDREN'S RIGHTS

Understanding that even the youngest children are equal in personhood to adults has profound implications for how we treat and teach them.

In 1996 – after some eight years of relentless policy initiatives and at the point of widely felt policy overload – I was beginning to feel that education was becoming something that was done *to* children rather than practised *for* or *with* children. It was work with Professor Tricia David and involvement in OMEP – the World Organisation for Early Childhood Education – that were responsible for this third 'thread' of research, for I came to realise the vital need to acknowledge and promote children's rights in the early years. In 1996 it is no exaggeration to say that I was startled at the scant attention paid to these issues, and to how little early childhood educators knew about the United Nations Convention on the Rights of the Child and of the part early education should play in realising those rights. I am still dismayed at the way young children's rights are often denied them – and this is no less true in education. For me, children's rights are not solely the responsibility of government but of every adult citizen.

Policy in the UK in the early 2000s has addressed issues of rights. *Every Child Matters* (DfES, 2003), *A Ten Year Childcare Strategy* (DfES, 2004) and even the *Early Years Foundation Stage* (DfE, 2017) can be seen, in some ways, to support the development of the key rights of young children: *prevention* of harm; *provision* of education and services; *protection* from abuse and exploitation; and *participation* in decisions that affect them. But is this enough? Can we honestly say that the basic rights of any human to be protected, consulted and to 'belong' is enough? For me, children's rights have to be central to early education where they learn in environments fit for the purpose, in the company of respectful educators who know they are working with capable young learners, and whilst children's rights research is the specific focus of Chapter 2, this is an overarching theme throughout the book, and rights issues are to be found in many of the chapters such as play (Chapter 4), poverty (Chapter 6), professionalism (Chapter 10), ethics of working and researching with young children (Chapter 12), languages (Chapter 15), and assessment (Chapter 17). Babies need to be securely attached to their key practitioners and toddlers need opportunities to learn in the company of older children (Page, 2016).

One of the most moving sights that I saw when working with artists and early years settings in Doncaster, England (Nutbrown and Jones, 2006) was a four-year-old boy in a day care setting, lovingly and patiently stroking the back of a 15-month-old toddler who was watching their game. Gently and intuitively, this four-year-old provided just that extra something: the necessary reassurance that it was OK to be part of this noisy game.

Rights include the right to belong, to behave as young and contributing citizens in a community of young learners, and rights for the youngest of children to the most experienced and well-educated educators. The youngest children have a right to learn in the company of highly educated adults, and that is why it is a rich privilege to work in higher education and see women and men progress from undergraduate through to Masters and Doctoral degrees, with the focus of their studies on young children, their lives and their learning. Fundamental to ensuring children's rights in early education is the cognate principle that those who work with them have, themselves, opportunities to learn and think and question. *Well educated educators is a matter of 'right' for children* (see Chapter 11).

And so this 'thread' has woven its way through all my research and teaching and is a fundamental basis from which other research threads have been spun.

ASSESSMENT

> Our systems of assessment are traditionally and credentially based on what children *cannot* do rather than on a celebration of their achievement.

In 1996 policy changes in early childhood education were not quite 'two-a-penny' but at least one every six months, and one policy which worried many was the imposition of state testing of four-year-olds. But what happened seven years later sent warning shots across the bows of all who believed that play should be at the core of early childhood education. In 1996, the government published *Nursery Education: Desirable Outcomes for Children's Learning on Entering Compulsory Education* (Oh what a title!), and this marked a distinct policy shift, stressing outcomes *above* process and *experience*. It was clear that the centrality of play in the early years had been systematically dismantled.

 Children's progress will be at different rates and individual achievement will vary. However, all children should be able to follow a curriculum which enables them to make maximum progress towards the outcomes. Children's whose achievements exceed the desirable outcomes should be provided with opportunities which extend their knowledge, understanding and skills. ... Other children will require continued support for achieving all or some of the outcomes after entering compulsory education. (SCAA, 1996: 1)

This heralded Baseline Assessment, which sought to reduce the rich learning in early childhood settings to a series of ticks in boxes on assessment sheets. For it was then becoming clear in this altered policy environment that the prevailing view in government was that outcomes could only be determined by measurement. So in 1997 we saw the first government imposed assessment of four-year-old children, as they entered school. And the battle about assessing young children has raged ever since.

> Baseline Assessment has two purposes: to provide information to help teachers plan effectively to meet children's individual learning needs; to measure children's attainment, using one or more numerical outcomes which can be used in later value-added analyses of children's progress …
>
> All children aged 4 or 5, admitted to a primary school … should be assessed. Assessment will be a requirement regardless of whether children attend full- or part-time, or whether they enter reception class or Year 1 …
>
> All schemes must include assessments of children's speaking and listening, reading and writing (these are aspects of language and literacy specified in the Desirable Outcomes), mathematics, and personal and social development. (SCAA, 1997: 2–8)

This was a flawed policy from the start, and was finally abandoned in 2002, though not before a huge amount of time, energy and money was wasted. Baseline Assessment put many reception teachers at the time in a position where their required practice ran counter to their better professional judgement in testing and reporting on their young pupils' performances in those tests. Little did we know, when Baseline Assessment was withdrawn in 2002, that there would be an attempt to resurrect this misguided policy in 2015 – with similar flaws and controversies and (again) an attempt to make one instrument provide information for teaching and learning *and* hold schools accountable for the achievement of the children that attend. I was prompted, in 2016, to write:

> Teachers in reception classes do not need a commercial assessment instrument to assess the learning of the children they work with. The 'broader assessments of children's development' that the government acknowledges teachers undertake are part of the business of daily teaching and learning in early childhood education. It's what teachers do – not with tests or a commercial package – but based on their own sound knowledge of high quality early years teaching. (Nutbrown, 2016)

The Better Without Baseline campaign (www.betterwithoutbaseline.org.uk) argued strongly and eloquently against this costly policy. Sadly, though there has been a pause, the policy drive towards Baseline Assessment is not over: a new consultation took place in March 2017, and the outcome now favours assessment at four years old. Unfortunately, despite practice and research attesting to the position that one-off assessments tell teachers nothing that they don't already know through their ongoing learning and teaching encounters with them, national policy insists on wasting teachers' time and ever-shrinking financial resources on ticking boxes to find out what is in young children's heads.

Baseline assessment created – I think for the first time – *failing* four-year-olds. To reiterate what seems obvious to me: assessment should show what children know and can do rather than what they can't yet do. And this minimalist approach to assessing young children's learning was an affront. Early education should be an orienteering expedition, not a route march, and assessment should be like conversations at different checkpoints along an interesting and personal journey with others to share the pleasure.

I suggest that there are three kinds of assessment: assessment for teaching and learning, assessment for management and accountability, and assessment for research. We need to be careful that the right tools are used for each and that the most important of these – assessment for teaching and learning – pays due respect to the riches of young minds. How can educators ensure that the efforts of *all* children are recognised? Children need adults who understand their learning and are insightful enough to try, respectfully, to show recognition of children's efforts and achievements, and to celebrate the success that children themselves identify. These themes are further considered in Chapter 17.

Recognition means acknowledgment of children's chosen goals and of their achievements as well as their needs, and a readiness to admit to their humanity, their tenacity, their rights, their language, their culture, their learning and their love.

EARLY 'EMERGENT' LITERACY

> Children 'read' their environment from their first moments; literacy should be no less natural – no less pleasurable.

Beginning in 1995, the Raising Early Achievement in Literacy (REAL) Project was a major study initiated by the School of Education at the University of Sheffield, and a significant development for the city of Sheffield. A long-term study which at one point involved over 50 schools and centres, the REAL Project aimed to develop meaningful ways of working with parents to promote the literacy development of their preschool children (and particularly those likely to have difficulties in the early years of school) and to improve their literacy development at school entry and afterwards.

Peter Hannon's direction of the project and partnership with schools, the university and the local authorities brought together hundreds of people all intent, in their different ways, on radically developing the systematic means to support families' participation in their children's early literacy development. We identified a broad conceptual framework which helped us to summarise parents' key roles in early literacy: providing *Opportunities*, showing *Recognition* of literacy achievements, *Interaction* around literacy events, and being *Models* of adult users of print. When the project ended 18 months later, parents told us that they truly valued being part of the work (Nutbrown et al., 2005).

Many people are part of this thread. The REAL Project involved hundreds of people: some 300 families, over 50 schools, over 100 teachers and nursery nurses, and countless other professionals (policy-makers, academics, secretaries,) who helped us at different points during the life of the Project. Some of the people who were key to this 'thread' were the project teachers: week after week for 18 months they visited parents and their children in their own homes, loaned literacy resources, planned interesting events and meetings for small groups of families and exchanged letters and cards with the children.

We learned that *all* children do some literacy activity at home (Nutbrown and Hannon, 2003) and – despite other research to the contrary – we learned that many fathers have active involvement in their children's early literacy development (Morgan et al., 2009). The studies relating to this thread of research are considered in Chapters 7 and 14, on parents and ECE, and on early literacy development respectively.

INCLUSION

Early childhood education provides the ground in which children will enjoy – and hence make an ideology of – a sense of inclusion.

 Respectful educators will include all children – not just children who are easy to work with, obliging, endearing, clean, pretty, articulate, capable, but every child – respecting them for who they are, respecting their language, their culture, their history, their family, their abilities, their needs, their name, their ways and their very essence. (Nutbrown, 1996: 54)

My 'thread' of inclusion – born directly, I now see, out of my concern for issues of rights in early childhood education – is fundamental to early childhood education. If we think about inclusion, often the first things that come to mind are issues of exclusion – who is *not* included – along with instances of learning difficulty and disability. Any exploration of what it might mean for settings actively to pursue the inclusion of all young children through approaches to curriculum and pedagogy should have, as their very core, the ethos of inclusion (Clough and Nutbrown, 2004). Inclusive educators and inclusive settings must examine their practices in terms of how the voices of *all* the children in those settings are listened to and how each and every child they work with could be said to be included – included as respected and belonging citizens of their early years communities (Nutbrown and Clough, 2004). Because inclusive *policies* are, in fact, only realised in acts of inclusive *practices, what* happens and *how* children are enabled to *belong* are crucial.

When we can see young children as citizens – in their settings, their communities and society – then perhaps we can call ourselves *inclusive*. Early childhood education practice and research has a strong thread of inclusion of children, inclusion of parents and inclusion of practitioners. But ultimately, fundamentally, and in all cases, inclusion is a matter of simple respect: respect for children, for families and for the people who work with and for them. and this research theme is further considered in Chapters 6 and 8, on poverty research, and on inclusion and diversity in ECE respectively.

Barbara Hepworth's words have long inspired me – she wrote:

> Perhaps what one wants to say is formed in childhood and the rest of one's life is spent trying to say it. (Hepworth, 1985: 3)

We need education and care in the early years that help children learn the importance of belonging, and of citizenship, so that the beliefs and values they form in childhood last them for the rest of their lives. And there remains a job to be done, by practitioners and policy-makers, and also, in the context of this book, by early childhood education researchers.

THE ARTS

Our primary sense of the world is aesthetic and our curricula for young children should maximise this essential characteristic.

Elliott Eisner wrote:

> The arts inform as well as stimulate, they challenge as well as satisfy. Their location is not limited to galleries, concert halls and theatres. Their home can be found wherever humans choose to have attentive and vital intercourse with life itself. This is, perhaps, the largest lesson that the arts in education can teach, the lesson that life itself can be led as a work of art. In so doing the maker himself or herself is remade. The remaking, this re-creation is at the heart of the process of education. (Eisner, 1998: 56)

There is common agreement that Christian Schiller, Robin Tanner and Alec Clegg (born between 1885 and 1909) from the 1920s onwards were amongst the grand architects of an Education and the Arts movement in the UK. Informed, no doubt, by the work of Rousseau, Pestalozzi and Froebel, they spoke and worked in a way that no one had done before in promoting a change in primary education which was radical and far reaching. From around 1930, Alec Clegg emphasised the importance of creativity in education, pioneering in-service courses for teachers, and between 1930 and 1974 he personally visited hundreds of schools, talking with teachers about their work and developing an extensive collection of children's art work. He noted that:

> there are two kinds of education: the education of the mind by imparting facts and teaching skills, and the education of the spirit, and the material to be worked on here is the child's loves and hates, hopes and fears, or in other terms, courage, integrity, compassion and other great human qualities. (Clegg, 1972: 23)

In 1977 HMI (Her Majesty's Inspector) Robin Tanner, in a lecture to teachers held in the University of Sheffield, said:

> children's sense of awe and wonder at the phenomena of the natural world should be central to their learning and ... in every school education should be primarily through the arts.

Because of the work of Clegg, Tanner and Schiller and others more recently – particularly in Creative Partnerships and other Arts Council England initiatives – there is a chorus running through recent history which lauds the arts and promotes creativity and discovery as essentials in learning. New generations somehow have to rediscover this truth, but the recurrent theme of arts and creativity in early education bears testimony to what is, I believe, an indisputable truth, that it is the arts which remind us of our humanity and the arts which offer us ways of expressing that humanity to others (Dissanayake, 1995; Nutbrown, 2013).

HISTORY

As professionals, we inherit traditions of practice, and we should be critically aware of where we have come from in order to justify our future acts.

Critical engagement with historical ideas and developments, influences on early childhood education, issues of policy development and implementation, and the impact of research on policy are essential. We can see where early childhood education has come from and where present policies fit, or do not fit, with the lessons of history. Awareness of the ways in which childhood has been constructed throughout recent history helps us to critique policies which have moved from the central aim of 'nurturing childhood' to a situation where 'raising educational achievement' is the main goal. With critical awareness we can also see how new policy-imposed terminologies have influenced early childhood practice.

Sheffield's history of early education is typical of many cities in the north of England. The city's Nursery Education Guidelines from 1987 include this overview:

> Nursery Education began in this country at the beginning of [this 20th] Century at the instigation of people who were concerned about the plight of children in industrial cities: Sheffield children were typical of these. The social climate was such that by the late 1920s Sheffield was beginning to suffer in the Depression: unemployment was rife and poverty was very real. In the centre of the city buildings consisted of many terraced houses and factories, with little opportunity for the children to grow and develop in a healthy environment.

> The local Women Councillors (in Sheffield) decided to fight for a nursery school and, although it was an uphill battle Denby Street Nursery School was opened in 1928 based on the McMillan open-shelter type. It was open from 8.30 am to 5.00 pm and holidays. There was practically no money, very little equipment and a skeleton staff.
>
> The emphasis was on physical care. The children were fed, washed, rested and loved. The food was simple and plentiful – buttered rusks, dripping toast, hash stew, shepherd's pie, lentil roast, milk puddings, custard and fruit and steamed puddings. The nurse and doctor visited regularly. Cod liver oil was administered and children monitored for impetigo, rickets, poor eyesight, etc. School became a haven especially if children were from families living in only one room, although the schools were very careful not to usurp the home.
>
> Outdoor play was robust and skilful as many of the children had played in the streets from a very young age. The imaginative play – particularly domestic play – was very real. The children were independent, practical, capable and resilient, many having to be so from a very young age, especially if they came from a large family. (Sheffield Local Authority, 1987: 2–3)

Learning from the past is one way of trying to ensure that new policies and investment do not repeat the mistakes of previous generations. But, as we know, policy-makers do not always learn from the past and ideas sometimes seem to return, are seemingly reinvented and appear in 'new clothes' but nevertheless bear distinctly familiar shapes (even if bringing new intentions) (Nutbrown and Clough, 2014).

Most recently, as has been the case over the centuries, many people have looked to the development of early years provision as a way of addressing (at least partially) social, economic and thus political difficulties (McMillan, 1925; Montessori, 1962; Field, 2010; Allen, 2011). We could identify the work of Robert Owen (1920) as pioneering provision that offered workplace education and care ensuring children learned whilst their parents worked. Alongside schooling for children was housing for workers and their families and classes in health and cooking for parents. Owen's work in New Lanark can be seen as the forerunner of Sure Start Centres, where provision for families connected to ensure children were safe and learning, and workers had a home and a reasonable (if not generous) wage.

Through the centuries, the work of many early childhood pioneers contributed to the weaving of a rich tapestry of understanding about young children's learning – and some of the threads I have woven in this chapter. This is something I shall return to towards the end of the book in Chapter 18. The point here is that whilst those who have their place in history made important contributions, it is up to us, and the researchers and practitioners of today, to take their work and craft it into our own work today. For as Christian Schiller wrote:

' There have been great men and great women whose vision and action have inspired a generation ... But they pass away – and their ideas pass with them unless these ideas are fashioned into new forms which reflect new circumstances and stand the test of new practices in the contemporary scene. The pioneers take such ideas and refashion and temper them in their daily work ... Patiently, day after day, week after week, year after year, they make the pathway from the past, through the present towards the future. (1951: xvii, in Griffin Beale, 1979: 57) '

SOME PRINCIPLES FOR EARLY CHILDHOOD EDUCATION

I want to conclude this introductory chapter by moving from the threads of research which have inspired me, to identify some principles for early childhood education.

YOUNG CHILDREN'S LEARNING

Young children are imaginative and capable learners – curricula should match their developmental needs and their patterns of learning.

We need to work with children's developmental stages, not battle against them. Research has repeatedly shown that real learning takes time, and the best way to help children be successful learners when they are five is to allow them to be three when they are three and four when they are four; rushing them on – too fast – means some will get left behind. Learning, as Vygotsky reminds us, is a social process, brought about when people communicate and test out and talk together. (We can only imagine the contribution his work would have made to our understanding if he had not died at the age of 38 years.)

PARENTS' ROLES

Early childhood educators need opportunities to share their pedagogy with parents in order to maximise opportunities for all young children.

Chris Athey (2007) argued that parents, professionals and pedagogy together were the three ingredients to support young children's thinking. From my own work and that of others found in this book, we know that parents are interested in their children and want to do all they can to help them. And they welcome the opportunity to learn more about how they might help.

CHILDREN'S RIGHTS

> Building early childhood education on the basis of children's rights will promote high quality experiences for all children.

In 1923, shortly before her death at the age of 81, Charlotte Mason wrote about children's rights in early education; written in 1922, her 'Principles of Education' (Mason, 1992) have also been referred to as a child's 'Bill of Rights', arguing for the involvement of parents, for learning outdoors, for high quality books and for a challenging and interesting curriculum: 'it stultifies a child to bring down his world to the child's level', she wrote (Mason, 1992: xxix).

Yet, as Chapter 2 demonstrates, a century on, those who work with young children still do not know enough about the UN Convention on the Rights of the Child and their part in realising those rights for every child, and governments still have much to do. It is the responsibility of every adult to consider their role in supporting and upholding children's rights.

ASSESSMENT

> Measurement and testing alone teach nothing; we need honest assessment for learning, and sensitive tools to identify what babies and toddlers and young children can do, and which do rich justice to their learning and their energy.

Despite research into the importance of appropriate assessment, despite numerous accounts of children learning creatively and holistically, we still have children who are over tested – certainly in England. The *fine mesh* of learning requires detailed, ongoing and sensitive observations of children as they play. The deep riches of children's learning can only be understood by patient, reflective adults who watch patiently and work hard to interpret what they see.

EARLY LITERACY DEVELOPMENT

> Literacy is key to learning – a key to the rest of the curriculum. Knowing the pleasure of the written word is an essential foundation for formal teaching.

We know from Yetta Goodman's work (1986) that young children need to understand something of how useful reading and writing are – the joy of books, rhymes and stories and the power of the written word – before they are formally taught segmented letters and sounds. Literacy *pleasure* comes first – and much of it can begin at home.

INCLUSION

Early education at its best is inclusive education, giving young children and their families a sense of belonging, of a citizenship worthy of the name, and of their own value in their learning communities.

These truths seem to me essential if children are to live in a future where the contribution of *all, everyone*, is valued. And I hold to a view of inclusion as a matter of respect and belonging for everyone – not confined solely to issues related to disability or learning difficulty but concerned with the broad range of issues that divide communities and nations. And as Comenius wrote in *The Great Didactic* in the 1600s:

 We are all citizens of one world, we are all of one blood. To hate a man because he was born in another country, because he speaks a different language, or because he takes a different view on this subject or that, is a great folly. Desist, I implore you, for we are all equally human. … Let us have but one end in view, the welfare of humanity; and let us put aside all selfishness in considerations of language, nationality, or religion. (Comenius, [1657] 1963: 91)

Different views and practices may be foreign to us, but understanding how they came to be puts us in a position to understand, or to challenge.

THE ARTS

The arts are an expression of our humanity – the arts can enhance children's learning in all aspects of their development and must be central to any early childhood curriculum.

Children need to work with artists – dancers, painters, musicians – and to see how new and amazing things can be created and enjoyed – they need to practise the skill of connoisseurship. And as Elliot Eisner reminded me when we viewed Egyptian jewellery in the Ulster Museum, *human beings must create things – it reminds us that we are human* … Early education needs to adopt a pedagogy of the arts, and allow young children's creativity to flow and flourish. International research in this area is sadly lacking and as researchers we need to do more to enhance understanding of young children's engagement in the arts.

HISTORY

We need to understand the history of early childhood education because it provides a 'rootedness' to our work.

It means we are building our work on solid ground and travelling along well-trodden paths. We can be inspired by some whose ideas came, as it were, before their time but yet were not reticent in articulating or realising their ideas. History can remind us that it is worth working for the things you believe in, and the study of history shows how important it is to record ideas and practices for those who follow to ponder.

History also reminds us that we all need others to help us do our work, that no one can stand alone.

But the important thing in early childhood education is not what Susan Isaacs, or Charlotte Mason or Katherine Bathurst might have said or done (inspiring though they were): the important thing is what those who live with, or work with and for young children in our present times and settings say and do. The important thing is that the new pioneers, those working in schools and nurseries and children's centres and elsewhere in the pursuit of the best provision for young children, take these ideas *into the future* (as Schiller would say) *and make them their own*. There is no better tribute to those who have gone than to remould, revisit and revise their ideas for a new today. This is why, in reviewing some of the most recent research in early childhood education, I reflect (in Chapter 18) on how historical perspectives have informed present practice.

***

Whilst I have presented these threads as distinct, they all in reality come together in an unfinished and imperfect weave – perhaps an untidy tangle! – but they *do* connect. Throughout this book there is a sense of connection, of relationships and of interaction between researchers and their participants. Connection and collaboration with other human beings is essential for every one of us; relationships feed our brain and nourish our intellect and our souls, and it is no different for young children. Children need to be able to make connections with other children and with close, sensitive, caring, loving adults – they need to learn in company with others. Frank Smith once wrote that 'we learn from the company we keep' (Smith, 1987: 9); and when researchers keep company with children, their families and their educators, new learning and new understanding bursts out from multiple perspectives. This book shows us what some researchers working around the world, in more recent times since the year 2000, have contributed to the field of early childhood education.

REFERENCES

Allen, G. (2011) *Early Intervention: The Next Steps: An Independent Report on the Early Years Foundation Stage to Her Majesty's Government*. London: Cabinet Office. www.gov.uk/government/publications/early-intervention-the-next-steps--2 (accessed 29 January 2018).

Athey, C. (2007) *Extending Thought in Young Children: A Parent–Teacher Partnership* (2nd edn). London: Paul Chapman Publishing.

Clegg, A.B. (1972) *The Changing Primary School: Its Problems and Priorities: A Statement by Teachers*. London: Chatto and Windus.

Clough, P. and Nutbrown, C. (2004) Special educational needs and inclusion: Multiple perspectives of preschool educators in the UK. *Journal of Early Childhood Research, 2* (2): 191–211.

Comenius, J.A. ([1657] 1963) *The Great Didactic of John Amos Comenius*. Translated and edited by M.W. Keatinge. London: A&C Black.

DfE (Department for Education) (2017) *Statutory Framework for the Early Years Foundation Stage: Setting the Standards for Learning, Development and Care for Children from Birth to Five*. London: Department for Education. www.gov.uk/government/publications/early-years-foundation-stage-framework--2 (accessed 29 January 2018).

DfES (Department for Education and Skills) (2003) *Every Child Matters* (Green Paper). London: HMSO. www.gov.uk/government/uploads/system/uploads/attachment_data/file/272064/5860.pdf (accessed 29 January 2018).

DfES (Department for Education and Skills) (2004) *Choice for Parents, the Best Start for Children: A Ten Year Childcare Strategy*. London: DfES.

Dissanayake, E. (1995) *Homo Aestheticus*. Seattle, WA: University of Washington Press.

Eisner, E. (1998) *The Enlightened Eye: Qualitative Inquiry and the Enhancement of Educational Practice*. New York: Teachers' College Press.

Field, F. (2010) *The Foundation Years: Preventing Poor Children from Becoming Poor Adults: The Report of the Independent Review on Poverty and Life Chances*. London: HMSO. http://webarchive.nationalarchives.gov.uk/20110120090128/http:/povertyreview.independ ent.gov.uk/media/20254/poverty-report.pdf (accessed 29 January 2018).

Goodman, Y. (1986) Children coming to know literacy. In W.H. Teale and E. Sulzby (eds), *Emergent Literacy: Writing and Reading*. Norwood, NJ: Ablex, pp. 1–14.

Griffin Beale, C. (ed.) (1979) *Christian Schiller in His Own Words*. London: A & C Black.

Hannon, P., Weinberger, J. and Nutbrown, C. (1990) A study of work with parents to promote early literacy development. *Research Papers in Education, 6* (2): 77–99.

Hepworth, B. (1985) *Hepworth: A Pictorial Biography*. London: Tate Publishing.

Mason, C. (1992) *Homeschool Series Volume 6: Towards a Philosophy of Education*. AmblesideOnline's Annotated Charlotte Mason Series. www.amblesideonline.org/CM/vol6complete.html#xxv (accessed 20 February 2018).

Mason, C. (2008) *Home Education* (5th edn). Radford VA: Wilder Publications.

McMillan, M. (1925) *Children, Culture and Class in Britain*. London: George Allen and Unwin.

Montessori, M. (1962) *Education for a New World*. Wheaton, IL: Theosophical Press.

Morgan, A., Nutbrown, C. and Hannon, P. (2009) Fathers' involvement in young children's literacy development: Implications for family literacy programmes. *British Educational Research Journal, 35* (2): 167–185.

Nutbrown, C. (ed.) (1996) *Respectful Educators – Capable Learners: Children's Rights and Early Education*. London: Paul Chapman Publishing.

Nutbrown, C. (2011) *Threads of Thinking: Schemas and Young Children's Learning* (4th edn). London: Sage.

Nutbrown, C. (2013) Conceptualising arts-based learning in the early years. *Research Papers in Education, 28* (2): 239–263. DOI:10.1080/02671522.2011.580365.

Nutbrown, C. (2016) After government U-turn on tests for four-year-olds, it's time to trust teachers. *The Conversation*, 11 April. https://theconversation.com/after-government-u-turn-on-tests-for-four-year-olds-its-time-to-trust-teachers-57498 (accessed 29 January 2018).

Nutbrown, C. and Clough, P. (2004) Inclusion in the early years: Conversations with European Educators. *European Journal of Special Needs Education, 19* (3): 311–339.

Nutbrown, C. and Clough, P. (2014) *Early Childhood Education: History, Philosophy and Experience*. London: Sage.

Nutbrown, C. and Hannon, P. (2003) Children's perspectives on family literacy methodological issues, findings and implications for practice. *Journal of Early Childhood Literacy, 3* (2): 115–145.

Nutbrown, C., Hannon, P. and Morgan, A. (2005) *Early Literacy Work with Families: Policy, Practice and Research*. London: Sage.

Nutbrown, C. and Jones, H. (2006) *Daring Discoveries: Arts Based Learning in the Early Years*. Doncaster: Creative Partnerships and the Arts Council.

Owen, R. (1920) *The Life of Robert Owen: Written by Himself*. London: G Bell and Sons.

Page, J. (2016) The legacy of John Bowlby's attachment theory. In T. David, K. Goouch and S. Powell (eds), *The Routledge Handbook of Philosophies and Theories of Early Childhood Education and Care*. London: Routledge, pp. 101–109.

SCAA (School Curriculum and Assessment Authority) (1996) *Nursery Education: Desirable Outcomes for Children's Learning on Entering Compulsory Education*. London: SCAA.

SCAA (School Curriculum and Assessment Authority) (1997) *The National Framework for Baseline Assessment: Criteria and Procedures for the Accreditation of Baseline Assessment Schemes*. London: SCAA.

Sheffield LEA (1986) *Nursery Education: Guidelines for Curriculum, Organisation and Assessment*. Sheffield: City of Sheffield Education Department.

Sheffield Local Authority (1987) *Guidelines for Nursery Education*. Sheffield: Sheffield LEA.

Smith, F. (1987) *Joining the Literacy Club: Further Essays into Education*. London: Heinemann.

Stachel, J. (ed.) (1987) *The Collected Papers of Albert Einstein*, Volume 1. Princeton: Princeton University Press.

PART I
CHILDREN

The coherence of this first part derives from a view of the children represented in the research as persons with inalienable characteristic rights: the rights – as absolute minima – to an optimal health of body and mind and spirit, and to the time and space for spontaneous play which reflexively develops these; and rights to the learning so developed that is heuristic and formative, and therefore personally engaged; and – in situations where we choose to include children in our research – rights to their informed and consenting participation.

The studies and writings that feature in each of the chapters are cited variously to realise a construction of 'childhoods' – the child, considered for the moment, and quite artificially, outside the concerns of adults, institutions and curricula. They seem to me to represent an unfolding narrative – well outside of psychology – of how young children can develop from rights to rightful reason through a curriculum which embodies the development of love and respect rather than any dictate of policy. But of course this does not always work for all children; and the last chapter of this first part of the book returns in its way to the first concerns with children's rights. For it seems to me that the logical – the moral, and above all *sentient* – response to the claims about children's rights (thus, rights *to* well-being and spirituality, rights to play, and to informed participation in their own learning and in research *with* them) is to look at where enacted policies and practices rupture, and are in default of those rights. Centre ground in this is the incidence of child poverty as one powerful index of that dereliction. It seems to me staggering beyond cliché that so many northern/western economies permit this; for example, the UK economy is ranked fifth globally, and yet acknowledges some 25 per cent of its children live in poverty, and this phenomenon is addressed explicitly or otherwise permeates so many of the studies I refer to in this part of the book. Without doubt child poverty reaches into many aspects of early childhood education research, and if not in the foreground is there, lurking, as a 'differentiating factor' or a 'subgroup of analysis', but these are real children, real lives and real issues that researchers, politicians and practitioners must not ignore.

So issues which seem to me to focus specifically on *children* open this book with research from many countries that illuminates the details of their experiences and learning – what supports them and what hinders them.

2

CHILDREN'S RIGHTS AND EARLY CHILDHOOD EDUCATION AND CARE

THIS CHAPTER WILL:

- describe the origin and purpose of the United Nations Convention on the Rights of the Child
- consider the 'child' in the UN Convention on the Rights of the Child
- discuss early childhood education and children's rights research
- discuss research into the area of children's rights education
- explore a children's rights-based curriculum
- speculate on the future for children's rights in early childhood education
- suggest some research questions on the topic of children's rights in ECEC
- provide some recommended reading to follow up the issues discussed.

Issues of children's rights were established in the drawing up of the UN Convention on the Rights of the Child in 1989, and to date 120 nations and recognised territories are signatories. Described by the UK, which signed the United Nations Convention on the Rights of the Child (UNCRC) in April 1990, as 'an international human rights treaty that grants all children and young people (aged 17 and under) a comprehensive set of rights' (DfE, 2015), the Convention underpins legislation and education in the UK and in many other countries around the world.

There are some notable exceptions, including the United States of America, but the broad agreement to this landmark United Nations (UN) initiative, which took over half a century to draft and agree, has given children in many parts of the world the right to freedoms, protections and conditions of life that are regarded as basic to all. This chapter looks briefly at what research tells us about the origins and achievements of the UNCRC. It then considers the nature of the 'child' in the UNCRC and how adults view the nature of childhood. This is followed by a discussion of research related to early childhood education and care (ECEC) and children's rights (a relatively under-developed field). This leads to consideration of how children come to learn about their rights through children's rights education. The section next explores the potential for curricula based on children's rights, and the chapter closes with some speculation on the future for children's rights in early childhood education.

THE ORIGIN AND PURPOSE OF THE UNITED NATIONS CONVENTION ON THE RIGHTS OF THE CHILD AND ITS RELATION TO ECEC

In 1996, I collaborated with a group of UK early childhood education experts to bring together in a book our thoughts about the implications of the UN Convention on the Rights of the Child for early education. At that time few thought much about the UN Convention and it was not unusual for education professionals to say that they had heard of the Convention but did not really know what it was all about – let alone to have given thought about the implication for ECEC. In the introduction to that book I wrote this:

> Children, from birth, must enjoy their rights and their parents, close adults and educators, working with and for children, must bear some additional responsibility for them and gradually teach them about the responsibilities that accompany rights and help them to learn how to assume and shoulder responsibility. To argue that because young children cannot shoulder responsibility they must not have rights is the position only of someone who continues to deny children the citizenship that is – rightfully – theirs. (Nutbrown, 1996: xiii)

In the 20 years since *Respectful Educators – Capable Learners* was published, the research base on children's rights in ECEC has been growing slowly, but as this chapter will show there is still a long way to go in establishing a critical, theoretically informed understanding of many aspects of children's rights as they relate to ECEC globally.

So, first a reminder of the origin and purpose of the UNCRC; I begin with the statement from UNICEF:

> The United Nations Convention on the Rights of the Child, or UNCRC, is the basis of all of UNICEF's work. It is the most complete statement of children's rights ever produced and is the most widely-ratified international human rights treaty in history. (UNICEF, 1989a)

UNICEF – the United Nations International Children's Emergency Fund – is a United Nations programme that provides humanitarian and developmental assistance to children and their families in developing countries and works for the realisation of the UNCRC.

Its mission states:

> The Convention has 54 articles that cover all aspects of a child's life and set out the civil, political, economic, social and cultural rights that all children everywhere are entitled to. It also explains how adults and governments must work together to make sure all children can enjoy all their rights.
>
> Every child has rights, whatever their ethnicity, gender, religion, language, abilities or any other status.
>
> The Convention must be seen as a whole: all the rights are linked and no right is more important that another. The right to relax and play (Article 31) and the right to freedom of expression (Article 13) have equal importance as the right to be safe from violence (Article 19) and the right to education (Article 28).
>
> The UNCRC is also the most widely ratified human rights treaty in the world – it's even been accepted by non-state entities, such as the Sudan People's Liberation Army (SPLA), a rebel movement in South Sudan. All UN member states except for the United States have ratified the Convention. The Convention came into force in the UK in 1992. (UNICEF, 1989a)

One of the most significant sections is Article 28, which states that:

> 1. States Parties recognize the right of the child to education, and with a view to achieving this right progressively and on the basis of equal opportunity, they shall, in particular:
>   (a) Make primary education compulsory and available free to all;
>   (b) Encourage the development of different forms of secondary education, including general and vocational education, make them available and accessible to every child, and take appropriate measures such as the introduction of free education and offering financial assistance in case of need;
>   (c) Make higher education accessible to all on the basis of capacity by every appropriate means;

(d) Make educational and vocational information and guidance available and accessible to all children;

(e) Take measures to encourage regular attendance at schools and the reduction of drop-out rates.

2. States Parties shall take all appropriate measures to ensure that school discipline is administered in a manner consistent with the child's human dignity and in conformity with the present Convention.

3. States Parties shall promote and encourage international cooperation in matters relating to education, in particular with a view to contributing to the elimination of ignorance and illiteracy throughout the world and facilitating access to scientific and technical knowledge and modern teaching methods. In this regard, particular account shall be taken of the needs of developing countries. (UNICEF, 1989b: 9)

In addition to Article 28 relating to education, the many Articles in the Convention relating to social justice issues including poverty, housing, safety, health and well-being also appertain.

In comparison to many other topics affecting early childhood education and care, issues of children's rights remain relatively under researched. Though there are studies of children's rights to participate in decisions that affect them in early childhood education, these are limited. Quennerstedt (2016) argues that rights research in early childhood education and care should pay particular attention to the lived experience of children under three, and encompass the experiences of children as well as those of the professionals who work with them.

THE 'CHILD' IN THE UN CONVENTION ON THE RIGHTS OF THE CHILD

Getting to the point where some 120 nations signed the UN Convention on the Rights of the Child was in itself a momentous recognition of the status of children as rightful world citizens where for children to have rights, adults must assume due responsibility. This was not always the case, as Devine (2008) reminds us:

Adult discourse on children and childhood has also undergone profound change in the Western world in the past one hundred and fifty years, and is most readily reflected in the partitioning of the child population through the introduction of state schooling. While the advent of mandatory schooling brought with it improvements in the health and general welfare of working class children in particular, the fundamental impact of removing children from the paid labour force significantly altered adult discourse on the role and usefulness of children in modern society. (2008: 16)

Devine considers the power relations between children and adults, and the ways in children are discussed, to have significantly influenced how we see children in society and how their rights are realised in the Irish education system. She traces the changing 'structures of domination' (2008: 16), which insisted on children being passive and denied 'voice' in matters that concerned them, where corporal punishment and religious ideology placed children as inferior and lacking status and recognition in society. Changes began in the early 20th century when, in the UK for example, the end of the Victorian era – where children were regarded (even dressed) as miniature, but immature, adults, 'seen and not heard' – marked changes in thinking about education, play and learning.

Herczog's (2012) review of the rights of the child and ECEC in Europe highlights the importance of well-being – that is action and investment for *now* – rather than well-becoming, or investment for the economy 20 years into the *future*. Herczog draws attention to the multi-disciplinary nature of the impact and responsibilities for children's holistic development, where action on housing, poverty, nutrition, social justice and well-being is as equally important as education. It is fair to say that if their basic needs of somewhere to live, citizenship, family and health are not in place then any education project will surely fail. In the UK, there will be many questions to ask about how children's rights will be preserved when the country leaves the European Union – because so many of these rights are enshrined in European law, supported by European Union networks, and a close eye will need to be kept on preserving, protecting and further enacting children's rights once the UK has left the European Union. Herczog, writing before the UK took the decision to leave the European Union, concluded that:

 In future, more research, data collection, analyses, monitoring and evaluation of the fast changing policies and practices would be needed. Conducting a pilot project on the implementation of GC7-based indicators on rights in early childhood could make a difference in all areas concerning children of 0–8 years of age and their parents. (Herczog, 2012: 554)

In 2017, as the UK prepared to leave the EU, this became even more poignant. Research is much needed in the field of children's rights. Indeed, the contested nature and perception of 'childhood' comes sharply into view when we take a pan-European perspective. Cultural, ideological and historical perspectives on childhood are brought to bear on how we 'see' children and therefore how policy and practice treat them in relation to a rights-based perspective. Reflecting on the 'now' or the 'for later' views of childhood we can draw on the work of Hazareesingh et al. (1989) who assert:

 This concept of the child as an 'unfinished' adult shifts the focus away from the child's own intentions, attachments and strivings – which might in fact open up many learning horizons for the adult, on to an end-product notion of adulthood which is unwisely equated with 'achieved knowledge'. It might be said that this represents a specifically western, rationalist approach to both childhood and learning which by separating the mind from the heart, effectively denies the essential unity of the child. (1989: 18) "

Our view on the 'child' in the UNCRC will shape and inform actions in relation to children's rights in early childhood education and care.

EARLY CHILDHOOD EDUCATION AND CHILDREN'S RIGHTS RESEARCH

Piaget's (1923) work on child development theory, and Vygotsky's (1978) thinking about learning as a social activity, contributed to developing approaches to nursery education for two- to six-year-olds, and the practical work in setting up nurseries and schools for young children – with play distinctively at the centre – brought about a different perspective on thinking about children as learners. Penn's (1999) view, that 'Adults control children's lives – how their time is spent and where it is spent – yet relatively little is understood about how children perceive and live within these constraints' (1999: 2), drew attention to the domination of a developmental psychology in early education that shaped goals and measures of achievements in ECE.

Today there is greater emphasis on the contribution children can make to their own learning (Dunphy, 2012) and, though by no means a universally shared perspective or fully adopted practice, we know more about how young children can construct their own learning. In the Reggio Emilia preschools of northern Italy, this is referred to as *The Pedagogy of Listening* (Rinaldi, 1999) where children's rights, community and the arts are central to pedagogic practice.

In the late 1990s remarkably few early childhood educators in the UK knew of, and fewer still were conversant with, the United Nations Convention on the Rights of the Child (UNCRC, xiii). Whilst this fact may have changed over the last 20 years there remains plenty to be done, as Kjørholt (2011) observes.

Yet the policy climate in England today seems to be driving a restricted pedagogy where *what* children learn and *how* they learn it are becoming increasingly constrained. And, in part because training and continuing professional development for early childhood practitioners are often lacking, due to limited funding, and because of poor pay and working conditions, the creative freedom to develop a rights-based approach to early childhood education seems to be increasingly difficult to achieve. In a study of practitioners' opinions about child poverty and their families in poverty in England and the US, Simpson et al. (2017) found that ECEC provision needs to continue to 'improve attempts to maximise the perspectives of children in poverty and their needs' (2017: 186). Further they argue that it is essential to re-state: 'the importance of [a] pedagogy of listening' to the perspectives of children affected by poverty if progress is to be made 'in reducing the attainment gap between children in poverty and their peers' (2017: 186).

Dunphy suggests that:

 Attuning to children's interests, concerns and experiences implies that the teacher must focus on the nature and contexts of children's experience and how these issues have impacted [on] children's perspectives. (2012: 292)

This, of course, requires well-educated education professionals, and adopting Dunphy's suggestion would make it possible to create learning opportunities that are meaningful, centred around children's interests and respectful of their motivation. Yet there is a tension when working in goal-oriented policy requirements on which funding and satisfaction ratings are based. As Dunphy points out:

 Goals can be agreed but educators must find the appropriate means of engaging all children in learning experiences which work towards these goals while still taking their individual perspectives into account. (2012: 293)

What, we might ask, would an early childhood setting that respects children's rights look like? How do education and care professionals work with young children when they take a rights-based position on their work? In Australia a study of young children's participation in their preschools showed that the policy establishing the right to participation – to express views, be listened to – was not matched with changes in practice (Theobald and Danby, 2011).

A Swedish study used observation to answer the question: 'How do children aged 1–3 enact their human rights in the preschool setting'. Quennerstedt (2016) developed a sensitive action-based methodological approach to observation and analysis of those observations to 'listen' to children, using three starting points:

1. that children's meaning-making (or voice) is observable in their actions
2. that children's actions provide first-hand information about their experiences in preschool
3. that the preschool context is a co-constructor of the children's actions. (2016: 9)

This attention to research design is an important lesson for researching young children's experiences.

The Swedish study observed 18 children aged 12 to 33 months, every day for three weeks, the focus being children's actions that could be 'reflected against a human right' (Quennerstedt, 2016: 9). Quennerstedt's findings highlight issues of ownership, influence and equal value and human rights in 'the functions of children's actions'. This fascinating study is an example of how close attention to the detail of what young children do is necessary if their evolving understandings of rights are to be understood. The author concludes that awareness of the everyday practices where human rights issues can be observed is essential for early childhood practitioners and researchers.

CHILDREN'S RIGHTS EDUCATION

If children's rights are to be realised in education, it is important that they have information and an opportunity to debate the issues. Children's rights education has been implemented in many countries as part of the monitoring of countries' progress on implementation of the UNCRC. Focusing mainly on primary schooling, Jerome identifies three roles for teachers: as implementers, as gatekeepers and collaborative agents, and as change agents – this latter role resulting in half of all state schools in Scotland gaining 'Rights Respecting Status' (Jerome et al., 2015). So what does children's rights education look like for the very young children in home and group settings?

Children's rights education is under researched – and we certainly need a greater understanding of processes and practices for the youngest children (Lundy, 2012). I suggest that this is bound up with researching 'voice' in early education and a consideration of young children's perspectives on the things that matter to them. This includes the setting they attend and what they do there. It includes their views on what and where to play, and on having their say on a range of things that impact on their lives. Though, as Lundy (2007) has it, 'Voice is not enough', and she argues that as well as 'listening' to children's views, adults must *act* on what they hear. An example of this is Nutbrown and Clough's (2009) work with early years practitioners in a study of young children's perspectives of 'belonging'. They cite many examples which demonstrate that young children have their own particular views of inclusion and belonging which are often different from those held by adults. Further, the examples of children's play and conversation illustrated how, given the opportunity to express their views, children can contribute their own unique viewpoints on situations in their early years settings.

Children's rights education requires educators to take a political position themselves, indeed Jerome (2016) argues that if children's rights education is to really tackle 'systemic inequalities and the marketisation of education', using children's rights education is a 'radical call to action' (2016: 152). This means taking a stance where government is challenged and will also require considerable professional development and support for early childhood professionals, to ensure that they have the confidence and knowledge to fully understand the radical changes that could be brought about when children really are at the centre of early childhood education and care. For Jerome (2016) this means rejecting any idea of:

'one size fits all' CRE (implemented from the top-down) for a series of locally negoti-
ated solutions, which address local problems in the context of local cultures, traditions
and resources – what Hopgood (2013) referred to as the 'democratization' of human
rights'. (2016: 152)

The challenge of teaching young children about their rights and of creating early education experiences which are rights-based is huge – research into children's participation in
their own learning can help, but this also needs professional and political momentum
with adults – professionals, politicians, parents and the general public – shouldering the
responsibility for realising those rights. In a review of children's rights and educational
policy across all European Union countries, Lundy suggests that:

 the education rights in the CRC provide a framework for transformation for those who
seek change and are committed to its values, an ever-open window of opportunity
that is hampered currently by a general lack of awareness of the CRC and its links to
domestic policy among educationalists. (2012: 409)

I argue that this is even more the case for the youngest children and this is a challenge to
those working in the early childhood education and care sector, and policy-makers and
parents.

A CHILDREN'S RIGHTS-BASED CURRICULUM

If as educators we are to push forward in developing pedagogy that embraces children's
rights, what must we do? What does a curriculum based on children's rights look like?
What pedagogical practices need to be employed? Dunphy suggests that:

From a rights-based perspective, there appears an obligation on the part of early
childhood educators to help young children to participate in their education setting
by enabling them to express their perspectives on issues related to curriculum and
pedagogy. (2012: 290)

And this is where the need for theory comes in. Educators need to be critically aware of
various theories of learning which are pertinent to young children. They need to be critical in their use and interpretation of those theories, and need to interrogate policies and
assessment practices in the light of those theories.

Perhaps the best way to explore this is through an example of young children as
autonomous learners where their educators adopt a schematic approach to pedagogy
(Athey, 2007). For example, Brierley and Nutbrown (2017) report on the schematic

behaviours of two-year-olds and highlight the importance of patient observation and open-ended activity to support children's self-initiated enquiry. The following observation of 29-month-old George shows how he uses what interests him in the outdoor environment whilst his educator watches patiently to learn from his actions:

> George was outdoors and busy in the sand; his attention seemed to be focused on the top of a plant pot. The plant pot was filled to the brim with sand and George seemed very intent on patting the sand down, using both his hands and at times a spade to pat and smooth the sand in line with the brim of the plant pot. George smiled at me seeming to acknowledge my presence, but showed no other signs of interest, quickly returning to his task with the sand and the plant pot.
>
> When the task had been completed to George's satisfaction, he left the sand pit and collected a watering can filled with water. He then began to water the plants that surrounded the wooden playhouse. After pausing to look at the plants, George continued to run his watering can along the window ledge of the playhouse. As he reached the end of the playhouse, George tipped the watering can, allowing the water to flow onto the floor. Continuing to walk, George made a water trail on the floor. The concentration on George's face suggested that this was not an accidental action.
>
> ...
>
> A large piece of driftwood measuring approximately 1 m in length × 0.5 m width × 0.5 m in height was positioned at the far side of the outdoor area. George displays an obvious interest in the piece of driftwood. George with his water-filled watering can, turned his attention to the driftwood and started to pour water into the nooks and holes in its surface.
>
> ... with obvious care and attention to detail George attempted to tip water into the small hollows and nooks of the bark. Rather than randomly tipping the water, George appeared to consider and plan where to place the water. It appeared he was methodically moving around the outer circumference of the log, seeking out the nooks and spaces he could fill with water.
>
> Throughout his investigation of the log George selected and used a variety of resources from which he was able to tip and pour water. Each time George had to stop to refill the container, he continued his investigation from his previous finishing place.
>
> Close observation of this investigation revealed the incredible and astonishing high level of accuracy displayed by a child of only 29 months old. (Brierley and Nutbrown, 2017: 145)

Working with George in this way is very different from planning for prescribed activities that are designed with specific learning goals in place. This, I suggest, is an example of George's practitioner listening to his 'voice' by watching his actions – not interfering to suggest new things or ask questions (often unnecessary if not banal), but actively listening to what George is 'saying' by his explorations.

THE FUTURE FOR CHILDREN'S RIGHTS IN EARLY CHILDHOOD EDUCATION

What do early childhood professionals need to do so as more fully to enact the UNCRC? It has been shown that whilst research into children's rights has addressed some important issues since the 1989 inception of the UNCRC, there remains a lack of theoretical grounding of the work (Quennerstedt, 2011). Indeed, Quennerstedt and Quennerstedt (2014) argue that the research field needs 'a fruitful and useful theoretical base for formulating research problems and undertaking research in children's rights in education' (2014: 115). They argue that:

> Research into children's rights in education needs sociological theory, pointing out the socially constructed and political character of childhood and clarifying children's active involvement and contributions in their own lives and to society. (2014: 130)

They put forward the argument that research should bring together educational theorising with theories of the sociology of childhood so that educational activities in early childhood settings can be subject to critical analysis from a rights perspective including: pedagogical approaches, curriculum content, relationships (between children and adults and children with other children) and how knowledge and confidence in rights is nurtured and grown.

As well as a theoretical lens, research into children's rights still needs particular crafting in terms of method and methodological approaches. As Nutbrown and Clough (2009) noted, any study which seeks to include young children's views – or listen for their meanings (be that through spoken language, body language, graphic images and so on) – must take issues of 'voice' as central to the methodology. Researchers must continue to develop ways to 'listen' to young voices and (as Lundy urges) act on what they say. Many of the views that young children offer can often be incorporated into changes in practices and settings that make them places of belonging, where the rights of the younger and older citizens who inhabit them are better understood and respected. There are ethical tensions too, and despite enhanced recognition of the rights of children to be heard, the adult view ultimately prevails in some instances – the irony is observed in this note on anonymity:

> We should like to thank the practitioners who allowed us to draw on aspects of their action research in the writing of this paper. We have respected their requests for anonymity. The children would have preferred us to include their real names – indeed all their names and several photographs – but for the moment, adult views of confidentiality and anonymity prevail – we thank them none the less. (Nutbrown and Clough, 2009: 203)

RESEARCH QUESTIONS ON CHILDREN'S RIGHTS IN ECEC

There is still much to learn about children's rights and early childhood education and care and research can play an important part. Signatory countries are committed to regular reporting on progress on children's rights, and though there is much to do, it appears that this macro level story is being told and researchers are able to use such reports to scrutinise and critique action. This chapter points to the need for greater understanding of how the UNCRC is impacting on ECE settings and informing pedagogy. So I suggest that it is the fine detail of what a children's rights-based curriculum looks like, and how children's rights-oriented practitioners practise in their daily work with children, which need our research efforts.

Some suggested research questions for early years practitioners and students might include:

- How do professional educators use the UNCRC to inform their work with young children?
  This question might involve interviewing a sample of early years practitioners to find out their views.

- How do young children experience children's rights in their preschool setting?
  Researching this question is likely to require close and sensitive observation or thoughtful conversation with young children. The younger the children, the less we can rely on spoken language, so it becomes necessary to watch what they do and how they respond to situations they experience.

- What impact does the UNCRC have on inclusion in a preschool setting?
  To research this question it will be important to decide whose views are important here; will the study include parents, children, practitioners, other professionals and volunteers? It is likely that discussion, perhaps focus group conversations and interviews, will be a key method for use with adults. Children might offer their views through drawings, play and talk.

- How do government policies support the development of children's rights in ECE in a particular country?
  To research this question it will be necessary to examine the policies of the chosen country and to carry out a documentary analysis for how policy connects with the UNCRC.

A NOTE ON RESEARCH ETHICS AND INTEGRITY

I suggest when researching children's rights issues there will be some particular ethical issues to show regard for. It will be important to remember that some children and their families may well have been through difficult and traumatic experiences – perhaps losing their nationality and homes due to war. The well-being of research participants is paramount, and paying due regard to their right to withdraw will be essential. Where the youngest children are concerned, it is difficult to obtain their informed consent but there are ways of gauging the assent of children and, of course, their parents will need to consent to their involvement. Researchers themselves will need to pay sensitive attention to the comfort and contentment of young children, babies and toddlers, and stop the process if they seem unhappy. Issues of anonymity and confidentiality need careful thought, as does faithful reporting of data and findings that pay due regard to the participants.

RECOMMENDED READING

Herczog, M. (2012) Rights of the child and early childhood education and care in Europe. *European Journal of Education*, 47 (4): 542–555.

This is a most useful review of rights of the child and ECEC in Europe, which foregrounds well-being and the need for multi-disciplinary action and investment to alleviate present difficulties with housing, poverty, nutrition, social justice, well-being and education.

Nutbrown, C. and Clough, P. (2009) Citizenship and inclusion in the early years: Understanding and responding to children's perspectives on 'belonging'. *International Journal of Early Years Education*, 17 (3): 191–206. DOI: 10.1080/09669760903424523.

This paper highlight projects which give due attention to children's views and concerns about their early years settings and shows how paying attention to children's perspectives can improve their learning environments. Important points are also raised about the ethics of research with young children.

Quennerstedt, A. (2016) Young children's enactments of human rights in early childhood education. *International Journal of Early Years Education*, 24 (10): 5–18. DOI: 10.1080/09669760.2015.1096238.

Focusing on a Swedish setting this paper argues that rights research in early childhood education and care should pay particular attention to the experiences of children under three, and encompass the experiences of children as well as those of the professionals who work with them.

UNICEF (1989) *The United Nations Convention on the Rights of the Child*. UNICEF: New York. https://downloads.unicef.org.uk/wp-content/uploads/2010/05/UNCRC_united_nations_convention_on_the_rights_of_the_child.pdf (accessed 30 January 2018).

Those working with and researching with young children and their families may well wish to read the UNCRC for themselves. This is the original text.

REFERENCES

Athey, C. (2007) *Extending Thought in Young Children: A Parent–Teacher Partnership* (2nd edn). London: Paul Chapman Publishing.

Brierley, J. and Nutbrown, C. (2017) *Understanding Schematic Learning at Two*. London: Bloomsbury.

Devine, D. (2008) Children: Rights and status in education – a socio-historical analysis. *Irish Educational Studies, 18* (1): 14–28. DOI: 10.1080/0332331990180105.

DfE (Department for Education) (2015) *United Nations Convention on the Rights of the Child* (UNCRC). How legislation underpins implementation in England. www.gov.uk/government/publications/united-nations-convention-on-the-rights-of-the-child-uncrc-how-legislation-underpins-implementation-in-england (accessed 2 March 2018).

Dunphy, E. (2012) Children's participation rights in early childhood education and care: The case of early literacy learning and pedagogy. *International Journal of Early Years Education, 20* (3): 290–299. DOI: 10.1080/09669760.2012.716700.

Hazareesingh, S., Simms, K. and Anderson, P. (1989) *Educating the Whole Child: A Holistic Approach to Education in Early Years*. London: Save the Children.

Herczog, M. (2012) Rights of the child and early childhood education and care in Europe. *European Journal of Education, 47* (4): 542–555.

Hopgood, S. (2013) *The Endtimes of Human Rights*. New York: Cornell University Press.

Jerome, L. (2016) Interpreting children's rights education: Three perspectives and three roles for teachers. *Citizenship, Social and Economics Education, 15* (2): 143–156. DOI: 10.1177/2047173416683425.

Jerome, L., Emerson, L. and Lundy, L. (2015) *Child Rights Education: A Study of Implementation in Countries with a UNICEF National Committee Presence*. Geneva: UNICEF PFP.

Kjørholt, A. (2011) Rethinking young children's rights for participation in diverse cultural contexts. In M. Kernan and E. Singer (eds), *Peer Relationships in Early Childhood Education and Care*. London: Routledge, pp. 38–48.

Lundy, L. (2007) 'Voice' is not enough: Conceptualising Article 12 of the United Nations Convention on the Rights of the Child. *British Educational Research Journal, 33* (6): 927–942.

Lundy, L. (2012) Children's rights and educational policy in Europe: The implementation of the United Nations convention on the rights of the child. *Oxford Review of Education, 38* (4): 393–411. DOI: 10.1080/03054985.2012.704874.

Nutbrown, C. (ed.) (1996) *Respectful Educators – Capable Learners: Children's Rights and Early Education*. London: Paul Chapman Publishing.

Nutbrown, C. and Clough, P. (2009) Citizenship and inclusion in the early years: Understanding and responding to children's perspectives on 'belonging'. *International Journal of Early Years Education, 17* (3): 191–206. DOI: 10.1080/09669760903424523.

Penn, H. (1999) *The Rights of Young Children*. Toronto: Childhood Resource and Research Unit, University of Toronto.

Piaget, J. (1923) *The Origin of Intelligence in the Child*. London: Routledge & Kegan Paul.

Quennerstedt, A. (2011) The construction of children's rights in education: A research synthesis. *The International Journal of Children's Rights, 19*: 661–678.

Quennerstedt, A. (2016) Young children's enactments of human rights in early childhood education. *International Journal of Early Years Education, 24* (1): 5–18. DOI: 10.1080/09669760.2015.1096238.

Quennerstedt, A. and Quennerstedt, M. (2014) Researching children's rights in education: Sociology of childhood encountering educational theory. *British Journal of Sociology of Education, 35* (1): 115–132. DOI: 10.1080/01425692.2013.783962.

Rinaldi, C. (1999) 'The pedagogy of listening'. Paper given in Reggio Emilia, Italy, 28 April.

Simpson, D., Loughran, S., Lumsden, E., Mazzocco, P., McDowall Clark, R. and Winterbottom, C. (2017) 'Seen but not heard': Practitioners work with poverty and the organising out of disadvantaged children's voices and participation in the early years. *European Early Childhood Education Research Journal, 25* (2): 177–188. DOI: 10.1080/1350293X.2017.1288014.

Theobald, M. and S. Danby. (2011) Child participation in the early years: Challenges for education. *Australasian Journal of Early Childhood, 36* (3): 19–26.

UNICEF (United Nations Convention on the Rights of the Child) (1989a) Adopted and opened for signature, ratification and accession by General Assembly Resolution 44/25 of 20 November 1989. London: UNICEF (UK). www.unicef.org.uk/what-we-do/un-convention-child-rights/ (accessed 1 March 2018).

UNICEF (1989b) *The United Nations Convention on the Rights of the Child*. UNICEF: New York. https://downloads.unicef.org.uk/wp-content/uploads/2010/05/UNCRC_united_nations_convention_on_the_rights_of_the_child.pdf (accessed 30 January 2018).

Vygotsky, L.S. (1978) *Mind in Society*. Cambridge, MA: Harvard University Press.

3

YOUNG CHILDREN'S WELL-BEING AND SPIRITUALITY

THIS CHAPTER WILL:

- describe the range of meanings that researchers have recently ascribed to the terms well-being and spirituality with regard to young children
- examine some of the findings of research studies on spirituality and ECEC
- discuss studies of well-being, spirituality and professional knowledge in early childhood education and care
- suggest some research question on the topic of young children's well-being and spirituality
- provide some recommended reading to follow up the issues discussed.

This chapter focuses on research in the field of young children's well-being and spirituality in early childhood education and care. With the rise of concerns around child mental health in the past decade, there is increasing concern over the well-being of young children more generally. There have been claims that the increased emphasis on higher levels of achievement and measurement of attainment has threatened that well-being, and in England in 2017, for example, there was expression of grave concern about these issues, leading to increased responsibilities in schools for child mental health.

Whilst researchers have for some time focused on these issues with regard to older children and young people, it is only really in the last decade or so that the idea of spirituality in young children has been the focus of research. Research is just not keeping up with the concerns of parents, educators and other professionals. This chapter is not about what happens when things go wrong in terms of children's well-being and mental health, but rather about what current research is telling us about young children's well-being and spirituality and how a greater appreciation of young children as spiritual beings has implications for early childhood education and care.

WHAT DO WE MEAN BY WELL-BEING AND SPIRITUALITY IN ECEC?

> the fruit of the Spirit is love, joy, peace, forbearance, kindness, goodness, faithfulness, gentleness and self-control. Against such things there is no law. (Epistle of St Paul to the Galatians, 5:22–23)

Spirituality might well be considered the core of human well-being (Hay and Nye, 2006), promoted in early childhood education and care through relationships between children and other children, and children and the adults with whom they live and who work with them in group settings (Hyde, 2008a).

As we saw in Chapter 2, the prominence of concern for children's well-being is an international concern with investment in well-being programmes for children around the world being a key concern of international children's charities such as UNICEF. Major policies in the UK, Australia and the US, to name but three countries, give importance to well-being, demonstrating how this is now a universal and multi-disciplinary concern and one for which educators (as front-line service providers for children) are expected to bear some responsibility. Though greatest concern is often focused on the most vulnerable children, in reality all children are vulnerable and all need to have their well-being secured and supported.

Whilst policy in recent years has begun to consider the importance of young children's well-being, few would disagree with the notion that defining well-being is difficult – although the term is much used – and reaching agreement about what spirituality means when it comes to young children is even more difficult. For as Taggart (2001: 323) noted, 'it is the nature of spirituality to be elusive', and Mata (2012) defines spirituality as:

an innate, human characteristic that allows us to connect with transcendence and/or the divine and feel part of the universe. Spirituality thus encompasses the individual capacity and the essence of life, providing humans with a greater consciousness and more profound understanding of being. (2012: 24)

Yet the difficulties around definition must not hinder a concern to address these important topics. Though researchers, it seems, have been slow to pick up on the need to consider young children in the exploration of this field, there remains a small but growing corpus of work that can be drawn on and built upon.

For Watson (2017) the concept of spirituality is not difficult to define. She puts forward an argument that early years practitioners need those who study spirituality to be clear about their terms, and concludes with a suggestion that 'post-secular' diversity must be acknowledged and 'spirituality' should signal the following key and shared cross-disciplinary values:

1. Spiritual diversity and inclusivity
2. Human rights and the right to spiritual voice
3. A critique of market-driven performativity and a focus on the whole child (and person)
4. Spiritual practice. (Watson, 2017: 12)

She argues that studies are needed to support practitioners:

because the spirituality of *each and every* child *still* matters: and what we really need to do *now* is to ensure that children and young people's spirituality – and adults' spirituality – is properly considered in professional practice and not ignored because it is too difficult to understand or pin down. (2017: 12)

Despite Watson's claim that spirituality need not defy definition, there is an argument that the very essence of spirituality, and its intensely personalised nature, means that it actually *should* be difficult to define, and the definition, of course, depends on who is asking whom! According to Bone (2008) spirituality is:

a means of connecting people to all things, to nature and the universe. Spirituality adds to my appreciation for the wonder and mystery in everyday life. It alerts me to the possibility for love, happiness, goodness, peace and compassion in the world. (2008: 244)

When it comes to children, according to Giesenberg's (2007) definition, spirituality:

 is an innate part of a person. It is an awareness or consciousness of the surrounding world, a sense of compassion and love towards this world and anything in it shown through wonder and through activities and relationship with peers and significant adults in the child's life. (2007: 270)

Mata-McMahon (2016) reviewed ten years of published empirical studies into children's spirituality, focusing mainly on children aged from birth to nine years, from 2005 to 2015, and whilst noting the relative scarcity of such work, identified three key themes: (1) spiritual meaning-making and relationships to/with God, (2) children's spirituality in education, and (3) identity formation and sense of self (2016: 142). Mata-McMahon's review suggests that, aside from any faith or non-belief, the presence of God seems strong for children in their early years, with children finding the notion of God comforting and important to their well-being and able to express a simple sense of a relationship to or with God. Further, in terms of spirituality and education, Mata-McMahon (2016) found that the greatest contribution to early childhood of the target studies was their support and challenge to education to improve experiences for children:

> in order to allow for the children to be happier (Wills 2011), by taking into account chil-
> dren's spiritual characteristic (Hyde 2008[a]), honouring the spirit of the child (Bone
> 2005), engaging children in creative arts within religious education curricula (Jacobs
> 2012; Mountain 2007), while allowing children to freely experience and express
> their spirituality in the classrooms in which they find themselves (Mata 2015).
> (Mata-McMahon, 2016: 146)

Finally, Mata-McMahon's review concludes that recent studies have highlighted spirituality as an important factor in their development of a 'worldview' and increasing happiness. The review points to the inconclusive nature of studies in relation to religion, faith and non-belief in terms of young children's developing sense of their 'spiritual selves' (2016: 148) and the failure of the studies to show how education can support these elements of their holistic development. Regretting the paucity of such studies of young children's spirituality, Mata-McMahon suggests that:

> The more we know about children's spirituality, directly from children, the better
> our chances to near the core of the issue, being able to better describe it, better
> define and better understand it. And thus, following, be better prepared to recognise,
> nurture and promote children's spirituality for future generations of young children.
> (2016: 149)

Calling for the study of young children's spirituality through a pluri-cultural perspective, and new ways of talking about the issues, Mata-McMahon argues that such a position would enable a focus on spirituality in a global context where multiple possibilities exist and where spirituality is not necessarily dependent upon, related to or limited by specific religious beliefs.

In terms of well-being, the evasiveness of a clear definition (despite the term featuring in many policy documents) can mask a lack of attention with regard to well-being. There is a danger that because policy speaks of well-being it must be assumed to be taken care of in educational settings. Whilst not focusing specifically on young children, Spratt (2016: 224) offers some policy insights that are perhaps even more incisive when considering the early years. She argues that whilst policy views well-being as necessary *for* learning, it should be seen as an *outcome* of learning. Placing her study in the Scottish educational context, Spratt demonstrated how the disciplines of medicine, psychology, social care and education feed into present day policy notions of well-being in Scottish educational policy with intercon-nected discourses of health promotion, social and emotional literacy, care and 'flourishing'. All of these things are inextricably linked in young children, and so give credence to Spratt's argument that well-being be considered a *prerequisite* and an *outcome* of education.

Having identified the difficulties in reaching agreement on how well-being and spiritu-ality might be defined in ECEC, the next section of this chapter will highlight some of the key issues from the relatively small number of studies that have been published recently.

RESEARCH ON SPIRITUALITY IN EARLY CHILDHOOD EDUCATION

Consider this true account of a mother talking with her young daugher:

'Why are we here mummy?' a five-year-old asked from the back seat of the car as they drove along the coast road, the waves high and white on the rocks. 'Well, we need to go the pet shop to buy some food for Peppy and then to the supermarket for some food for us' replied her mother. Not content with the response the child continued 'No! No! – I mean why are *we* – why are we *here*?'. Her mother paused before replying – realising that her daughter was asking a much bigger question that the purpose of the car journey – and in the space of her hesitation her child continued 'Do you know why we are here? With *this* sea and *this* sky? What are we here – *for*?' He mother replied that she didn't know – but that it was a good question, that sometimes she wondered about it too. 'So, only *God* knows why we are here then?' the five-year-old offered. 'Perhaps that's so' was all her mother could say, as she contemplated the vastness of the ocean and her own smallness in comparison.

Drawing on work conducted in the UK, Nye (2013) defines spirituality thus:

Children's spirituality is an initially natural capacity for awareness of the sacred quality of life experiences. This awareness can be conscious or unconscious, and sometimes fluctuates between both, but in both cases can affect actions, feelings and thoughts. In childhood, spirituality is especially about being attracted towards 'being in relation', responding to a call to relate to more than 'just me' – i.e. to other, to God, to creation or to a deeper inner sense of Self. This encounter with transcendence can happen in specific experiences or moments, as well as through imaginative or reflective activity (thoughts and meaning making). (2013: 6)

Some children show a sense of being in touch with the big questions of human existence, and have a quest for answers. This seems to be less obscure in the early years because children have not yet learned to edit out their thinking to conform to what they think adults approve of.

Perhaps one of the most obvious approaches to early childhood education where spirituality is to the fore is Steiner Waldorf education, where Steiner's 'anthroposophy' posits that humans are made up of three equal parts: body, soul and spirit (Steiner, 1963), and in this way spirituality is seen as innate. Some within this and kindred movements hold that because children have only recently left the angels, where they were before their birth, they have a closeness to the spiritual world that adults must work to regain. Montessori's writings also stress the spiritual nature of the child, a fundamental and intrinsic part of their development which needs to be nurtured as are other aspects of development. Whilst modern policy documents might mention spirituality, there is less of a sense of what this actually means and how this might be nurtured in early childhood education and care.

Bone's (2008) focus is on relationships within early childhood settings, with spirituality to be found in connectedness and belonging between people. Drawing on work in New Zealand ECE settings, Bone uses the term 'everyday spirituality' – which brings a kind of *ordinariness* to the concept. Finding ordinariness in what others consider *ethereal* might be helpful in establishing what spirituality looks like – or perhaps we should say *feels like* – in ECEC practices. But perhaps it is the ordinary alongside the ethereal that is the reality of spirituality in ECEC, and that could be what makes the discussion and the evolution of practice difficult to grasp; that, and the lack of a real shared language with which to express spirituality in practice.

Unsurprisingly, perhaps, music has been found to be an important channel for developing 'connectedness' in young children (Nortjé and van der Merwe, 2016). In a study of a music group for 15 four- to five-year-olds in Potchefstroom, South Africa, the authors used a series of music sessions to foster *Ubuntu*, the 'essence of being human', through connectedness with others using the medium of music. Using a hermeneutic phenomenology, Nortjé and van der Merwe identified seven themes, defined by quotes from the children: love for music: 'music is the best'; corporeality: 'my body dances'; spatiality: 'music takes me places'; relational interaction: 'we can play together'; relationality connection: 'you and me'; relationality transformation: 'I feel better'; and spiritual virtues: 'you can have mine'. A prominent finding of this study is the sheer pleasure children derived from the music sessions, and their growth in terms of interconnectedness with their peers: the use of their body in moving to music, changing their place in a space, change in themselves through the experiences they shared through music, and enhanced giving, caring and loving.

Generally, it is the creative opportunities (such as music) offered to children that open up possibilities for nurturing well-being and spirituality. In a study of 20 two- and three-year-old children in an English preschool setting, Goodliff (2013) explored how these young children expressed spirituality in their imaginative play. Linking creativity and spirituality, Goodliff shows how exploration of open-ended materials and connections with other children and adults fosters (or gives expression to) young children's spirituality through creativity. Goodliff suggests that:

> The everyday imaginative spaces they create and inhabit become spaces rich with potential for listening to, and hearing languages of spirituality ... [and] ... includes moments of care and compassion, inner-reflection, transcendence and the meaning-making of identity, these elements combine in a rich interplay. (2013: 1067)

Goodliff warns of the misguided action of removing a spiritual dimension from the English Early Years Foundation Stage (DfE, 2012), arguing that this is an important part of nurturing children's humanity and that developing 'languages of spirituality' (Goodliff, 2013: 1068) is as important as the development of other, empirical languages.

In a similar vein, Harris (2016) conducted a study of how outdoor play spaces, specifically public parks, contribute to children's spiritual development through the experiences of nature, pretend play and storytelling with parents and grandparents. For Harris, 'Just as each child has unique strengths, personality traits and temperaments, the meaning of spirituality for each child is also distinctive' (2016: 91). The accounts in Harris's study indicate how freedom to move and make noise, and explore nature and play spaces, was found to enable children to give expression to curiosity, awe and wonder in ways that indoor space cannot offer; and she adds that families can play and explore informally together whilst following children's leads:

> This openness to pedagogy of listening creates opportunities for the child and family to construct ideas and knowledge. When this happens, acceptance to nature can occur; spiritual awareness is receptive by making learning conscious and intentional for the child. This richness makes learning meaningful. New adventures have the potential to nurture a child's spiritual development. (2016: 92)

Children's shared joy is evident in the vignettes used by Harris to describe her interpretations of their spirituality in outdoor spaces. She argues that young children's spiritual development can be nurtured through playing in outdoor spaces where their interests, strengths, creativity and family bonding are facilitated.

Drawing on two studies, one in Cyprus (Loizou et al., 2011) and one in the US (Mata, 2015), Mata-McMahon (2017) highlights the importance of kindness, caring, compassion and relationships (in the Cyprus-based study) and joyfulness and delight (in the US study). Using rich vignettes from data gathered in the two studies, Mata-McMahon demonstrates how the expression of joy was in itself a spiritual experience, as were expressions of compassion and kindness in relating to others. Loizou et al. used drawings and interviews with 23 kindergarten children to explore their creativity and humour. Bringing these two studies together Mata-McMahon suggests that there are distinct connections between spirituality and humour, with humour being one of many ways of expressing the 'spiritual self' (2017: 175) and concludes:

> it might be that humour and kindergarteners' ability to identify, differentiate and create humourous stories is related to their spiritual self, as it is expressed through imaginative play and experiences of joyfulness and delight. (2017: 175)

The implications of this analysis for ECEC are that humour and imagination should be nurtured, with opportunities for children to create funny stories and drawings and – quite simply – to laugh.

Adams et al. (2016) review some of the literature on spirituality and early childhood and ask in conclusion: 'What is early years spirituality?'. They offer eight key themes: spirituality as being innate; relationality; identity; connectedness; creativity; transcendence; spiritual experience; and awe and wonder (2016: 768). Their review of the research highlights, perhaps not unexpectedly, that play is a central factor in children's demonstration (and perhaps exploration and discovery) of their spirituality. Because play features to greater and lesser degrees in most educational philosophies and pedagogies, the inevitability of play as a means of spiritual exploration is clear. And to return to Giesenberg's thinking: 'young children express their spirituality in everything they do, say and are' (2007: 261). Taking this view, how do adults make decisions about what to take forward and what to leave fallow? Whilst, as Adams et al. (2016) state, a clear understanding of the distinctiveness of young children's spirituality is essential, there are dangers of 'inferring too much from data, requiring considerable attention to limit researcher bias' (2016: 770), and this must be the case when practitioners themselves seek to examine and study elements of their own practice. Adams et al. urge more empirical studies which help us to learn from young children what spirituality is, so as to provide a stronger base for future practice. Such work would also support the development of policy and it may even be helpful to acknowledge that there is ambiguity across multiple understandings of spirituality in early childhood, and so open up discussion and the development of spiritually sensitive practice. Working in the Australian context of diversity, Bone and Fenton (2015: 88) suggest an approach that is intended to support practitioners to 'recognise and value the spiritual dimension of children's lives'. They provoke an awareness of 'good' and 'bad' spiritual care of young children and identify:

> the responsibility of teachers to take a more political view of the spiritual, and to advocate for the right to a safe, holistic and non-abusive spirituality that gives a possibility for healing (Dei 2011) rather than hurt. (Bone and Fenton, 2015: 92)

An example of this comes from Bone and Fenton, whose work seeks to offer clarity of thinking to aid practice around protecting young children's spirituality through a strengths approach. Bone and Fenton discuss examples of what might be called 'poor care', which they suggest is 'spiritual abuse' where compassion is lacking. In such situations we could ask about how the spirituality of the practitioners is nurtured and supported in order that they create spiritually safe environments for the children they work with.

Given the openness and inconclusive nature of researchers' attempts to define spirituality, and the relatively narrow definitions of policy, practitioners are often left to decide for themselves how they define and nurture spirituality and well-being in early childhood.

WELL-BEING, SPIRITUALITY AND PROFESSIONAL KNOWLEDGE IN EARLY CHILDHOOD EDUCATION AND CARE

Though research about well-being and spirituality in ECEC remains sparse, what is clear from the studies reviewed to date is the crucial role that adults who work with young children play in these aspects of their growth and development. An Australian study (Davis et al., 2012) involving interviews with 13 family day care educators indicated that whilst they were content to consider children's social and emotional well-being they were less confident when it came to early signs of mental health problems. The study showed that promotion of children's mental health was, in the main, informal and relied on individuals rather than being part of a planned service-wide system. The study points to the need for more support and resources for training in child mental health.

Mata (2012) argues that spirituality should form part of initial teacher education and that early years teachers should be supported in their development of both their definitions of spirituality and of practical schema to nurture children's spirituality. Ten of the eleven student teachers in Mata's (2014) US study deemed spirituality to be important in early childhood education: 'Appreciation of nature, reflection and pondering, meditation practices and yoga were the suggested strategies made by teacher candidates, in order to incorporate and nourish children's spirituality in the classroom' (2014: 118).

Work in the UK (Nye, 2103) has led to the proposal of six criteria which form the basis of nurturing children's spirituality: Space, Process, Imagination, Relationship, Intimacy and Trust (SPIRIT). This calls for uninterrupted space in which to explore relationships in an atmosphere of calm and security, something which the business of ECEC settings often neglects, but which is most definitely achievable and would surely be of benefit to early years practitioners as well as the children they share those spaces with.

So, whilst a definition of spirituality with regard to young children might be elusive, its expressive presence in young children is wholly perceptible to everyone who acknowledges that dimension of being, and who seeks to develop it. Working with children's spirituality requires some openness and awareness of our own spirituality, and, I suggest, a willingness to work with uncertainties. The words of Khalil Gibran's *The Prophet* offer a fitting conclusion to this chapter:

and if you would know God, be not therefore a solver of riddles,

Rather look about you and you shall see him playing with your children.

And look into space; you shall see him walking in the cloud, outstretching arms in the lightening and descending in rain.

You shall see him smiling in flowers, then rising and waving His hands in trees. (Gibran, 1923: 21)

RESEARCH QUESTIONS ON YOUNG CHILDREN'S WELL-BEING AND SPIRITUALITY

There is a distinct lack of empirical studies in the area of well-being and spirituality, so studies conducted with this focus, however small, would make an important contribution to developing practice and enhancing dialogue and understanding. Perhaps because of its characteristically ethereal nature – in comparison with other aspects of young children's growth and development – spirituality evades the jargon of clear definition. And perhaps that's the point; that individual practitioners must decide for themselves what *they* mean by 'spirituality', and coming to their own view of what spirituality is *for them* takes them a step further in understanding something of children's spirituality and how that might be nurtured.

Some suggested research questions for early years practitioners and students:

○ How do early years practitioners in your setting define spirituality?
  This question might be investigated by talking with individuals or in focus groups. Where, like Mata (2014), individual definitions are explored and discussed.

○ What are parents' views on nurturing spirituality? Do they believe that ECEC settings have a role in supporting this aspect of children's development ?
  Seeking parents' views on this topic is something that studies seem yet to do. Talking with a small number of parents, asking for examples of what they think depicts their child's spirituality, say, would give important insights.

○ What practices nurture young children's spirituality?
  Thinking about Steiner and Montessori practices, and spirituality supportive practices (such as the work of Nye, 2013), how can settings create space for

spirituality in ECEC? This will of course depend on how settings define 'spirituality' and useful perspectives and examples of practice could be uncovered .

○ How do ECEC policies nurture young children's well-being and spirituality in an ECEC setting?
This question would necessitate a detailed examination for the policy and careful examination of practice – perhaps through a combination of observation and discussion.

A NOTE ON RESEARCH ETHICS AND INTEGRITY

Themes of spirituality and well-being are highly personal and may require additional sensitivities. It will be important to bear in mind that spirituality is not *necessarily* related to a specific faith or religion, though of course for some people it is. Working on spirituality requires sensitivities with regard to families' perspectives and expectations. It will be important to give as much clarity as possible about what the aims of any study are and how it might impact on children, their families and other practitioners.

RECOMMENDED READING

Adams, K., Bull, R. and Maynes, M. (2016) Early childhood spirituality in education: Towards an understanding of the distinctive features of young children's spirituality. *European Early Childhood Education Research Journal*, 24 (5): 760–774. DOI: 10. 1080/1350293X.2014.996425.

This paper reviews some of the literature on spirituality and early childhood to define the topic in terms of eight key themes: spirituality as being innate; relationality; identity; connectedness; creativity; transcendence; spiritual experience; and awe and wonder. The paper makes the case for more empirical studies of spirituality and young children to provide a stronger base for future practice.

Mata, J. (2014) Sharing my journey and opening spaces: Spirituality in the classroom. *International Journal of Children's Spirituality*, 19 (2): 112–122. DOI: 10. 1080/1364436X.2014.922464.

Based on data from ten student teachers in a US study, this paper argues that core attention should be given to young children's spirituality and implications for practice during training and initial qualifications.

REFERENCES

Adams, K. (2017) Towards an interdisciplinary approach to understanding and nurturing spirituality and the whole child. *International Journal of Children's Spirituality*, *22* (1): 1–3. DOI: 10.1080/1364436X.2017.1279726.

Adams, K., Bull, R. and Maynes, M. (2016) Early childhood spirituality in education: Towards an understanding of the distinctive features of young children's spirituality. *European Early Childhood Education Research Journal*, *24* (5): 760–774, DOI: 10.1080/1350293X.2014.996425.

Bone, J. (2008) Creating relational spaces: Everyday spirituality in early childhood settings. *European Early Childhood Education Research Journal*, *16* (2): 343–356. DOI: 10.1080/ 13502930802292122.

Bone, J. and Fenton, A. (2015) Spirituality and child protection in early childhood education: A strengths approach. *International Journal of Children's Spirituality*, *20* (2): 86–99. DOI: 10.1080/1364436X.2015.1030594.

Davis, E., Priest, N., Davies, B., Smyth, L., Waters, E., Herrman, H., Sims, M., Harrison, L., Cook, K., Marshall, B. and Williamson, L. (2012) Family day care educators: An exploration of their understanding and experiences promoting children's social and emotional wellbeing. *Early Child Development and Care*, *182* (9): 1193–1208. DOI: 10. 1080/03004430.2011.603420.

Dei, G.J.S. (2011) Introduction. In G. J. S. Dei (ed.) *Indigenous Philosophies and Critical Education*. New York: Peter Lang. pp. 1–15.

DfE (Department for Education) (2012) *Statutory Framework for the Early Years Foundation Stage*. London: DfE. http://webarchive.nationalarchives.gov.uk/20130404110654/ https://www.education.gov.uk/publications/standard/AllPublications/Page1/DFE-00023-2012 (accessed 28 February 2018).

Gibran, K. (1923) *The Prophet*. NewYork: Alfred A. Knopf.

Giesenberg, A. (2007) 'The phenomenon of preschool children's spirituality'. PhD thesis, Queensland University of Technology, Australia. http://eprints.qut.edu.au/16519/1/ Anna_ Giesenberg_Thesis.pdf (accessed 2 February 2018).

Goodliff, G. (2013) Spirituality expressed in creative learning: Young children's imagining play as space for mediating their spirituality. *Early Child Development and Care*, *183* (8): 1054–1071. DOI: 10.1080/03004430.2013.792253.

Harris, K.I. (2016) Let's play at the park! Family pathways promoting spiritual resources to inspire nature, pretend play, storytelling, intergenerational play and celebrations. *International Journal of Children's Spirituality*, *21* (2): 90–103. DOI: 10. 1080/1364436X.2016.1164669.

Hay, D. and Nye, R. (2006) *The Spirit of the Child*. London: Jessica Kingsley.

Hyde, B. (2008a) The identification of four characteristics of children's spirituality in Australian Catholic primary schools. *International Journal of Children's Spirituality*, *13* (2): 117–127.

Loizou, E., Kyriakides, E. and Hadjicharalambous, M. (2011) Constructing stories in kindergarten: Children's knowledge of gender. *European Early Childhood Education Research Journal*, *19* (1): 63–77.

Mata, J. (2012) Nurturing spirituality in early childhood classrooms: The teacher's view. In M. Fowler, J. D. Martin, and J. L. Hochheimer (eds), *Spirituality: Theory, Praxis and Pedagogy*. Oxford: Inter-Disciplinary Press, pp. 239–248.

Mata, J. (2014) Sharing my journey and opening spaces: Spirituality in the classroom. *International Journal of Children's Spirituality*, *19* (2): 112–122. DOI: 10.1080/1364436X.2014.922464.

Mata, J. (2015) *Spiritual Experiences in Early Childhood Education: Four Kindergarteners, One Classroom*. New York: Routledge.

Mata-McMahon, J. (2016) Reviewing the research in children's spirituality (2005–2015): Proposing a pluricultural approach. *International Journal of Children's Spirituality*, *21* (2): 140–152. DOI: 10.1080/1364436X.2016.1186611.

Mata-McMahon, J. (2017) Spirituality and humour: Making connections for early childhood education. *International Journal of Children's Spirituality*, *22* (2): 170–178. DOI: 10.1080/1364436X.2017.1287681.

Nortjé, E. and van der Merwe, L. (2016) Young children and spirituality: Understanding children's connectedness in a group music class. *International Journal of Children's Spirituality*, *21* (1): 3–18. DOI: 10.1080/1364436X.2016.1138932.

Nye, R. (2013) *Children's Spirituality: What It Is and Why It Matters* (3rd edn). London: Church House Publishing.

Spratt, J. (2016) Childhood wellbeing: What role for education? *British Educational Research Journal*, *42* (2): 223–239. DOI: 10.1002/berj.3211.

Steiner, R. (1963) *The Life, Nature and Cultivation of Anthroposophy*. London: Rudolf Steiner Press.

Taggart, G. (2001) Nurturing spirituality: A rationale for holistic education. *International Journal of Children's Spirituality*, *6* (3): 325–339.

Watson, J. (2017) Every child still matters: Interdisciplinary approaches to the spirituality of the child. *International Journal of Children's Spirituality*, *22* (1): 4–13. DOI: 10.1080/1364436X.2016.1234434.

Wills, R. (2011) The magic of music: A study into the promotion of children's well-being through singing. *International Journal of Children's Spirituality*, *16* (1): 37–46.

PLAY IN EARLY CHILDHOOD EDUCATION AND CARE

THIS CHAPTER WILL:

- introduce the international context of research on play in ECEC
- consider definitions of play from children's perspectives
- discuss research on risky play
- discuss the contribution of international studies to understanding of new forms of play with 21st century digital technologies
- suggest some research questions on the topic of play in ECEC
- provide some recommended reading to follow up the issues discussed.

Many conceptions of play have included taken-for-granted and often uncontested beliefs that play is 'good', 'innocent' and contributes to children's learning and development. From early studies of child development and the pioneering work of Susan Isaacs in documenting her work with children playing, we have records of what children over the last century have played with, what they have said about play, and what play can be said to achieve. Uninterrupted play is a fundamental part of the Steiner Waldorf kindergarten, where natural materials and objects (not plastic or digital toys) are used by the children with the only limit being their own imaginations.

Early childhood education and play have, in the past, been synonymous. But recently, increased state control over the early years curriculum and increasing interventions around pedagogy have led to the introduction of 'planned purposeful play' – with its implication that unplanned play might not be purposeful!

The literature on play is rich and diverse, and this chapter cannot cover it comprehensively. Rather it looks at the themes that have dominated early childhood education research during the 21st century; these include expanding and contested definitions of play, the notion of free play and choice, and teacher involvement in play.

Because play is all pervasive in ECEC this chapter does not cover aspects of play which are addressed in other chapters. Chapter 5 examines aspects of children's 'voice', which links with the section in this chapter on children's perspectives on play. Elements of gender and play are considered in Chapter 8 where issues of inclusion research are the focus. Play also features in Chapter 13 on curricular approaches. Digital play and literacy are the focus of Chapter 16.

THE INTERNATIONAL CONTEXT OF RESEARCH ON PLAY IN ECEC

A comprehensive and rigorous review of early years research conducted in the UK (Payler and Wood, 2017) included a review of play research (Wood and Chesworth, 2017) which includes some 40 peer-reviewed papers and research books that together represent the following nine themes: play, learning and development; play, literacy and communication; play and mathematics; information and communication technologies and digital play; agency, diversities and identities; play and metacognition; outdoor play; play, pedagogy and curriculum; policy–practice tensions. This chapter does not attempt to replicate or replace that review of UK research, but rather offers an international complement which in many ways mirrors the UK report. The global foci of research on play are broadly similar to those found in UK-based studies, and the tensions and conflicts around play and policy continue. The focus on children as central – 'what play *is*' – and policy on play in learning – 'what play achieves' so far as policy outcomes are concerned – often conflict in the literature.

Peer-reviewed papers reporting studies in a number of countries have many and varied points of interest, demonstrating that play in ECEC is ubiquitous and draws in many researchers who may not define themselves as play scholars, but their substantive topic of interest – for example, 'race' (MacNevin and Berman, 2017); gender (Lynch, 2015; Børve

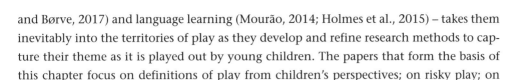

and Børve, 2017) and language learning (Mourão, 2014; Holmes et al., 2015) – takes them inevitably into the territories of play as they develop and refine research methods to capture their theme as it is played out by young children. The papers that form the basis of this chapter focus on definitions of play from children's perspectives; on risky play; on new forms of play with 21st century digital technologies; and on play and learning

DEFINITIONS OF PLAY FROM CHILDREN'S PERSPECTIVES

CHILDREN'S PERSPECTIVES ON THEIR PLAY

What children understand about and how they interpret their play can be very different from the meanings adults construct from watching or engaging in children's play. This is why it is crucial to gain children's own perspective on their play. Several studies have sought to do this, using mainly small samples of children in single settings to record and interpret the fine details of play though children's eyes. The studies reviewed here build on the work discussed in Chapter 3 relating to children's voices and pedagogy.

Breathnach et al.'s (2017) ethnographic study with 25 five-year-old children in Brisbane, Australia, examined children's understandings of play using children's accounts and video-recorded observations. They found that 'teacher-framed agendas' influenced children's participation but children also were able to choose some activities for themselves as they developed their own spaces for play. This study raises interesting questions about what children regard as 'play' and 'work' in a school setting, and demonstrates how they exercise agency in their play.

In England, Chesworth (2016) reported on a small-scale, interpretive study of play in a reception class with five children aged between four and five years. Three-hour play episodes were filmed each week for eight months, and the film was used to provoke discussion with children, parents and teachers. Chesworth found that children drew on their own funds of knowledge gleaned from their home and community, from classrooms, and from popular culture to play out and manipulate materials to their own purposes, showing sophisticated understanding of the imaginary as well as the real. Echoing Hedges et al. (2011), Chesworth (2016: 303) observes that: 'funds of knowledge offer a lens for engaging with and responding to children's interests in relation to their social and cultural experiences …', whereby children construct a 'bridge' between their home and school cultures. Implications of this study include the importance of:

> [t]he availability of flexible, un-prescribed classroom materials, such as blocks, fabric and play-dough, [which] offered multiple affordances for children to draw upon their interests and construct meaning in their play. Hence, the findings support the proposition

that such resources offer more inclusive opportunities than realistic play props for
children to explore their interests and make meaning of their diverse identities.
(Chesworth, 2016: 303)

Taking a 'funds of knowledge' approach as in Chesworth's study provides an alternative
perspective on play and sees children as knowledgeable participants as they construct
their own play. How much knowledge children have in their fund, and what that knowledge is, can amount to different amounts of differently valued 'cultural capital' (Bourdieu,
1986) and so there remains space for children to include and exclude on these bases, as
has been found in other studies.

Film data have become a popular method of data collection for observing play and for
stimulating participant conversations about play. Robson (2010) used video and audio recordings to examine the activities of 12 three- and four-year-olds, across three London settings,
with a focus on their self-regulation and metacognition, which she finds are often governed
or influenced by social contexts. Robson shows how children are able to articulate considerable awareness of what they are doing during play and other setting-based activities, and data
uncover the knowledge children bring into their play from home and group setting contexts.

'FREE' PLAY?

Wood (2014) argues that freedom in play – both free play and free choice – is constrained
by policy structures and systems which impose rules and expectations on children. She
argues that:

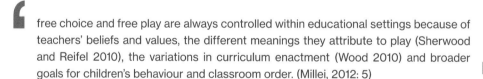

free choice and free play are always controlled within educational settings because of
teachers' beliefs and values, the different meanings they attribute to play (Sherwood
and Reifel 2010), the variations in curriculum enactment (Wood 2010) and broader
goals for children's behaviour and classroom order. (Millei, 2012: 5)

Further, Hedges' (2010) study of teachers' knowledge and children's interests sets out a
clear difference between play interests and enquiry-based interests. For Hedges, the teachers can miss the depth of children's interests by paying scant attention to children's funds
of knowledge gleaned from outside the school setting which enable children to engage
deeply in some serious issues through their own serious enquiry. Hedges demonstrates
how such enquiry can sit alongside play activities. Lack of involvement in children's free
play was also a concern identified in a phenomenological study of four teachers of five-
and six-year-old children in Turkey (Aras, 2016), who saw children's free play time as an
opportunity to complete routine daily paperwork.

In the context where choice and freedom in play are controlled by 'outcomes-led' policy, Wood's (2014) study of ten children's play choices in an Early Years Foundation Stage

setting in England shows how children can subvert rules, how they include and exclude their peers with honed strategies, and how freedom may advantage some children but disadvantage others. She concludes that:

> by paying attention to microanalyses of play, alternative meanings and interpretations become accessible, which open the possibility for deeper engagement with the socio-political dimensions of children's play cultures and practices. (2014: 16)

That children use their play to exercise their autonomy was also a finding of Howe's (2016) study of 11 children in a large English city, which found that when children were able to be autonomous in deciding on their activity, they were more engaged, but that autonomy with teacher involvement produced a more focused learning encounter. Similarly Fleer (2015), working in an Australian context, makes the case for teacher involvement in children's play as *inside* players rather than *outside* observers. She suggests that:

> when the teacher is part of the imaginary play, she/he has an opportunity, from inside of the play, to develop the play further, introducing complexity and, I would suggest, genuinely using learning goals that are detailed in curriculum to help solve the tensions in imaginary situations. (2015: 1812)

Policies in many countries appear to be manipulating and disrupting 'free' play and driving an outcomes model of practice in early childhood education settings in ways which appear to be threatening the introducion of what Gunnarsdottir (2014) describes as 'schoolification' in Icelandic preschools. Such a move infiltrates and threatens to usurp play pedagogy.

RISKY PLAY

A focus, internationally, on where children play highlights a preoccupation with the outdoors and with risk. What in recent years has become termed 'risky play' often takes place outdoors, with what might be considered traditionally child-like pursuits of running, climbing and hiding all now carrying 'new' elements of risk in today's risk-averse world (Gill, 2007). In Australia, Little (2017) investigated outdoor play provision in terms of space, resources and planning for risk-taking in play. Whilst she found settings to be well resourced in terms of outdoor play opportunities, settings varied in the opportunities they provided – or permitted – for risk-taking play with teachers' individual practices being the main governor of risk. Many teachers imposed rules to reduce risk – such as how high the wooden blocks could be built – which Little argues demonstrates a need for pre- and in-service training of providing for children's risk-taking in outdoor play.

In an ethnographic study of children's power, Haywood-Bird (2017) focused on the risky play of 25 two-and-a-half- to five-year-old children in a 'Waldorf-inspired' kindergarten setting. Like many authors Haywood-Bird recollects how she herself had outdoor freedom as a child whilst her own daughter does not. Changes in environment, concerns about child safety, fear of child abduction, the built environment, and more have led to restrictions on children in many parts of the world, which have in turn constrained children's opportunity to take risks in their play and to play out of the gaze of adults. Elsewhere, as UNICEF (2016) reports, some children play in contaminated water or on rubbish heaps because the poverty and deprivation of their locale offers them little choice.

Many ECEC settings recreate a more 'natural' outdoor environment to replicate, in safe practice, the natural risks of woods and rivers. 'Forest Schools' have more recently become popular in introducing children to the outdoors and the safe use of tools for wood-cutting and fire. Haywood-Bird's (2017) US study emphasises the outdoors as a channel for exercising 'free-will', where children's emotions and the exercise of power were clear in their explorations of outdoor phenomena. Risk aversion is often practised in a number of different countries, by practitioners who fear for children's safety and who must also operate within strict health and safety codes of practice, and views of what is 'risky' vary according to culture and expectation. In a review of professional attitudes to children's risk-taking, van Rooijen and Newstead (2017) summarise thus:

> Constructs of children as vulnerable and in need of protection are unlikely to involve notions of risk-competence (defined as children's skills to recognize, engage and evaluate risks in play in order to protect themselves). In some cases this may result in professionals underestimating children's risk-assessment capabilities and overriding children's legitimate decisions about appropriate levels of risk in their play, thus undermining children's own efforts to make decisions for themselves. (2017: 949)

In parallel with this the 'real world' experiences of children raise different kinds of risk. In the US context of gun violence, Delaney (2017) explores how the use of guns, as seen by children in real life or on the media, infiltrates their play. She uses the term 'playing at violence' to describe pretend play which centres around violent themes such as shooting, and a 'darker' side of life – death, war, fear – and argues that these are important and powerful parts of play; they form part of the process that children engage in as a way of making sense of the things they witness or see in the media. Focusing on a group of four-year-olds and their teacher, Delaney explores how a teacher offers 'acceptable' playing at violence, and raises issues of power tensions and control in play. Of course play has always been a site of resistance, where children switch expertly from the real to the imaginary and back again, knowing when they are 'playing' and when what they do is 'real' – and sometimes reminding adults who misread the cues that 'this is pretend'. Delaney concludes that whilst teachers and parents might be fearful of violence in children's play, it is important to try to understand what meanings children ascribe to those types of play. The need to manage play – especially risky play – was the focus of a Belgium-based project where risky play activities were introduced into a three-month programme for two classes of four- and six-year-olds (Lavrysen et al., 2017). The programme was shown to improve risk perception and competence in young children through intensive opportunities for risky play activities at school and appropriate 'training' in risk detection.

NEW FORMS OF PLAY WITH 21ST CENTURY DIGITAL TECHNOLOGIES

As with all generations, children evolve play practices to incorporate the materials and tools they have available to them, and as the last two decades have seen digital technologies develop apace, so children have taken these technologies into their play (Marsh, 2010). Thus, the literature on digital play has some way to go to catch up with over a century of studies of other forms of children's play, and early years practitioners need support themselves to better understand how children come to learn about the use of the various digital tools and devices (Aubrey and Dhal, 2014).

According to Nikolopoulou and Gialamas (2015) information and communications technology play have largely replaced 'traditional' play in Greece, but the integration of ICT in ECE remains under developed. Findings from a questionnaire survey of 190 early years teachers indicate that enhanced teacher confidence, understanding the impacts on classroom practices, and professional development to support them in this are much needed.

Studies of digital play are now gaining an established place in the play scholarship literature and acknowledged to have a place in early childhood education. This has led to a challenge for early childhood practitioners to develop new or adapted pedagogies which facilitate digital play. In Australia, Bird and Edwards (2015) have taken a socio-cultural framework for digital play to help educators to frame their pedagogies in digital contexts. Focusing on still cameras, iPads and computers, Bird and Edwards mapped 'device-specific' behaviours in play relevant to different technologies. They note:

 exploratory behaviours were associated with framing images in the viewfinder for cameras; or seemingly random tapping of the screen for iPads. Ludic behaviours were more strongly associated with using technologies to create deliberate symbolic play, like a doll's house scenario on the iPad and/or the creation of pretend play scenarios and then using technologies to digitally record planned play, e.g., Joyen creating and recording a puppet show on the iPad. (2015: 1153)

Bird and Edwards' Digital Play Framework provides a summary of the observable behaviours of children learning to use various devices through play thus forming a framework for developing practice to extend learning. Edwards' (2016) Melbourne-based study, with 20 ECE practitioners and 40 child 'experts', focused on her concept of 'web-mapping'

which 'represents the blurring boundaries between children's traditional and converged play as co-constituted' (2016: 515). Edwards identified five main influences of web-mapping, whereby web-mapping:

- promotes an in-depth focus on children's interests
- provides a visual aid for observing children's play interests
- means teachers plan play-based experiences typically considered 'unsuitable'
- promotes intentional teaching
- aligns children's digital experiences and knowledge with play-based learning experiences.

Edwards (2016) discovered that the practitioners in the study found the process helpful in understanding the 'technology, digital media and popular-culture aspects of children's life-worlds' and thus found them more acceptable in the classroom as shared knowledge within the group of children. This, and a subsequent report (Edwards and Bird, 2017), points again to the importance of professional development and support for teachers to incorporate children's uses of technology and their knowledge of digital devices into their pedagogy.

Reporting on another Australian study, Nuttall et al. (2015) move on from the identification of a professional development need (which they regard as largely unsuccessful) to argue that the limited take up of digital technologies in children's play in the early years curriculum can be reframed to focus on children's play. They argue for professional development as a 'form of consciousness raising', and further conclude that since how teachers feel influences how they behave, there needs to be a planned 'space' for teachers to articulate their concerns and excitements about the incorporation of new technologies into children's new digital play.

RESEARCH QUESTIONS ON PLAY IN ECEC

In recent years much research on children's play has used film to generate data that are then viewed and discussed by the children themselves and their ECE practitioners and parents. The relative ease with which film can be generated now means that technologies can be used by children themselves to film their play. New digital technologies offer new ways of researching children's play with them as meaningful participants in generating meaning from these data. Though play has been the focus of research throughout the 20th century, the new developments around risk and digital play that have arisen in the 21st century still offer many avenues for study.

Some suggested research questions for early years practitioners and students include:

○ What are the views of ECE practitioners on children's play using digital technologies? This question could be researched using a questionnaire survey, interviews or focus groups; breadth of coverage would need to be balanced by the opportunity that a smaller number of participants might offer to generate deeper insights.

○ How do children move between real and imaginary worlds in their play?

Video recording is probably the best way to capture episodes of play that might shed light on children's actions, and when viewed by the children their own meanings can be further elicited and interpreted.

○ What are parents' views of children taking risks in their outdoor play?

Talking with a small number of parents about their views around risky play will give a good understanding of the issues as they see them. Face-to-face interviews on a one-to-one basis or small focus groups are the best ways to find out how parents see this aspect of their children's play.

○ How do practitioners strike a balance between national curriculum policies and the provision for free, child-led play?

Discussion with practitioners is probably the best way to learn about practitioners' concerns and strategies. Using Skype or other social media and internet facility might make it possible to involve participants from a number of countries.

A NOTE ON RESEARCH ETHICS AND INTEGRITY

As with any research involving young children – especially when using images and film – there are many things to consider around confidentiality, anonymity, choice to withdraw or not participate, and aspects of informed consent. Care needs to be taken not to intrude on children's time without meaningful engagement with them and the subtle cues which might signal non-participation need to be heeded and respected.

RECOMMENDED READING

Chesworth, L. (2016) A funds of knowledge approach to examining play interests: Listening to children's and parents' perspectives. *International Journal of Early Years Education*, 24 (3): 294–308. DOI: 10.1080/09669760.2016.1188370.

This chapter provides an interesting insight into children's 'funds of knowledge' using video of children playing.

Delaney, K.K. (2017) Playing at violence: Lock-down drills, 'bad guys' and the construction of 'acceptable' play in early childhood. *Early Child Development and Care*, 187 (5–6): 878–895. DOI: 10.1080/03004430.2016.1219853.

Challenging orthodoxy around 'what' children play and how this is 'accepted' or not, this paper addresses issues of the knowledge of violence that children introduce into their play.

Fleer, M. (2015) Pedagogical positioning in play – teachers being inside and outside of children's imaginary play. *Early Child Development and Care*, 185 (11–12): 1801–1814. DOI: 10.1080/03004430.2015.1028393.

Considering teachers' positioning in play and their roles as insiders and outsiders, with insightful use of data this paper reflects on teacher interventions and assumptions about what is being played.

Wood, E. and Chesworth, L. (2017) Play and pedagogy. In J. Payler and E. Wood (eds), *BERA-TACTYC Early Childhood Research Review 2003–2017*. London: British Educational Research Association. www.bera.ac.uk/wp-content/uploads/2017/05/BERA-TACTYC-Full-Report.pdf?noredirect=1 (accessed 29 January 2018).

This chapter reviews the most recent literature on play and pedagogy in the UK.

REFERENCES

Aras, A. (2016) Free play in early childhood education: A phenomenological study. *Early Child Development and Care*, 186 (7): 1173–1184. DOI: 10.1080/03004430.2015.1083558.

Aubrey, C. and Dahl, S. (2014) The confidence and competence in information and communication technologies of practitioners, parents and young children in the Early Years Foundation Stage. *Early Years*, *34* (1): 94–108.

Bird, J. and Edwards, S. (2015) Children learning to use technologies through play: A Digital Play Framework. *British Journal of Educational Technology*, *46* (6): 1149–1160. DOI: 10.1111/bjet.12191.

Børve, H.E. and Børve, E. (2017) 'Rooms with gender: physical environment and paly culture in kindergarten'. *Early Child Development and Care, 187* (5–6): 1069–1081. DOI: 10.1080/03004430.2016.1223072

Bosacki, S., Woods, H. and Coplan, R. (2015) Canadian female and male early childhood educators' perceptions of child aggression and rough-and-tumble play. *Early Child Development and Care, 185* (7): 1134–1147. DOI: 10.1080/03004430.2014.980408.

Bourdieu, P. (1986) The forms of capital. In J. Richardson (ed.), *Handbook of Theory and Research for the Sociology of Education*. New York: Greenwood, pp. 241–258.

Breathnach, H., Danby, S. and O'Gorman, L. (2017) 'Are you working or playing?': Investigating young children's perspectives of classroom activities. *International Journal of Early Years Education, 25* (4): 439–454. DOI: 10.1080/09669760.2017.1316241.

Chesworth, L. (2016) A funds of knowledge approach to examining play interests: Listening to children's and parents' perspectives. *International Journal of Early Years Education, 24* (3): 294–308. DOI: 10.1080/09669760.2016.1188370.

Delaney, K.K. (2017) Playing at violence: Lock-down drills, 'bad guys' and the construction of 'acceptable' play in early childhood. *Early Child Development and Care, 187* (5–6): 878–895. DOI: 10.1080/03004430.2016.1219853.

Edwards, S. (2016) New concepts of play and the problem of technology, digital media and popular-culture integration with play-based learning in early childhood education. *Technology, Pedagogy and Education, 25* (4): 513–532. DOI: 10.1080/1475939X.2015.1108929.

Edwards, S. and Bird, J. (2017) Observing and assessing young children's digital play in the early years: Using the Digital Play Framework. *Journal of Early Childhood Research, 15* (2): 158–173. DOI:10.177/1476718X1579746.

Fleer, M. (2015) Pedagogical positioning in play – teachers being inside and outside of children's imaginary play. *Early Child Development and Care, 185* (11–12): 1801–1814. DOI: 10.1080/03004430.2015.1028393.

Gill, T. (2007) *No Fear: Growing Up in a Risk Averse Society*. London: Calouste Gulbenkian Foundation.

Gunnarsdottir, B. (2014) From play to school: Are core values of ECEC in Iceland being undermined by 'schoolification'? *International Journal of Early Years Education, 22* (3): 242–250. DOI: 10.1080/09669760.2014.960319.

Haywood-Bird, E. (2017) Playing with power: An outdoor classroom exploration, *Early Child Development and Care, 187* (5–6): 1015–1027. DOI: 10.1080/03004430.2016.1223070.

Hedges, H. (2010) Whose goals and interests? In L. Brooker, and S. Edwards (eds), *Engaging Play*. Maidenhead: McGraw-Hill/Open University Press, pp. 25–38.

Hedges, H., Cullen, J. and Jordan, B. (2011) Early years curriculum: Funds of knowledge as a conceptual framework for children's interests. *Journal of Curriculum Studies, 43* (2): 185–205.

Holmes, R.M., Romeo, L., Ciraola, S. and Grushko, M. (2015) The relationship between creativity, social play, and children's language abilities. *Early Child Development and Care, 185* (7): 1180–1197. DOI: 10.1080/03004430.2014.983916.

Howe, S. (2016) What play means to us: Exploring children's perspectives on play in an English Year 1 classroom. *European Early Childhood Education Research Journal, 24* (5): 748–759. DOI: 10.1080/1350293X.2016.1213567.

Lavrysen, A., Bertrands, E., Leyssen, L., Smets, L., Vanderspikken, A. and De Graef, P. (2017) Risky-play at school: Facilitating risk perception and competence in young children. *European Early Childhood Education Research Journal, 25* (1): 89–105. DOI: 10.1080/1350293X.2015.1102412.

Little, H. (2017) Promoting risk-taking and physically challenging play in Australian early childhood settings in a changing regulatory environment. *Journal of Early Childhood Research, 15* (1): 83–98. DOI: 10:1177/1476718X15579743.

Lynch, M. (2015) Guys and dolls: A qualitative study of teachers' views of gendered play in kindergarten. *Early Child Development and Care, 185* (5): 679–693. DOI: 10.1080/03004430.2014.950260.

MacNevin, M. and Berman, R. (2017) The Black baby doll doesn't fit the disconnect between early childhood diversity policy, early childhood educator practice, and children's play. *Early Child Development and Care, 187* (5–6): 827–839. DOI: 10.1080/03004430.2016.1223065.

Marsh, J. (2010) Young children's play in online virtual worlds. *Journal of Early Childhood Research*, 8: 23–39.

Millei, Z. (2012) Thinking differently about guidance: Power, children's autonomy and democratic environments. *Journal of Early Childhood Research*, 10 (1): 88–99. DOI: 10.1177/1476718X11406243.

Mourão, S. (2014) Taking play seriously in the pre-primary English classroom. *English Language Teaching Journal*, 68 (3): 254–264. DOI: 10.1093/elt/ccu018.

Nikolopoulou, K. and Gialamas, V. (2015) ICT and play in preschool: Early childhood teachers' beliefs and confidence. *International Journal of Early Years Education*, 23 (4): 409–425. DOI: 10.1080/09669760.2015.1078727.

Nuttall, J., Edwards, S., Mantilla, A., Grieshaber, S. and Wood, E. (2015) The role of motive objects in early childhood teacher development concerning children's digital play and play-based learning in early childhood curricula. *Professional Development in Education*, 41 (2): 222–235. DOI: 10.1080/19415257.2014.990579.

Payler, J. and Wood, E. (eds) (2017) *BERA-TACTYC Early Childhood Research Review 2003–2017*. London: British Educational Research Association. www.bera.ac.uk/wp-content/uploads/2017/05/BERA-TACTYC-Full-Report.pdf?noredirect=1 (accessed 29 January 2018).

Robson, S. (2010) Self-regulation and metacognition in young children's self-initiated play and reflective dialogue. *International Journal of Early Years Education*, 18 (3): 227–241. DOI: 10.1080/09669760.2010.521298.

Sherwood, S.A.S. and Reifel. S. (2010) The multiple meanings of play: Exploring preservice teachers' beliefs about a central element of early childhood education. *Journal of Early Childhood Teacher Education*, 31 (4): 322–343. DOI: 10.1080/10901027.2010.524065.

UNICEF (United Nations Children's Fund) (2016) *The State of the World's Children 2016: A Fair Chance for Every Child*. UNICEF: New York.

van Rooijen. M. and Newstead, S. (2017) Influencing factors on professional attitudes towards risk-taking in children's play: A narrative review. *Early Child Development and Care*, 187 (5–6): 946–957. DOI: 10.1080/03004430.2016.1204607.

Wood, E. (2010) Developing integrated approaches to play and learning. In P. Broadhead, J. Howard, and E. Wood (eds), *Play and Learning in the Early Years: From Research to Practice*. London: Sage, pp. 9–26.

Wood, E.A. (2014) Free choice and free play in early childhood education: Troubling the discourse. *International Journal of Early Years Education*, 22 (1): 4–18. DOI: 10.1080/09669760.2013.830562.

Wood, E. and Chesworth, L. (2017) Play and pedagogy. In J. Payler and E. Wood (eds), *BERA-TACTYC Early Childhood Research Review 2003–2017*. London: British Educational Research Association. www.bera.ac.uk/wp-content/uploads/2017/05/BERA-TACTYC-Full-Report.pdf?noredirect=1 (accessed 29 January 2018).

5

CHILDREN AS PARTICIPANTS IN THEIR OWN LEARNING AND IN RESEARCH

THIS CHAPTER WILL:

- consider the lessons from research onto children's perspectives of what they do in ECEC settings
- discuss studies focusing on children's involvement in assessment of their own learning
- suggest some research questions on the topic of children's perspectives on their learning and in research
- provide some recommended reading to follow up the issues discussed.

The Victorian maxim that children should be 'seen and not heard' somehow still pervades policy and practice in early childhood education and care – despite decades of work which has argued that the 'voice' of the child is important to matters that affect them and their lives. Whilst many might agree that, of course, it's important to listen to children – in the ways that the UN Convention on the Rights of the Child highlights – there are still many instances where young children are effectively silenced. Their perspectives are not taken into account, sometimes lip-service is paid to their views, and the notion of equality where children's perspectives are concerned still has a long way to go.

This chapter examines some of the small but growing studies that have focused on children's perspectives – on their play, their learning and the assessment of that learning. It highlights the power of children's voices when their perspectives are genuinely elicited, and the difficulties facing many adults – including early childhood educators – in really placing children's perspectives at the centre of their practice.

The chapter draws on recent studies to show how powerful it can be to work from a children's perspectives approach and how this can illuminate learning in ways that imposed outcomes measures never can.

CHILDREN'S 'VOICES' AND PEDAGOGY

Imagine early childhood settings where practice was based on what children said and how they perceived their worlds. Whilst many settings might claim to operate with respectful concern from children's perspectives, in reality, few can claim to hold children's voices and children's perspectives as central. In England, and many other countries, this is because national policies around, for example, curriculum and pedagogy, are outcomes focused, and pay little attention to the specific needs and interests of individual children. In 2017, the government in England was not alone in proposing a school readiness test, to check children's skills (particularly in reading) on entry to school. Similar tests were proposed by policy-makers in parts of Australia and the US, in part as a way of judging school effectiveness based on progress of children later on in their school careers. Such an approach to assessment leaves little, if any, room for children's voices and in the main sets out what children can't do rather than what they can do and what interests them. So, what might a setting based on children's views of what is important look like? How might a setting develop curriculum, pedagogy and assessment practices, which are truly child centred? It is true that there have been some fine examples of such approaches; the Reggio Emilia preschools and infant-toddler centres in Northern Italy provide us with one world-renowned example. But it is fair to say that such settings are exceptions – one reason why thousands of people seek to learn about Reggio Emilia approaches. Where national policies often push against initiatives (such as child-centred practices and pedagogies) the job of practitioners who want to develop a more subtle approach to pedagogy, which takes account of and is based around children's perspectives, is all the harder. Working with young children in a system where there are imposed 'one size fits all' outcomes-based policies – with their accountability measures, inspections and audits – and seeking to balance this with a proper respect for young children's capabilities and concerns is a tricky business, but one that many early years practitioners find themselves confronting day in, day out. They try to fulfil the conditions of their employment whilst also balancing the needs of the children.

Many policies are drawn up from the perspectives of 'what do we need this generation to be able to do when they are 5, 15, 25, 50 years old?'. Few policies are drawn up by focusing first on the young children themselves, at a particular 'now' point in time, and so beginning with questions such as: Who is this young person? What is he interested in? What worries her? What upsets him? What does she enjoy? What can he do? What does she do at home? What makes this child 'belong'?

Taking questions such as these as starting points means that there is a greater likelihood of pedagogical approaches that are relevant to each individual child and, as such, inclusive of *all* who join the setting community. Taking questions such as these as beginnings of pedagogy means that parental and community involvement are necessities. Taking questions such as these as starting points requires a high level of practitioner knowledge, understanding, skill and sensitivity. Settings where children's voices and children's perspectives are attended to by practitioners as the lead motivations in pedagogy would, it seems, offer early years experiences which are relevant, inclusive and sensitive to capabilities and needs. As Sommer et al. (2013) put it:

> instead of arguing for a certain programme to early years education, we try to focus attention to certain features and aspects that could be of importance for a child's right to education. (2013: 549)

They argue that there is an important distinction between 'child perspective' – where adults seek to understand children's perceptions but can only reach an approximation from their own (adult) perspective – and 'children's perspectives' – whereby children's own experiences and meaning making in their world are the focus of adult understanding. Sommer et al. have argued that working with children's perspectives has important implications for professional knowledge:

> First, top-down theorising stemming from the so-called 'grand developmental' period in psychology becomes external to a child perspective by objectifying the child. Second, some recent contributions from the 'new child view' reflect a genuine child perspective, while others appear conceptually somewhat fluffy. (2013: 463)

There is no doubt that sensitivity to and evolving practices that embrace children's perspectives require enhanced professional knowledge, skills and understanding and a deep and respectful sense of and attitude to humanity.

This chapter examines recent studies and theoretical perspectives that have attempted, to different degrees, to advocate or develop pedagogy that stems from listening to the voices of young children, however young they may be, and by whatever means they use to express themselves.

RESEARCH ONTO CHILDREN'S PERSPECTIVES OF WHAT THEY DO IN ECEC SETTINGS

What children themselves think about how they spend their time and what they do in preschool settings has been a matter of growing interest over the last two decades.

A small but growing number of research projects have fashioned innovative and inclusive research methods and approaches to gain a greater understanding of how children perceive their childhood worlds. Generating rich seams of data, they tell the detail of children's fine grain experiences, what's meaningful to them, and what matters are of most importance in their days. There are still not enough of these studies, but those that have been published recently make insightful contributions, which create a window on children's learning worlds and their broader lives.

An ethnographic study with five-year-old children in Australia (Breathnach et al., 2017) used children's accounts and video observation to investigate how they understood play in their classroom. They found that 'teacher-framed agendas' influenced what children thought and did, and the extent to which teachers afforded children the agency 'to engage in self-chosen activities and to design and negotiate their play spaces' (2017: 1). In a context where, like so many countries, academic achievements are increasingly given higher value as outcomes of ECEC, this study sought to understand the ways in which young children aged 4.5 years to 5.5 years (13 girls and 12 boys) in one Brisbane classroom, 'accounted for and engaged in classroom activities' (2017: 4).

Breathnach et al. (2017) identified three themes: (1) 'children frame their activities within adult agendas' – of timetables, routines and activities set by the teachers, (2) 'children value agentic opportunities in classroom activities' – whereby they could choose and take come control over what they did, but these opportunities were somewhat limited, and (3) 'children initiate self-described 'work' practices' – which tended to occur when children were free to choose (and often included practices such as writing – which they indicated they preferred not to do when it was teacher prescribed). Breathnach et al. propose that children's definitions of 'work' and 'play' suggested that 'work' involved the teacher, whereas play – and 'choice' – occurred during self-initiated activity. The authors conclude that:

> Planning with children – rather than for children – can provide opportunities for educators and children to identify together possibilities to support children's agentic participation in classroom activities. Affording children agentic opportunities may also promote their self-initiated participation in activities in more meaningful and flexible ways. This consideration means a re-focusing of teacher–child talk around classroom activities in the context of agentic opportunities for children rather than the framing of activities as distinct pursuits. (2017: 12)

Taking time to find out what children think about how they spend their time, and what they think about the play and learning activities they are provided with, can lead to insights that will help teachers create curriculum contexts where children have more agency, and potentially more enjoyment and motivation, in what they do. As Breathnach et al. (2017) point out, writing as a set activity by the teacher and writing in the context of self-initiated play may look like very similar activities – but the addition of agency may well mean that children's ownership of and motivation for the task are enhanced. They point out the value of children's 'insider knowledge' which, if adults can access it, may help to reduce the assumptions that adults often make about what children think, and provide greater insight into how they respond to 'work' and 'play' in the early years classroom.

Given the quantity of research publications about play and early learning, the number focusing on the children's own perspectives on what they do that *we* call 'play' remains low. Despite a growing commitment to what is often referred to as 'the voice of the child', stemming from developments since the UN Convention on the Rights of the Child, there remain relatively few studies that actually *listen* to what it is that children themselves are saying. Too many studies still seek to measure, count and evaluate through adult frameworks and perspectives, the actions, words and play of young children. Colliver and Fleer (2016) sought to address this concern in a study of 28 two- to five-year-olds' perspectives on what they learned when playing. Drawing on a rich data set, including children's comments and observed play episodes, they demonstrated what children across the full age range of their participants, including the two-year-olds, knew about their own learning – one could say some were experts in their own learning.

The findings of this study offer a fresh view of understanding young children's thinking and provoke a challenge to educators to see through different lenses, which seem to magnify the detail of children's thought. What Colliver and Fleer (2016) give us in this study is the confidence to interpret, with a better understanding, children's perspectives and their learning. Looking differently at what children do and listening with attentiveness to what they say can give educators a more robust way of engaging with children in their playful learning so that they, in turn, can challenge the children with more tuned-in guidance and interaction. This study offers a challenge to rigid outcomes-driven frameworks for the early years curriculum, which are being imposed in many parts of the world.

Let's focus on a child for a moment:

Arnold was playing alone using some small wooden bricks of different colours and shapes. Kneeling, surrounded by the bricks, he reached and stretched and crawled, he searched around him – until he found the brick he wanted next. He sometimes turned them over in his hand … before placing them. He whispered quietly to himself as he examined, moved and placed each brick in the place he selected for it. He worked quite slowly, seemingly working out a plan as he went along. Nothing appeared to distract him, even quite noisy play by a group of children nearby … Quite what he was doing was not clear … he frowned slightly as he paid diligent attention to his self-chosen task. To any adult – the task was not clear. Eventually … he sat back on his heels and a barely detectable smile came to his face … The bricks were clustered – some quite high – in six multi-coloured configurations of a range of shapes. They varied in height, breadth and form. Arnold was watching his bricks – still sitting on his heels – smiling gently when a passing adult (who had not been watching Arnold) said – 'Hi Arnold – I like the way you sorted out the bricks' as she walked by. Arnold looked a bit puzzled … A few seconds later he left – making his way outdoors.

We have no clue as to what Arnold was thinking – but from close observation of what he was doing, his full immersion in his self-chosen task was palpable. Unless Arnold chooses to tell, we shall never know what he was thinking – and we should not assume that we do. Arnold was not – I think – simply sorting the bricks, he was engaged in something much more complex. When we focus on children – rather than pre-determined and imposed outcomes – sometimes we must be patient, and sometimes we must live with a degree of not knowing – and trust them.

STUDIES FOCUSING ON CHILDREN'S INVOLVEMENT IN ASSESSMENT OF THEIR OWN LEARNING

In the last decade or so, it has become an accepted (but by no means universally expected) part of early years practice to involve children in thinking about and compiling evidence of their own learning. This practice is known by many different names – each having their own distinctive traits – but essentially all aim to involve children, to different degrees, in compiling a document which sets out what they have learned in a given period of time. Such documents are intended to be personal, child friendly and to feature the things the children themselves see as significant to them. Research studies in recent years have varied in their approach, but as this section will demonstrate, there remains a considerable amount of work to do if children are truly to be equal and valued participants in documenting their learning.

Perhaps the pioneering approach to children's involvement in documenting their learning is Margaret Carr's work in New Zealand on children's 'learning stories' (Carr, 2001). This takes a socio-cultural approach to recording children's learning by involving the children, their parents and practitioners in compiling a picture of children's learning disposition – not necessarily 'accomplishments' but their positioning for, or approach to, learning. For Carr, a child's learning story includes description, decision-making, discussion and documentation. Children first work with their parents to describe what they can do or have done. They then participate in a decision-making process to select what, from their learning engagements, is included in their personal 'learning story'. This includes discussion of their achievements, likes, dislikes, ambitions, with an adult (and sometimes other children), and finally the selected item (account, drawing, photo or a combination of all of these) is added to the learning story in a process of documentation – often led by the adult.

Carr (2001: 92) writes that learning stories are 'participation repertoires', each of which encompasses 'skills + knowledge + intent + social partners and practices + tools + motivation'; thus children's active involvement in this process is stressed. For Carr, the learning stories process is inclusive in that children's words and perspectives (and those of their families) are central and their own cultural capital is foregrounded. Carr's approach to assessment is one that places assessment in a complete learning cycle, which is used to inform next steps. Carr (2011) has continued to emphasise shared dialogue between teachers and young children as part of the learning and reflection process, which includes open-ended questions that genuinely invite children's engagement.

In England, Garrick et al. (2010) examined children's experiences of the foundation stage at that time – focusing on 146 three- to five-year-olds in 15 English early years settings, funded by the Department for Children, Schools and Families. This fitted with the UNCRC requirement that governments consult children on the things that mattered to them and provided an indicator, at least, that the then government had an interest in the young children's perspectives. Focusing, amongst other things, on children's involvement in their learning records, Garrick et al. concluded that:

 Many children we spoke to did not recognize the setting record as their own and some children were unhappy that they could not understand the written information. (2010: 39)

This suggests that although children have personalised files which documented what they had achieved, the children themselves did not take full ownership of those documents, did not have a full say in their contents, and that these were, on the whole, documents for staff accountability rather than personalised archives of an individual child's learning. The children were reported to have expressed some unhappiness about this lack of ownership.

Bath (2012) uses data from the Garrick et al. (2010) study on children's experiences of the Early Years Foundation Stage (DCSF, 2008).

Bath argues that children's participation in pedagogical documentation:

> should be to enable adult and child communicative cooperation, rather than to provide statements about children's progress which feed into the 'discourses of quality in early childhood. (2012: 190)

Taking the findings of Garrick et al. (2010), Bath asks: 'How can we achieve a pedagogy which involves children in documentation?' (2012: 200). She concludes that this requires a pedagogical process where 'knowledge-building by all of the participants' is continuous and recognises that it takes place in a context of 'acceptance of uncertainty and the importance of different and simultaneous perspectives' of those involved. She calls for a climate where adults and children 'work together on documenting learning and develop ever more varied and expressive ways of communicating' (2012: 200).

This, of course, requires highly skilled and sensitive professionals who have learned how to tune in such that they can attempt to see things from children's perspectives. Dayan and Ziv (2012) suggest that this might begin with involving student early childhood practitioners in children's perspectives research – so that – from the beginning – a focus on children's views is established through initial training and development.

TAKING CHILDREN'S VIEWS SERIOUSLY IN ECEC PEDAGOGY AND PRACTICE

Perhaps it was working with children's perspectives that was the intended meaning of the Plowden Report, *Children and their Primary Schools*, which recommended future development for primary education for children in England and Wales in 1967. Some 50 years later, these words still hold a truth worth remembering:

> At the heart of the educational process lies the child. No advances in policy, no acquisitions of new equipment have their desired effect unless they are in harmony with the nature of the child, unless they are fundamentally acceptable to him [sic]. (The Plowden Report, 1967: Part 2, Chapter 2, para 9)

So how do we do all this? How do we create practices and research where children's perspectives are core? And will we know it when we see it? The research featured in this chapter gives some indication of the attempts to understand and, in some cases, enact pedagogies that value or (rarely) are driven by children's perspectives on their worlds. Sommer et al. (2013) set out five criteria, which also form a clear set of values, in response to a similar question:

1. Seeing the child as a person.
2. Empathic participation with the child.

---

3. An interpretative attitude of respecting the child's utterances and world of meaning.
4. Guiding the child in a sensitive way by adjusting and expanding their initiatives
5. Early care and education is a dialogical process between the child and the carer/teacher, where both contribute to the learning objective

Of course, such criteria necessitate a good deal of working through in any setting so that shared understandings can be established, and clarity about how practices that adhere to each value are developed. According to Sommer et al., working with the five criteria requires the following:

> To meet each child in their experience means to see both the child's experience uttered 'in action,' which can be observed by the teacher, and as a 'mental act,' which demands more effort and willingness to interpret the child's perspective and see the child as a subject, a unique person. (2013: 468)

It seems at present that too many policies leave little room for practitioners to develop practices that hold children's perspectives as central. There remains, in many national policies across several countries, a 'top-down' didactic response to early childhood pedagogical practices and a lack of understanding about children's perspectives. This chapter has shown what can happen when children are the centre of the pedagogies of their early childhood settings and how research which includes children's perspectives can be enriched by their contribution. There are important contributions to be drawn from some Scandinavian research, but on the whole, there is much more for research to do and one important contribution that research could make would be to provide policy-makers with insightful examples of pedagogy based on children's perspectives. This, of course, necessitates a value position where policy-makers take children's views seriously and move away from a view that childhood is for making adults who are economically contributing citizens, rather than seeing the importance of nurturing childhood *for now* which will in turn equip them *to be* the adults they eventually grow into.

RESEARCH QUESTIONS ON CHILDREN'S PERSPECTIVES ON THEIR LEARNING AND IN RESEARCH

Whilst there has been an increase in involving children in research and thinking of children as agents and architects of their own learning, it is important to be clear that fundamentally researchers must not waste children's time. Some important insights have been generated by researchers who make sensitive use of evolving methodologies (and technologies) to

(Continued)

(Continued)

learn more about children's perspectives on their own learning and on things that matter to them. Such studies offer a most useful and growing catalogue of children's perspectives that, taken together, contribute much to our understanding, which can be used to evolve practices that better fit young children's learning.

Some suggested research questions for early years practitioners and students:

- How do early years practitioners interact with children in ways that allow children to lead the learning and bring their perspective to that learning?
  A study of this kind could involve interviewing of some sort but might also need to include observation.

- What do children say about their play and learning?
  Focusing on this as a research project would mean that it is necessary to make close observations of children, and probably video record the children playing. Playing back the film to the children and asking them to talk about what they were doing can open up some important understandings.

- In what ways do planned learning outcomes support and suppress children's agency in learning?
  A study focusing on this question would need an analysis of the policy documents that set out planned learning outcomes. It would also need to include thoughtful and reflective observations of children playing and a good analysis of the adult interactions and their rationale for the decisions they make about whether or not to 'steer' the children's learning.

- How might assessment practices in a setting include children's perspectives on their learning and achievements?
  This sort of study would need to try things out, it would need to develop ways of identifying learning moments that were meaningful to individual children and find ways of recording them which allowed the children to retain ownership over their record.

A NOTE ON RESEARCH ETHICS AND INTEGRITY

Any work with young children requires patient and sensitive data collection approaches. Of course the permission of parents is needed, but it is crucial in studies where children are involved in giving their views, that they are given an opportunity to understand what they are participating in and to refuse whenever they wish. Research reporting children's perspectives must also be faithfully reported, so as to report the uncovered truths and their intended meanings.

RECOMMENDED READING

Colliver, Y. and Fleer, M. (2016) 'I already know what I learned': Young children's perspectives on learning through play. *Early Child Development and Care*, 186 (10): 1559–1570. DOI: 10.1080/03004430.2015.1111880.

A qualitative case study which involved 28 two- to five-year-old children in a Brisbane preschool. Methodologically clear and respectful, this study draws out the perspectives of the children on what they believed they were learning when they played. Taking a cultural–historical theory stance towards analysis, the paper challenges the view that children are not aware and expert in their own learning.

Sommer, D., Pramling Samuelsson, I. and Hundeide, K. (2013) Early childhood care and education: A child perspective paradigm. *European Early Childhood Education Research Journal*, 21 (4): 459–475. DOI: 10.1080/1350293X.2013.845436.

This paper defines 'child perspectives' and 'children's perspectives' and sets out, with exemplars, five basic assumptions behind a child perspective-oriented approach in practice.

REFERENCES

Bath, C. (2012) 'I can't read it; I don't know': Young children's participation in the pedagogical documentation of English early childhood education and care settings. *International Journal of Early Years Education, 20* (2): 190–201. DOI: 10.1080/09669760. 2012.715242.

Breathnach, H., Danby, S. and O'Gorman, L. (2017) 'Are you working or playing?' Investigating young children's perspectives of classroom activities. *International Journal of Early Years Education, 25* (4): 439–454. DOI: 10.1080/09669760.2017.1316241.

Carr, M. (2001) *Assessment in Early Childhood Settings: Learning Stories*. London: Sage.

Carr, M. (2011) Young children reflecting on their learning: Teachers' conversation strategies. *Early Years: An International Journal of Research and Development, 31* (3): 257–70.

Colliver, Y. and Fleer, M. (2016) 'I already know what I learned': young children's perspectives on learning through play. *Early Child Development and Care, 186* (10): 1559–1570. DOI: 10.1080/03004430.2015.1111880.

Dayan, Y. and Ziv, M. (2012) Children's perspective research in pre-service early childhood student education. *International Journal of Early Years Education, 20* (3): 280–289. DOI: 10.1080/09669760.2012.718114.

DCSF (Department for Children, Schools and Families) (2008) *The Early Years Foundation Stage: Setting the Standards for Learning, Development and Care for Children from Birth to Five*. London: DCSF.

Garrick, R., Bath, C., Dunn, K., Maconochie, H., Willis, B. and Wolstenholme, C. (2010) *Children's Experiences of the Foundation Stage.* Report RR071. London: DfE.

The Plowden Report (1967) *Children and their Primary Schools: A Report of the Central Advisory Council for Education (England).* London: Her Majesty's Stationery Office.

Sommer, D., Pramling Samuelsson, I. and Hundeide, K. (2013) Early childhood care and education: A child perspective paradigm. *European Early Childhood Education Research Journal, 21* (4): 459–475. DOI: 10.1080/1350293X.2013.845436.

6

POVERTY IN CHILDHOOD AND THE IMPACT OF EARLY CHILDHOOD EDUCATION AND CARE

THIS CHAPTER WILL DRAW ON INTERNATIONAL RESEARCH TO:

- think about what 'equality' means in early childhood education and care
- consider some recent research findings by leading charities on international child poverty
- suggest some research questions on the topic of childhood poverty and ECEC
- provide some recommended reading to follow up the issues discussed.

This chapter focuses on research into poverty in childhood. and the impact of ECEC on the effects of poverty. This is such a wide-ranging topic that this chapter can only begin to scratch the surface. The wide range of international research means that this chapter cannot provide anything approaching a comprehensive overview but rather offers an urgent sense of the deep issues that poverty in childhood can lead to, and the contribution that research can make to reduce the perpetuation of inequalities. The broad geo-political issues of war and natural disasters such as flood and famine lead to drastic changes in the living circumstances and health of families, bringing poverty, struggle and death. Families forced to leave their homelands to seek asylum elsewhere, fleeing their home countries as refugees, means that by circumstance children can move from a place of comfort and safety to the utter vulnerability that leaving everything behind can lead to.

This chapter considers some of the research by major charities about global poverty.

WHAT DOES 'EQUALITY' MEAN IN ECEC?

Inequity imperils millions of children and threatens the future of the world. (UNICEF, 2016: xi)

So reads the opening statement of UNICEF'S 2016 report on the world's children. It continues:

> Before they draw their first breath, the life chances of poor and excluded children are often being shaped by inequities. Disadvantage and discrimination against their communities and families will help determine whether they live or die, whether they have a chance to learn and later earn a decent living. Conflicts, crises and climate-related disasters deepen their deprivation and diminish their potential. (UNICEF, 2016: xi)

The global picture includes all forms of inequity, some of which need adequate funding to alleviate by providing health care, infrastructure and other interventions. Whilst all effects of inequity need a strong political will, some aspects of poverty may be at least reduced by removing the impoverishment brought about by a lack of education and proper care in early childhood.

Down the years, early childhood education has been seen as a panacea for many inequalities in society, not solely in relation to learning but also in areas of health, well-being and participation. Indeed, early intervention within ECEC has often been the 'go to' to address inequalities and promote equality. The renowned economist Heckman (2000) and sociologist Esping-Andersen (2009) have both supported the view that work with preschool-age children makes an important contribution to equalising societies. Many philosophers have paid considerable attention to the nature and imperative of equality, the nature and meaning of opportunity and the morality of relative advantage and disadvantage, which there is not space for here; however, Morabito and Vandenbroeck (2015) provide an overview and discussion of these issues as the basis for their argument about equality of opportunity as a continuum ranging from Responsibility-oriented Equality of Opportunity (REOp) to Circumstances-oriented Equality of Opportunity (CEOp), and argue that focusing on circumstances is a more effective way of addressing equality in early childhood. These authors suggest that:

> there is concurrence in defining the *equalisandum* as opportunities, as goods, services, needs, resources, enabling individuals to freely choose and pursue their life plans. The opportunities to equalise are those that are unequally distributed due to 'circumstances' beyond the individual's responsibility. As a result, equalising opportunities means compensating those who suffer from negative endowments (by neutralising or maximising the minimum), so that difference in life achievements will be the result of individual responsibility, preference, and free choices. (2015: 459)

In 2017, in a small, pretty village in northern England, the secretary of the local school went to the foodbank to collect food for a young mother, too ashamed and frightened to go herself, so that she could feed her young children. When families suffer inequalities due to poverty, this means the children in those families do too. Those families living in poverty or on low incomes are likely to be less able to give their children the opportunities that families on higher incomes can provide. Yet redistribution of wealth is not the usual policy option; rather, policies seem to focus on enhanced provision for young children so as to enhance equal opportunities in the future. This returns us to the issue of investment in childhood *for the now* versus investment in children *for the future*, which was discussed in Chapter 3. Indeed two major reports for the UK government drew attention to the view that income was not the only issue in tackling child poverty and closing the poverty gap. The Field Review on poverty and life chances (Field, 2010) was sub-titled *Preventing Poor Children Becoming Poor Adults*, and drew extensively on research in many fields to argue for early intervention programmes for children living in poverty. Field argued that:

> Even if the money were available to lift all children out of income poverty in the short term, it is far from clear that this move would in itself close the achievement gap. (2010: 16)

And continued:

> To do this, it is necessary to shift the focus of the child poverty strategy so that it also addresses the factors that affect life chances, with the ultimate aim of achieving a programme of childhood interventions which can overcome the influence of income and social class. (2010: 27)

The following year the Allen Review (2011) focused on early intervention with a startling cover image of CT scans of the brains of two three-year-olds, one labelled as 'normal', the other of a child who experienced 'extreme neglect'; this emphasised a key theme of the report that the period from birth to three years was crucial for development and growth, and:

> In that period, neglect, the wrong type of parenting and other adverse experiences can have a profound effect on how children are emotionally 'wired'. This will deeply influence their future responses to events and their ability to empathise with other people. (2011: xiii)

Both these government reports were arguing for intervention to change behaviours as a means to addressing future inequalities rather than redistributing wealth or enhancing the income of poor families; thus this favours the child *now* who might benefit from early childhood education as an early intervention to enhance the chances of the same child in the *future*, as a citizen able to contribute to the economy because their life chances are enhanced. Whilst this can go some way to breaking the cycle of future inequalities, it does little to address the misery of poverty for the child in the *now*.

Morabito and Vandenbroeck (2015) challenge this position:

> Another often forgotten, yet important issue is that interventions or investments at an early age are expensive if one wishes to have both the high quality that is needed for effective impact on children's development and the assurance that provision reaches poor families. The earlier one starts, the more expensive early childhood education is (Barnett and Masse, 2007). This is especially the case when one wishes to achieve universal access, since comparative studies show that regions with universal access have higher enrolment rates by families in poverty than regions with targeted provision, even when targeted at the poorest families (Van Lancker, 2013). Generating the necessary public funding therefore requires substantial taxation. (2015: 466)

It is this necessary public investment that will go some way to creating equal opportunities, but further, to achieving *realised* equality, where children can take up and benefit from the opportunities on offer, leading to tangible outcomes where inequalities are minimised.

As many recent research studies have demonstrated, poverty is a key factor in underachievement in education (Ayoub et al., 2009; De Feyter and Winsler, 2009; Cooper, 2010; Mistry et al., 2010). In a US study of 'persistence in the face of academic challenge', which involved 103 disadvantaged preschool children attending Head Start programmmes, Brown (2009) concluded: 'Some poor children, it seems, will face an academic double jeopardy: school entry cognitive skill gaps coupled with a lack of persistence in the face of challenge' (2009: 182).

Focusing on children in Europe, Leseman and Slot (2014) recommend that higher quality ECEC provision with greater attention given to culturally relevant curricula is needed in order to support children's needs adequately where they are living in poverty. This, alongside multi-disciplinary provision, they argue, combined with family support and bilingual support, will enhance the inclusiveness of ECEC and go some way to 'breaking the cycle of poverty' in Europe.

RECENT RESEARCH FINDINGS ON INTERNATIONAL CHILD POVERTY

 Unless the world tackles inequity today, by 2030,

- 167 million children will live in extreme poverty (UNICEF, 2016: 3)
- 60 million children under age five will die between 2017 and 2030 – half of them babies (United Nations Inter-agency Group for Child Mortality Estimation, 2017)
- 60 million children of primary school age will be out of school (UNICEF, 2016: 3).

The statistics on poverty are shocking, and it seems to be the research by major charities that informs us best. Compared to the richest children, the poorest children are 1.9 times as likely to die before age five (United Nations Inter-agency Group for Child Mortality Estimation, 2017). Of course income (or wealth) is a significant factor in the effects of poverty and moving out of poverty, but so is the education of the mother:

 Across much of South Asia and sub-Saharan Africa, children with mothers who received no education are almost three times as likely to die before age 5 as children of mothers with secondary education. Education enables women to delay and space births, secure access to maternal and child health care and seek treatment for children when they fall ill. (UNICEF, 2016: 3)

UNICEF identifies education as 'one of the most effective drivers of development and the greatest equalizer of opportunity'. Its 2016 report clearly states:

 Without quality education, disadvantaged children are far more likely to be trapped as adults in low-skilled, poorly paid and insecure employment, preventing them from breaking intergenerational cycles of disadvantage. But a greater focus on early childhood development, on increasing education access and quality, and on providing education in emergencies will yield cascading benefits for both this generation and the next. (2016: 6)

The responsibility of early childhood educators is huge, and given that we know high quality provision for the youngest children can make such a positive difference to the life chances of young children in their childhoods, and in their futures as parents themselves, it is a both a clear moral and a prudent economic responsibility of governments to properly and securely resource such provision.

Moving from the global picture to the UK, the number of children living in poverty has increased in recent years with 30% of children living in poverty (Joseph Rowntree Foundation, 2017). The Institute for Fiscal Studies forecasts a rise in child poverty to some 5 million children by 2020, and a non-working, one-parent family is predicted to be worse off by £2800 a year by 2020 (Department of Work and Pensions, 2017). With more than one in four children in the UK living in poverty we need to be aware of the impacts of poverty on children's lives and well-being, and the UK figures are so appalling that it is important to rehearse them repeatedly. Consider that:

- Children from poorer backgrounds lag at all stages of education.
- By the age of three, poorer children are likely to experience a gap of some nine months of development and learning, between them and children from more wealthy backgrounds (Shelter, 2006).
- By the end of primary school, pupils receiving free school meals are estimated to be almost three terms behind their more affluent peers academically.
- Children's whose families are poorer, may miss out on events, parties, trips and other community experiences (Child Poverty Action Group, 2018).
- The majority of children who die at birth or in early childhood are born into poorer families (CPAG, 2018).
- Poorer families usually live in poor housing which brings with it stress, ill health and threats to general well-being (Shelter, 2006).

In the US, the picture is no less alarming: out of the 11 million babies and toddlers under three years of age 5.2 million live in low-income families (45%) and 2.6 million live in poor families (23%) (Jiang et al., 2017). And of course, one of the largest groups living in poverty are children from immigrant families. In the US, Latino families make up the largest immigrant group, and some 37% have been estimated to be living in poverty, and at risk of many health difficulties as well as vulnerable when it comes to 'school readiness' (Ansari and Winsler, 2012). Due to poverty, many Latino children do not achieve as well as their white-American peers (Galindo and Fuller, 2010). Given the gap in well-being and achievement from birth, children such as these, who live in poverty and whose families struggle on little or no income, have been found to do well in terms of social-emotional skills and behaviour (De Feyter and Winsler, 2009), and so perhaps balance their lack of curriculum capital with skills in social, emotional and behavioural strengths. This, according to Magnuson et al. (2006), bodes well when they begin school, perhaps because they are not a problem in terms of taking up teacher time to deal with difficult behaviour, even though they may struggle with the curriculum. However, not all young children are able to access preschool provision that might support them and boys, more than girls, struggle considerably on entry to school, a starting point for a lifetime of struggle due to perpetual under-achievement (Koh and Neuman, 2009).

TACKLING THE INJUSTICE OF POVERTY

This chapter has touched on some of the research on child poverty and ECEC. In doing so it has only skimmed the surface of the complex and human issues that often invite discrimination as a result of poverty. Of the issues highlighted here it is important to acknowledge that simply by virtue of their age, some young children often face discrimination: they often do not have a real 'voice' and are dependent upon adults to identify and meet their needs. This is particularly so in the case of babies and toddlers, many of whom, because their early years practitioners are low paid and work in poor conditions of service, suffer an unequal start in their life journey.

A recent review of early childhood education research in England and Wales (Payler and Wood, 2014) urged that all early years practitioners should:

 have a core understanding of social inequalities and cultural differences, and their impact on families, and [be] able to look at the world from a parent's point of view, whilst still maintaining fully professional relationships that allow them to carry out safeguarding functions. (2014: 6)

Understanding the meaning of poverty and the impacts of inequalities is indeed 'core' to the work of early years practitioners. According to Ridge (2003):

an understanding of childhood poverty that is grounded in the lives and experiences of children is an essential part of addressing the intractable nature of child poverty and has the potential to add considerably to our capacity for addressing social and structural inequalities within childhood. (2003: 9)

Therefore, if ECEC is to meet the high demands placed on it to contribute to achieving equality, addressing inequalities and challenging discrimination, further investment is needed, for three reasons. First, to enhance the equality of staff in many aspects of provision where profit margins often mean that pay is low and where there are few – if any – highly qualified staff who attract higher salaries (a factor that has been shown to make a difference to children's development and progress) (Early et al., 2007). Second, investment is needed to provide ongoing professional development for all staff if early attendance in an early years setting is really to count as meaningful and effective early intervention.

Finally, hungry and frightened children can't learn; tackling the inequalities of poverty requires commitment at the highest political level to lift whole families out of the poverty trap so that whilst their young children attend high quality provision, they and their families – at the same time – are not hungry, not cold, not homeless, not ill and not depressed. Inequalities cannot be tackled on the cheap, and equality requires investment and global political commitment. It's not impossible.

RESEARCH QUESTIONS ON CHILDHOOD POVERTY AND ECEC

In a study involving practitioners in urban and rural settings in the US and England, Simpson et al. (2017) discuss the importance of a 'Pedagogy of Listening' in relation to the negative effects of childhood poverty on children's preparedness for school. They argue that listening helps practitioners to understand children's vulnerabilities as well as their dynamic and curious approaches to learning, and also argue that:

> Listening is central to foundational and contemporary theories and approaches in the early years – 'having at their heart' the importance of 'intense listening and a desire to tune into children' … Listening therefore potentially allows practitioners to become sensitive to the impact of inequality and to gain an understanding of disadvantaged children's priorities, interests and concerns therefore allowing children to have some participation within the construction of pedagogical space. (2017: 179)

In their study they asked practitioners to think about children they worked with who they considered to be living in poverty and to assess seven aspects of their development (social development, emotional development, health, motor skills, cognitive skills, respectfulness, and ability to stay on-task) on a scale of 1–9 (1 being 'below average' and 9 being 'above average'). Practitioners' rankings were described as pessimistic, but importantly their 'recognition of poverty status did not feature prominently in shaping the interactions of practitioners with children' (Simpson et al., 2017: 182). Thus if children are treated similarly, regardless of their living conditions, differentiation according to need is less likely to happen. Simpson et al. warn against the 'organising out' of young children's voices, thus leading to a lack of attention being paid to their particular needs and capacity to make choices in ECEC settings. Importantly the study concludes that: 'Listening potentially contributes to resilience building but reform of practice is essential and will not fully materialise until it is recognised that such a pedagogical approach is about rights' (2017: 187).

Research continues to identify the 'attainment gap' between children disadvantaged by poverty and their non-disadvantaged peers (Mathers and Smees, 2014). This is often blamed on the inadequate quality of ECEC environments, but clearly more needs to be done to enable children disadvantaged by poverty to take advantage of the opportunities presented to them just as their non-disadvantaged peers are already poised to exploit what is offered to them.

Some suggested research questions for early years practitioners and students:

○ What are the perceptions of early years practitioners on working with children disadvantaged by poverty?

This question will require dialogue with practitioners, by questionnaire or some form of interview. The format could follow something similar to the study by Simpson et al. (2017) or it could ask different questions about whether practitioners work with children living in poverty and what they think the effects of poverty are on children's learning.

○ How do early childhood practices specifically support children disadvantaged by poverty?

Some answers to this question could be obtained by talking with practitioners or by observational studies.

○ What are the effects of poverty on children living in the local area?

This question could be explored by focusing on specific children; due regard would need to be given to the considerable ethical issues but just because it is difficult to do this, it is not a reason to avoid the question. An alternative way to investigate this question is to look back at childhood from, say, the school leaving figures of the current year and trace childhood poverty trends using school achievements data, pupil premium data, and other reports on medical and housing data to identify the effects of poverty on achievement on leaving school.

A NOTE ON RESEARCH ETHICS AND INTEGRITY

Researching inequality inevitably gives rise to the need to be acutely sensitive to the potential vulnerabilities of those who participate. It will be important when focusing on the effects of poverty, and other issues of disadvantage, to approach the studies with great care. This does not simply mean attending diligently to issues of anonymity and confidentiality, but it will be important to 'do no harm'. Opening up a discussion on the disadvantages experienced by families, or of how practitioners are alert to and try to mitigate effects of disadvantage, can call for considerable attention to be paid to the feelings and effects on individuals.

RECOMMENDED READING

Jiang, Y., Granja, M.R. and Koball, H. (2017) *Basic Facts About Low-Income Children: Children Under 3 Years, 2015*. New York: National Centre for Children in Poverty.

A report on low income and poverty in the US, highlighting the impact on young children, and in particular on immigrant families living in poverty.

Leseman, P.P.M. and Slot, P.L. (2014) Breaking the cycle of poverty: Challenges for European early childhood education and care. *European Early Childhood Education Research Journal*, 22 (3): 314–326. DOI: 10.1080/1350293X.2014.912894.

Focusing on children in Europe, this study recommends that higher quality ECEC provision with greater attention given to culturally relevant curricula is needed in order to support children's needs adequately where they are living in poverty. This paper also argues for multi-disciplinary provision, family support and bilingual support to enhance the inclusiveness of ECEC and contribute to the work needed to 'breaking the cycle of poverty' in Europe.

Simpson, D., Loughran, S., Lumsden, E., Mazzocco, P., McDowall Clark, R. and Winterbottom, C. (2017) 'Seen but not heard': Practitioners work with poverty and the organising out of disadvantaged children's voices and participation in the early years. *European Early Childhood Education Research Journal*, 25 (2): 177–188. DOI: 10. 1080/1350293X.2017.1288014.

This paper provides an important perspective on the importance of active listening to young children's experiences of the effects of poverty. It draws attention to the negative effects of childhood poverty on children's preparedness for school. In this US/English study the authors argue that listening helps practitioners to understand children's vulnerabilities as well as their approaches to learning.

UNICEF (2016) *The State of the World's Children: A Fair Chance for Every Child.* New York: UNICEF.

This report by one of the major charities challenging and tackling child poverty highlights the state of child poverty globally and provides important statistics country by country. It points out the importance of education and also of the need for infrastructures which enable young children to take advantage of education provision.

REFERENCES

Allen, G. (2011) *Early Intervention: The Next Steps. An Independent Report to Her Majesty's Government.* London: The Cabinet Office/HM Government.
Ansari, A. and Winsler, A. (2012) School readiness among low-income Latino children attending family childcare versus centre-based care. *Early Child Development and Care*, *182* (11): 1465–1485. DOI: 10.1080/03004430.2011.622755.

Ayoub, C., O'Connor, E., Rappolt-Schlictmann, G., Vallotton, C., Raikes, H. and Chazan-Cohen, R. (2009) Cognitive skill performance among young children living in poverty: Risk, change, and the promotive effects of Early Head Start. *Early Childhood Research Quarterly*, *24* (3): 289–305. DOI: 10.1016/j.ecresq.2009.04.001.

Barnardo's (2017) Child poverty statistics and facts. www.barnardos.org.uk/ what_we_do/our_work/child_poverty/child_poverty_what_is_poverty/child_poverty_ statistics_facts.htm (accessed 7 February 2018).

Barnett, W.S. and Masse, L.N. (2007) Comparative benefit-cost analysis of the Abecedarian Program and its policy implications. *Economics of Education Review*, *26*: 113–125.

Brown, E.D. (2009) Persistence in the face of academic challenge for economically disadvantaged children. *Journal of Early Childhood Research*, *7* (2): 173–184. DOI: 10.1177/1476718X09102650.

Child Poverty Action Group (2018) *The Impact of Poverty*. Available at: http://cpag.org.uk/ content/impact-poverty (accessed 11 March 2018)

Cooper, C.E. (2010) Family poverty, school-based parental involvement, and policy-focused protective factors in kindergarten. *Early Childhood Research Quarterly*, *25* (4): 480–492. DOI: 10.1016/j.ecresq.2010.03.005.

De Feyter, J. and Winsler, A. (2009) The early developmental competencies and school readiness of low-income, immigrant children: Influences of generation, race/ethnicity, and national origins. *Early Childhood Research Quarterly*, *24*: 411–431.

Department of Work and Pensions (2017) *Households Below Average Income: An Analysis of the UK Income Distribution: 1994/95–2015/16*. London: DWP. www.gov.uk/government/ uploads/system/uploads/attachment_data/file/600091/households-below-average-income-1994-1995-2015-2016.pdf (accessed 7 February 2018).

Early, D., Maxwell, K., Burchinal, M., Bender, R., Ebanks, C., Henry, G., Iriondo-Perez, J., Mashburn, A.J., Pianta, R.C., Alva, S., Bryant, D., Cai, K., Clifford, R.M., Griffin, J., Howes, C., Jeon, H., Peisner-Feinberg, E., Vandergrift, N. and Zill, N. (2007) Teachers' education, classroom quality, and young children's academic skills: Results from seven studies of preschool programs. *Child Development*, *78* (2): 558–580.

Esping-Andersen, G. (2009) *The Incomplete Revolution: Adapting Welfare States to Women's New Roles*. Cambridge: Polity Press.

Field, F. (2010) *The Foundation Years: Preventing Poor Children Becoming Poor Adults. The Report of the Independent Review on Poverty and Life Chances*. London: HMSO. http://webarchive. nationalarchives.gov.uk/20110120090128/http:/povertyreview.independent. gov.uk/media/20254/poverty-report.pdf (accessed 29 January 2018)

Galindo, C. and Fuller, B. (2010) The social competence of Latino kindergarteners and growth in mathematical understanding. *Developmental Psychology*, *46* (3): 579–592.

Heckman, J. (2000) Policies to foster human capital. *Research in Economics*, *54*: 3–56.

Jiang, Y., Granja, M.R. and Koball, H. (2017) *Basic Facts About Low-Income Children: Children Under 3 Years, 2015*. New York: National Centre for Children in Poverty.

Joseph Rowntree Foundation (2017) *UK Poverty 2017 A Comprehensive Analysis of Poverty Trends and Figures*. London: Joseph Rowntree Foundation Analysis Unit. Available at: https://www.jrf.org.uk/report/uk-poverty-2017 (accessed 21 June 2018)

Koh, S. and Neuman, S.B. (2009). The impact of professional development in family child care: A practice-based approach. *Early Education and Development*, 20 (3): 537–562.

Leseman, P.P.M. and Slot, P.L. (2014) Breaking the cycle of poverty: Challenges for European early childhood education and care. *European Early Childhood Education Research Journal*, *22* (3): 314–326. DOI: 10.1080/1350293X.2014.912894.

Magnuson, K., Lahaie, C. and Waldgofel, J. (2006) Preschool and school readiness of children of immigrants. *Social Science Quarterly*, *87* (5): 1241–1262.

Mathers, S. and Smees, R. (2014) *Quality and Inequality: Do Three- and Four-year Olds in Deprived Areas Experience Lower Quality Early Years Provision?* London: Nuffield Foundation.

Mistry, R.S., Benner, A., Biesanz, J.C., Clark, S.L. and Howes, C. (2010) Family and social risk, and parental investments during the early childhood years as predictors of low-income children's school readiness outcomes. *Early Childhood Research Quarterly*, *25* (4): 432–449. DOI: 10.1016/j.ecresq.2010.01.002.

Morabito, C. and Vandenbroeck, M. (2015) Equality of opportunities, divergent conceptualisations and their implications for early childhood care and education policies. *Journal of Philosophy of Education*, *49* (3): 456–472.

Payler, J. and Wood, E. (2014) *Early Years: Policy Advice and Future Research Agendas*. A BERA Early Childhood Special Interest Group/TACTYC: Association for the Professional Development of Early Years Educators Collaboration. London: BERA and TACTYC.

Ridge, T. (2003) Listening to children: Developing a child-centred approach to childhood poverty in the UK. *Family Matters*, *65*: 4–9.

Shelter (2006) 'Chance of a Lifetime: The impact of bad housing on children's lives'. Available at: http://england.shelter.org.uk/_data/assets/pdf-file/0016/39202/Chance_of_a_Lifetime.pdf (accessed 11 June 2018)

Simpson, D., Loughran, S., Lumsden, E., Mazzocco, P., McDowall Clark, R. and Winterbottom, C. (2017) 'Seen but not heard': Practitioners work with poverty and the organising out of disadvantaged children's voices and participation in the early years. *European Early Childhood Education Research Journal*, *25* (2): 177–188. DOI: 10.1080/1350293X.2017.1288014.

UNICEF (2016) *The State of the World's Children: A Fair Chance for Every Child*. New York: UNICEF.

United Nations Inter-agency Group for Child Mortality Estimation (2017) *Levels & Trends in Child Mortality – Report 2017*. New York: UNICEF.

Van Lancker, W. (2013) Putting the child-centred investment strategy to the test: Evidence for the EU27. *CSB Working Paper*, No. 13/01.

REFLECTION ON PART I
RESEARCH FOCUSING ON CHILDREN

This section (of five chapters) has reviewed ECE research published since 2000 organised around the broad theme of *Children*. In this reflection I have identified what stands out for me, and highlighted a paragraph from each of the chapters in this part of the book and identified what I see as needed next to take these issues forward.

ON CHILDREN'S RIGHTS

The challenge of teaching young children about their rights and of creating early education experiences which are rights-based is huge; obviously research into children's participation in their own learning can help, but this also needs professional and political momentum with adults – professionals, politicians, parents and the general public – shouldering the responsibility for realising the rights of young children.

NEXT STEPS

The teaching of children's rights to the youngest children needs to be adequately resourced and practitioners charged with this responsibility need to be better equipped. The teaching of children's rights should be moved way up the research agenda.

ON WELL-BEING AND SPIRITUALITY

Given the openness and inconclusive nature of researchers' attempts to define spirituality, and the relatively narrow definitions of policy, practitioners are often left to decide for themselves how they define and nurture spirituality and well-being in early childhood.

NEXT STEPS

The well-being and spirituality of early childhood practitioners themselves need to be valued and supported. Researchers, in collaboration with ECE practitioners and parents can, with appropriate resources, uncover more to aid our understanding of this under-researched area of children's lives in relation to ECE.

ON PLAY

Changes in environment, concerns about child safety, fear of child abduction, the built environment and more have led to restrictions on children in many parts of the world, which have in turn constrained children's opportunity to take risks in their play and to play out of the gaze of adults. Elsewhere, as UNICEF reports, some children play in contaminated water or on rubbish heaps because the poverty and deprivation of their locale offer them little choice.

NEXT STEPS

Inequity in terms of where it is safe to play has to be addressed, but we will come to that later. The issue of adult fears inhibiting children's opportunities to play 'out of the gaze of adults' is one that needs further thought. Whilst we can and must charge politicians and individuals with the task of making society and communities safe, researchers need to continue to address ways of giving children space to play which enables them to experience freedom.

ON CHILDREN'S PARTICIPATION

A small but growing number of research projects have fashioned innovative and inclusive research methods and approaches to gain a greater understanding of how children perceive their childhood worlds. Generating rich seams of data, they tell the detail of children's fine grain experiences, what's meaningful to them, and what matters are of most importance in their days. There are still not enough of these studies, but those that have been published recently make insightful contributions which create a window on children's learning worlds and their broader lives.

NEXT STEPS

Children are experts on children. They are experts in their own lives. Asking them about the things they do and the things that are important to them is crucial. Most studies, however, are small scale and few are well funded. The next step needed here is for a recognition that children's contributions to research are important; that they provide exclusive forms of data which enlighten and which can importantly inform policy. We must build on studies that raise children's diverse 'voices' and learn from them to develop policy and practice.

ON POVERTY IN CHILDHOOD

The statistics on poverty are shocking, and it seems to be the research by major charities that informs us best. Compared to the richest children, the poorest children are nearly twice as likely to die before age five ((United Nations Inter-agency Group for Child Mortality Estimation, 2017). Of course income (or wealth) is a significant factor in the effects of poverty and moving out of poverty, but so is the education of the mother.

NEXT STEPS

This must stop. That people are starving and children die from starvation does not need research: it needs food. Political will to commit more funding to feeding people is what is needed here. Given that most of the research on poverty is carried out by major charities, we should ask why governments are not sufficiently interested in the effects of poverty to properly fund this themselves; but in truth we don't need research into the effects of poverty – we need to end poverty . We need to ensure that people around the world have somewhere to live, food to eat and clothes to wear, and all the basic things that bring human dignity. So let's not face a future where we continue to read studies of the impact of poor housing on young children's lives – we know poor housing is bad and brings many ill-effects. Let's face a future where all young children and their families live somewhere good, and safe, and conducive to their well-being and growth. So, the next step is not more research on the impact of poverty – the next step is to heed the lessons from existing research and act on what our own eyes tell us – to end poverty.

PERSONAL REFLECTION AND PLANNING

Use the questions below to make some notes and/or discuss in groups, and consider:

- What stands out for you? Which piece of research would you award a prize to? What gave you the biggest surprise? And what may be particularly useful to you as a practitioner? Did anything made you feel, 'Yes, but ... so what?'
- Are there any research findings here that you suspect, or doubt? Or that you strongly disagree with? Is this 'just a hunch' or do you have evidence – from your own life- and practice-experience, or from other reading – to support that view?
- Is there something (that you've come across) missing from this account?
- Which of the researchers reported would you most like to meet, and what would you want to ask them?

In the next five years ...

- What do *you* think are the most important topics for future research around young children?
- What does your experience and reading of the literature suggest are likely to be the barriers to the development of work with and for young children's ECE in these years?

PART II
ADULTS

In Part I of the book, I posited a notion of *children* artificially detached from what are, in fact, the only ways we come to understand them: the *adult* ways of our constructions of children, as parents or professionals; the ways professional training in setting practice, in policy, management and curriculum define and police those constructions; and the ways in which those constructions are mediated by ethical and moral concerns. In this next section of the book, I introduce research into some of those major forces on the 'construction' and development of children.

I start, of course, with the child's first educator(s) – the parents/carers for whom the 'curriculum' is a lived 24-hour affair (and whose role in realising Maslow's (1943) untarnished *hierarchy of needs* is a defining and transcendent necessity). The evidence shows that for many, we are a long way from achieving a state where even all basic physiological and safety needs are met, let alone those human needs further up the hierarchy. And we are a still a long way from realising this, despite the burgeoning evidences of a failure to do what is needed. The many research studies that focus on the effects of new initiatives on 'disadvantaged' families and children beg a bigger question. To be sure, we need to know if, and why, initiatives and interventions 'worked' for children, but the bigger question – and one not often asked, it seems, by researchers – is 'Why?' Why are we still, in the 21st century, working in contexts of disadvantage? Why are early years settings closing when the need for provision for young children is high in so many countries in the world? Why are the people who work with young children mostly poorly paid, with limited opportunities (for many) for professional development? Why do politicians tell us that funds are short? Why do they do this when, it seems, funds for wars – when the need is perceived – are forthcoming? I use the notion of *failure* here, not to refer to those parents, children, practitioners who are in fact *failed by* national policies, by settings and by systems, and our collective lack of grasp – but on *the will*, notably the political will, to meet them. This perspective led me to the next chapter focusing on the diverse heterogeneity of family constructions, the needs which they experience, and the institutions which variably include and exclude them at a cost; and in turn to the wide variety of professional services which attempt *inter* and *intra alia* to minimise the exclusive tendencies of traditionally patriarchal systems. The following two chapters take us thus to research into the identities of practitioner education and effects, before the final chapter in Part II explores the variable sets of ethics which underpin (or otherwise) the issues and practices of adult constructions and realisations of education and care.

My own enduring view, after reviewing many of the recent international studies on these themes, is that we must invest in the adults who live and work with and for young children. We must value parents, such that they can bring up their children without struggle. We must value early years professionals whatever their role, to ensure they are well qualified and properly remunerated. We must value researchers and ensure that they can investigate the hard questions that inform and challenge flawed and failing policies. For whilst we have policies which do not do justice to living and working with young children, we shall not easily overcome a sedimented tendency to manage with what we have. We need to argue for much more: for a situation where there is no need to research 'disadvantage' or 'inequity' or 'literacy difficulties' because there will be none. For now we must continue to argue for a situation where the rights of children to live their lives with their basic needs met are realised, with families properly resourced to support them. We must further argue for the rights of children to learn in ways that nurture them towards their full potential to be realised, by fully and properly rewarding their educators.

REFERENCE

Maslow, A.H. (1943) A theory of human motivation. *Psychological Review*, 50 (4): 370–96.

7

PARENTS AND EARLY CHILDHOOD EDUCATION AND CARE

THIS CHAPTER WILL:

- describe recent research on aspects of parental partnership, involvement and engagement programmes
- discuss some studies focusing on parents facing disadvantage
- consider recent studies of parents' roles in early literacy development
- explore studies addressing fathers' roles and involvement
- suggest some research questions on the topic of parents in relation to ECEC
- provide some recommended reading to follow up the issues discussed.

This chapter focuses on research on the roles and contributions of parents in early childhood education and care. As increased numbers of children in many parts of the world spend time outside of their own homes, many settings have developed ways to share information about professional practices and work in partnership with parents to understand and meet the needs of their young children. This chapter draws on the international literature to consider studies on aspects of parental partnership, involvement and engagement programmes; research which considers the experiences of parents facing disadvantage; enquiries into parents' roles in early literacy development; and a growing research interest in fathers' roles and involvement in early childhood education.

RESEARCH ON ASPECTS OF PARENTAL PARTNERSHIP, INVOLVEMENT AND ENGAGEMENT PROGRAMMES

Whilst the engagement of parents in ECEC, and recognition of their vital role as educators of their own children, are not new, today's practitioners might be surprised to learn that there was a time in the not too distant past when it was not common practice to involve parents in their children's learning – or to set foot in the nursery or school setting.

Despite the efforts of Margaret McMillan in the 1920s to engage mothers in learning more about nutrition and their children's health, by the 1970s school and home seemed to be separate entities with limited engagement between teachers and parents as a regular and expected practice. Several studies in the last two decades have been concerned with effectiveness of a variety of programmes designed to involve parents to improve children's outcomes, whilst other work has identified and opened up other issues that parents face in relation to ECEC.

The very many parental partnership programmes established around the world are designed and provided as a means of addressing either particular needs of children, or as a way of focusing parents' attention more generally on their children's development and their relationship with them and involvement in their learning. Several programmes focus in particular on work with parents whose children are identified as having a specific and special educational need. One of the most well-known interventions involving one-to-one, home-based work with parents is the Portage home visiting programme. For many decades Portage home visiting has supported parents of children with additional needs and, though difficult to evaluate due to its highly individualised nature, many families interviewed by Russell (2007) reported that they valued the programme because they saw how it helped their child. The home visiting element of the Portage programme has since been used for a range of interventions, not solely for children with additional support needs, and it is this individualised and home-based support that enables relationships to be established, and these parent–professional relationships are essential. A New Zealand study of parent 'agency' applied the concept of an 'affordance network' for engaging with families focusing on developing parent engagement with a setting or programme through opportunities that are *available, inviting* and *personalising* as a way of enhancing involvement and engagement by families (Clarkin-Phillips and Carr, 2012). It is clear that relationships are crucial to successful parental partnership programmes, as a US study to engage parents in playing with their children showed (Kellar-Guenther et al., 2014). Indeed Kellar-Guenther et al. conclude that 'communication, and by extension the parent–provider relationship, may be more critical to parent involvement than the venue for the services' (2014: 90). However, given the success of home visiting in many programmes it could well be the case that relationships are more easily formed when professionals have time and space to work on a one-to-one basis with parents, and their own home is often the best place for this to develop.

Of course, present day technologies have also influenced the development of support for parents, and Head Start, a well-established US intervention, has long held parental involvement to be crucial to children's learning. Hurwitz et al. (2015) evaluated a programme to send text messages to parents giving them advice on parenting and how to involve themselves in their children's learning. Two hundred and fifty-six parents of children enrolled in Head Start programmes participated in the text message study with half receiving text messages for six weeks. Parents who received the texts reported that they were more involved in their children's learning, it being particularly successful with fathers and with parents of boys. Interestingly, the parents said they were very happy with the text advice service. However, Hurwitz et al. suggest that text-based intervention programmes should be seen as supplementary to face-to-face family engagement.

It is important to remember that there are cultural norms and many different practices and expectations in families depending on their cultural perspectives and their backgrounds and experiences. Huntsinger and Jose (2009) explored three types of parental involvement which involved: 1) communicating, 2) volunteering at school, and 3) learning at home, with Immigrant Chinese and European-American parents of young children in the US. They found that European-American parents tended to volunteer more in schools, whilst Chinese-American parents engaged in their own children's learning (often being quite systematic in their teaching) at home. Chinese-American parents tended to be intent on receiving graded reports on children's progress, and favoured (and sustained) their formal teaching at home. The authors conclude that teachers of young children would be wise to appreciate the efforts of Chinese-American parents to teach their children at home, and suggest that 'parents are not likely to quickly abandon a cultural tradition that has worked so well for several thousand years' (2009: 408) despite the belief of many Americans that children in their early years are too stressed by early academics (Elkind, 2001). The study serves as a reminder that cultural norms and traditions are powerful influences which need to be understood when planning and developing parental involvement programmes and strategies. This was also an outcome of another US study (Keels, 2009), which focused specifically on mothers, representing a range of cultural groups and also identified a greater readiness in European-American mothers to engage in school-based involvement.

STUDIES FOCUSING ON PARENTS FACING DISADVANTAGE

Reviewing the literature on parental involvement in minority group families, Kim (2009) sought to identify the barriers which some parents from some minority groups experience in relation to their involvement in schools. The study identifies teachers' perceptions about the effectiveness of some minority group parents, and their perceptions concerning those parents' capacity to support their children. Kim also identified that barriers existed concerning teachers' beliefs in the effectiveness of parental involvement and developmental philosophy. Other issues inhibiting minority parents' engagement included: school friendliness and positive communication, the diversity of parental involvement programmes, school policies and school leadership. Not surprisingly Kim suggested that better understanding about the nature of the involvement of minority parents in their children's ECEC settings would contribute positively to home–school partnership and successful parental involvement in the longer term. Kim concluded:

> Shaping a broad perspective that parental involvement embraces not only parental involvement at school but also at home; parental involvement at home and at school can be limited by school resources as well as parents' resources; and parental involvement at home and at school can be improved by school efforts [which] may reduce the negative perceptions of teachers and administrators about minority parental involvement. (2009: 92)

Pointing to the understanding that parental involvement has sometimes tended to be lower amongst economically disadvantaged families, Wang et al. (2016) identify that the reasons for this are unclear. Why are family economic status and parents' involvement in their children's education linked? Why might involvement of parents on lower incomes be lower than that of more affluent families? Wang et al. focused on a large sample (N = 12,724) of low-income families from north-western China to consider the influence of high expectation for children's educational attainment and perceived barriers, including parents' level of education. They suggest that parents' expectations can have an impact on parental involvement, regardless of economic status, especially where mothers were well educated. The study indicates that the effects of economic status and parents' level of education are not simple, and that whilst family economic status is a factor in parental educational involvement in Chinese families, it is not the only factor, and parents' (particularly mothers') own educational level is significant.

As Bruner (1975) reminded us:

> With respect to virtually any criterion of equal opportunity and equal access to opportunity, the children of the poor ... are plainly not getting as much schooling, or getting as much from their schooling as their middle-class age mates. (1975: 43)

Clearly poverty reaches into all aspects of families' lives, and low income in households can, of course, affect parents' capacity to focus on wider issues. However, what is clear is that there is no simple relationship between poverty and disadvantage and parents' willingness to get involved in their children's learning. Indeed, in many instances, parents who themselves did not do well in school show considerable determination to do all they can to support their children so that they benefit from their education and do not have the experiences of their parents.

Drawing on the findings of the 'Effective Pre-school, Primary and Secondary Education' research (EPPSE) (Sylva et al., 2014) on the educational pathways of nearly 3000 English children, Sylva (2014) shows the impact of high quality preschool experiences on children's learning. Drawing on the concept of 'resilience' Sylva highlights the importance of 'hard' (cognitive) and 'soft' (non-cognitive) skills to their future attainment and notes that: 'Resilient children have been shown to engage in planning for the future in ways that non-resilient children do not' (2014: 682). Picking up on Bruner's (1975) paper, Sylva notes that children whose lives are disadvantaged by poverty and its multiple effects have been thought to be less resilient than their peers who do not suffer such disadvantages. This is because children from poorer families have more stress in their lives and so more to cope with and fewer opportunities to develop the resilience they need. She goes on to highlight the important role that high quality learning environments can play in enhancing children's chances and how early childhood education can narrow the achievement gap if the quality of learning experiences is high.

PARENTS' ROLES IN EARLY LITERACY DEVELOPMENT

As with involvement of parents in general, it was not until the 1980s that involving parents in home–school collaboration around reading began to be established, and it was researchers who fostered these developments.

One of the first studies to do this was the pioneering home reading model PACT (Parents and Children and Teachers) whereby children regularly took books home from school to read to their parents (Hewison and Tizard, 1980). Several schemes were introduced in the 1980s, in the UK, focusing on linking school and home reading, and introducing the concept of 'parents as educators' (Topping, 1986). The Haringey Reading Project (Tizard et al., 1982) was influential in schools beginning to send children's reading books home on a regular basis. Later, the Belfield Project (Hannon, 1987) in Rochdale, England, encouraged daily book borrowing, and supported parents in reading with their children. Innovative at the time, the study showed that many working-class parents were keen to read with their children at home in the early years of school and that this was strongly associated with later reading attainment.

Whilst for some families, reading at home predates formalisation in school practice, the bringing together of home and school around reading was new in the 1980s.

Evidence from the Mass Observation Archive (www.massobs.org.uk) shows that some children, who missed school due to long periods of illness and could not read and write, were taught at home in order to catch up. One female correspondent wrote about her grandmother (1888–1972):

> [She] educated my mother and uncle at home for a year or two, because they were ill with childhood illnesses (scarlet fever and diphtheria) and could not go to school at the proper age of 5. Uncle went to school when he was 6, and my mother did not go until she was 7. Grandma therefore taught them to read and write a little before they went to school, so as not to let them get behind. Both Grandma and Grandpa L encouraged their children to value education, and the three who survived infancy did fairly well at school. (A2212, female, living in Watford, born 1956, writer. Autumn/Winter 1995 Directive: Mothers & Literacy in the early 1900s)

The Basic Skills Agency raised awareness in 1994 that literacy development at home differs widely between families, which led to a model of 'family literacy' (Brooks et al., 1997, 1999). This work also contributed to the growing argument that parents should be supported and encouraged to engage in their children's learning in the preschool years in order to help reduce the achievement gap at school start age (Hannon, 1996).

In the US, Sim et al. (2014) investigated the effects of two shared reading interventions on children's language and literacy skills. Parents of 80 five-year-old children participated in one of two eight-week home reading interventions: 1) dialogic reading, and 2) dialogic reading with the addition of print referencing. A three-month follow-up showed that children in both programmes made gains in comparison to the control group, thus the authors suggest that there is potential for short duration home-based interventions to promote children's emergent literacy.

In contrast, the UK's Raising Early Achievement in Literacy (REAL) Project (1997–2005) in Sheffield was a low intensity, long duration intervention whereby families received a visit once every three weeks or so, for the 18 months before children reached five years old and began formal schooling. The REAL Project identified ways of working with families in their own homes to effectively support parents in enhancing their own children's literacy development in the preschool years (Nutbrown et al., 2005). The randomised control trial showed how home visiting, lending resources and giving parents key information about how literacy develops were effective in raising the literacy achievement in young children, most particularly those children whose mothers reported having no formal educational qualifications (www.real-online.group.shef.ac.uk/aboutreal-text.html). Follow-up tests were carried out some two years after the programme ended in contrast to the Sim et al. study where the follow-up was after three months, thus we do not know if, or for how long, the gains of children in the short-term study were sustained. Chapter 15 will pick up the family literacy theme again.

FATHERS' ROLES AND INVOLVEMENT

It has long been the case that mothers have been the main focus of parental involve-ment in early childhood education, and even though programmes over the decades have referred to 'parental involvement' in reality they have been 'mother involvement' pro-grammes. Because of growing emphasis on the importance of involving fathers in their children's early learning, a number of programmes and initiatives have been developed in recent years aimed at the specific involvement of fathers. It is particularly good to see these programmes being evaluated so that successful features of these initiatives can be adopted and developed and the less successful elements are not repeated in future work.

Whilst many parental involvement programmes have sought to engage families in a variety of formats to positively affect the ways in which parents interact with their young children, it is typically mothers that have been reached by such initiatives (DeBruin-Parecki and Krol-Sinclair, 2003). Overall, mothers provide more literacy activities, more frequently, at home than do fathers, yet where fathers do provide such activities they have been found to be particularly important for the academic development of children, especially those whose mothers are below degree level (Foster et al., 2016). Parent–child reading studies have traditionally focused on mothers (Malin et al., 2014), but in recent years fam-ily literacy programmes have made specific efforts to involve fathers.

In a study of over 5,000 two-year-olds, Baker (2013) found 'that both fathers' and moth-ers' home literacy involvement positively contributed to children's cognitive and social emotional development' (2013: 1) and more home literacy involvement (such as reading stories together) led to better outcomes for children in terms of their attention span and behaviour. Findings led Baker to conclude that programmes aimed at 'increasing family literacy involvement can have positive benefits for children's cognitive and social emo-tional skills during the developmentally important early childhood years' (2013: 194).

In the US, a study with fathers of children in a Head Start/Early Head Start programme suggested a lack of 'fit' between fathers' perspectives on their roles and programme aims and strategies, which may hinder engagement, but a good 'fit' could enhance father involvement. Anderson et al. (2015) also point to the importance of practitioners valuing fathers, promoting children's learning and enjoyment, and supporting fathers' develop-ing parenting skills in order to impact positively on their relationships with their children. These factors appeared to change how fathers saw their role and their later engagement in a programme. The authors conclude that:

> Fathers' enjoyment, coupled with seeing their children's competencies improve, having their role valued by the programme, and having opportunities to develop new parenting skills seemed to facilitate the fathers' sense of efficacy and expanded their views of their roles as fathers, further motivating them to engage in programme services and their children's learning. Early childhood practitioners may face unique challenges when encouraging fathers to engage in early childhood programmes and with their

> young children, but by being responsive to how fathers construct their roles, early childhood practitioners can support fathers in 'finding their own selves' and contributing to their young children's development. (Anderson et al., 2015: 374)

In a similar vein, Duursma et al. (2008) argue that little is known about fathers reading with their children, especially in low-income families. Their study examined the frequency of low-income fathers reported reading to their children. As part of the US national evaluation of Early Head Start (EHS), fathers were recruited via mothers for the study – a further indicator, if one were needed, of the dominance of mothers in early childhood education involvement. Fathers were interviewed, in their own homes, and an assessment of their two- to five-year-old children's cognitive and language development was carried out. The study suggests that there was considerable variation in how often fathers read to their children, with use of English as a home language and fathers having a high school education being factors that positively influenced more reading – children with well-developed language skills were also read to more. Duursma et al. found that frequency of reading with their children was a predictor of children's language outcomes, 'but only for children whose fathers had at least a high school education' (2008: 351). However, there was no focus on the quality of reading interactions, something which would also affect children's developmental gains. The authors concluded that 'fathers in families enrolled in Early Head Start program were less likely to read infrequently to their children' (Duursma et al., 2008: 362). However, they draw an interesting conclusion about the role of mothers in supporting fathers' engagement with their children, which deserves some reflection. They say that:

> It is likely that when mothers are actively involved in an early intervention program, the effect of the program carries over to fathers as well. When mothers are encouraged to read to their children, they may also support fathers in reading to their toddlers, making it more of a family affair. (Duursma et al., 2008: 362)

There is an interesting assumption here that father involvement programmes may depend on mothers' involvement on several levels from recruitment to participation, to be successful. This raises the question of fathers' participation in and of their own right, and may well raise questions about programme design.

Ihmeideh (2014), in a study involving 258 fathers whose three- to five-year-old children attended kindergarten in Amman, Jordan, argues that many fathers have no 'voice' in early years education. Fathers' perspectives of their own contribution to their children's learning was found to be low, but, in keeping with other studies, fathers' level of income and their education were factors related to the frequency and quality of engagement with their children's learning. Traditionally, Jordanian mothers have held the main responsibility for young children's learning, yet in recent years, as more mothers have worked outside the home, mothers have begun to think more about their children's fathers having a role in their young children's development (UNICEF, 2009).

As Ortiz (2001) and Karther (2002) have demonstrated, fathers of low socio-economic status (SES) are willing and able to learn how to support their children's early literacy development and are prepared to develop the skills they need to do so. Bauman and Wasserman (2010) have argued that it behoves educators to develop programmes that are designed to support fathers in these circumstances in helping their children and to evaluate their effectiveness. Importantly, DeBruin-Parecki (2009) calls for programme design to be culturally relevant so that there is a 'fit' between the programme and the programme participants. Programmes should incorporate and build on the culture of communities in which they are used, including those of local tradition, faith and heritage; and they need to have relevance to all intended participants, which also means interventions must be meaningful to fathers as well as mothers. This is because:

 Fathers may be an untapped, and potentially highly influential, resource for fostering academic competence in their preschool age children, especially for families who are experiencing risk factors associated with low parental education or low socioeconomic status, a priority group for many early intervention efforts. (Foster et al., 2016: 1859–1860)

Studies have shown how attempts to involve fathers in their young children's literacy could benefit their children. In the UK, the Sheffield REAL Project successfully involved fathers, often unseen by professionals, in supporting their children's learning at home (Morgan et al., 2009) where the authors report that:

 Although largely invisible to outsiders, in many families the fathers' presence in their children's literacy became apparent to teachers in the project. As one teacher commented: *Whatever Beth makes or does, she likes to show dad (although I have never met him). He obviously takes a keen interest in activities she has done.* It would be regrettable if educators, researchers and policy makers were to underestimate this, often unseen, contribution of fathers to their young children's early literacy development. (2009: 183)

Similarly, in England and Wales, the FLiP (Family Literacy in Prisons) Project has had considerable success in involving imprisoned fathers in their children's early literacy development (Nutbrown et al., 2017). Several international studies have identified the important and beneficial effects on children's learning and development, and their fathers' well-being and resolve towards desistance, where fathers and children remain in contact (Steinhoff and Berman, 2012; Roettger and Swisher, 2013; Thulstrup and Karlsson, 2017).

In the US, some 20 years ago the critical role of men in children's learning was highlighted by the National Center for Education Statistics (1997), which stated that 'children do better in school when their fathers are involved in their schools, regardless of whether their fathers live with them' (1997: 77). Since then, and particularly in the last decade, greater efforts have been made – particularly in the US and UK, and also elsewhere – to develop programmes specifically to involve fathers, by creating programmes designed to be attractive to men, culturally relevant, and in some cases targeting fathers of boys which both addressed the lack of father involvement and sought to narrow the gap between boys' and girls' literacy (Bauman and Wasserman, 2010; Malin et al., 2014; Foster et al., 2016).

ATTITUDES, VALUES AND PRACTICES IN WORKING WITH PARENTS

The research reviewed in this chapter has made clear that attitudes and values around working in partnership with parents are central to successful collaboration and success for children and their families.

The vital role of parents as educators of their children is now widely recognised and their presence in early years settings is now expected and commonplace for many. Yet there remains work to do to ensure that *all* parents are welcomed and feel welcome and able to make a contribution in their children's settings if they wish to do so.

There are now many programmes aimed at engaging parents in their children's learning, as this chapter has shown, and whilst effectiveness varies, they, on the whole, show that parents are keen and interested in supporting their children. We can see that, as well as overcoming the challenges of engaging a small minority of parents who don't feel confident getting involved in group settings, there is work to do with teachers and other ECEC professionals to continue to build positive attitudes and create welcoming schools and early years settings so that home–school collaboration around reading and many other aspects of young children's learning and development becomes better established.

Work on involving fathers is only just beginning to gain recognition, and the stereotype of the involved mother and disengaged father is beginning to be challenged with important and effective initiatives designed to be inclusive of all parents. Such programmes incorporate and build on the culture of their local communities and create meaningful synergies between families and early years practitioners.

RESEARCH QUESTIONS ON PARENTS IN RELATION TO ECEC

Settings need to consult parents on many issues and it is also important to evaluate existing initiatives from time to time to ensure that their intended impact is being achieved. When involving parents in studies of parental involvement it is important, as shown in the examples in this chapter, to be sensitive to cultural traditions and expectations, and to ensure that families are included if they wish to be in such evaluations and consultations. Families are more likely to participate where there are opportunities to communicate in their home language and there is a sensitivity to parents' literacy abilities; such issues are important considerations if evaluations are not to exclude parents, thus ensuring that multiple perspectives are gathered.

Some suggested research questions for early years practitioners and students include:

- How does a setting involve parents?

  This question would first require some form of audit of parental involvement activity, and a search of the literature to show how what is provided fits with other involvement possibilities.

- How do parents feel about having ECEC professionals from the setting visiting them at home to help them support their children's learning?

  This would involve talking with parents about the possibility of home visiting, and perhaps the development of a pilot programme to try out home visiting initiatives. If the setting has a home visiting programme, parents who are so involved could be asked for their views.

- What do parents think of the opportunities to be involved in their child's early years setting?

  Finding out from parents how they perceive opportunities to get involved in their child's setting is useful information for those planning new initiatives. A questionnaire or focus groups will provide useful information.

- What are the perspectives of early childhood professionals on involving parents in their setting? How equipped are ECEC professionals to work with parents in the setting or in their own homes?

  The focus here is on the professionals' own views. It will be important to elicit the views of all who are working in the setting, perhaps through focus groups.

A NOTE ON RESEARCH ETHICS AND INTEGRITY

Issues of confidentiality will be important for parents so that they can offer negative as well as positive views on the provision presently available without feeling that they might in some way be penalised for expressing less than positive views. Where views of professionals in the setting are part of the data gathering, it will be important to reach a shared understanding that people are free to express their views in order to reach a shared consensus on parental involvement and engagement in the setting.

RECOMMENDED READING

Hannon, P., Morgan, A. and Nutbrown, C. (2005) Parents' experiences of a family literacy programme. *Journal of Early Childhood Research*, 4: 19.

This paper evaluates a preschool parental involvement in literacy programme (the REAL Project) from parents' perspectives.

Hewison, J. and Tizard, J. (1980) Parental involvement and reading attainment. *British Journal of Educational Psychology*, 50: 209–215.

A report on the pioneering parental involvement in reading programme.

REFERENCES

Anderson, S., Aller, T.B., Piercy, K.W. and Roggman, L.A. (2015) 'Helping us find our own selves': Exploring father-role construction and early childhood programme engagement. *Early Child Development and Care*, *185* (3): 360–376. DOI: 10. 1080/03004430.2014.924112.

Baker, C. (2013) Fathers' and mothers' home literacy involvement and children's cognitive and social emotional development: Implications for family literacy programs. *Applied Developmental Science*, *17* (4): 184–197. DOI: 10.1080/10888691.2013. 836034.

Bauman, D.C. and Wasserman, K.B. (2010) Empowering fathers of disadvantaged preschoolers to take a more active role in preparing their children for literacy success at school. *Early Childhood Education Journal*, *37* (5): 363–370. DOI: 10.1007/s10643-009-0367-3.

Brooks, G., Gorman, T., Harman, J., Hutchison, D., Kinder, K., Moor, H. and Wilkin, A. (1997) *Family Literacy Lasts*. London: Basic Skills Agency.

Brooks, G., Harman, J., Hutchison, D., Kendall, S. and Wilkin, A. (1999) *Family Literacy for New Groups*. London: Basic Skills Agency.

Bruner, J.S. (1975) Poverty and childhood. *Oxford Review of Education*, *1* (1): 31–50.

Clarkin-Phillips, J. and Carr, M. (2012) An affordance network for engagement: increasing parent and family agency in an early childhood education setting. *European Early Childhood Education Research Journal*, *20* (2): 177–187. DOI: 10.1080/1350293X. 2012.681130.

DeBruin-Parecki, A. (2009) Establishing a family literacy program with a focus on interactive reading: The role of research and accountability. *Early Childhood Education Journal*, *36* (5): 285–292.

DeBruin-Parecki, A. and Krol-Sinclair, B. (eds) (2003) *Family Literacy: From Theory to Practice*. Newark, DE: International Reading Association.

Duursma, E., Pan, B.A. and Raikes, H. (2008) Predictors and outcomes of low-income fathers' reading with their toddlers. *Early Childhood Research Quarterly*, *23* (3): 351–365. DOI: 10.1016/j.ecresq.2008.06.001.

Elkind, D. (2001) *The Hurried Child: Growing Up Too Fast Too Soon* (3rd edn). Cambridge, MA: Perseus Publishing.

Foster, T.D., Froyen, L.C., Skibbe, L.E., Bowles, R.B. and Decker, K.B. (2016) Fathers' and mothers' home learning environments and children's early academic outcomes. *Reading and Writing*, *29* (9): 1845–1863 DOI 10.1007/s11145-016-9655-7.

Hannon, P. (1987) *The Belfield Reading Project Final Report*. London: National Children's Bureau and Belfield Community Council.

Hannon, P. (1996) School is too late: Preschool work with parents. In S. Wolfendale and K. Topping (eds), *Family Involvement in Literacy: Effective Partnerships in Education*. London: Cassell, pp. 37–49.

Hewison, J. and Tizard, J. (1980) Parental involvement and reading attainment. *British Journal of Educational Psychology*, *50*: 209–215.

Huntsinger, C.S. and Jose, P.E. (2009) Parental involvement in children's schooling: Different meanings in different cultures. *Early Childhood Research Quarterly*, *24* (4): 398–410. DOI: 10.1016/j.ecresq.2009.07.006.

Hurwitz, L.B., Lauricella, A.R., Hanson, A., Raden, A. and Wartella, E. (2015) Supporting Head Start parents: Impact of a text message intervention on parent–child activity engagement. *Early Child Development and Care*, *185* (9): 1373–1389. DOI: 10. 1080/03004430.2014.996217.

Ihmeideh, F.M. (2014) Giving fathers a voice: Towards father involvement in early years settings. *Early Child Development and Care*, *184* (7): 1048–1062. DOI: 10. 1080/03004430.2013.842562.

Karther, D. (2002) Fathers with low literacy and their young children. *The Reading Teacher*, *56*: 184–193.

Keels, M. (2009) Ethnic group differences in early Head Start parents' parenting beliefs and practices and links to children's early cognitive development. *Early Childhood Research Quarterly*, *24* (4): 381–397. DOI: 10.1016/j.ecresq.2009.08.002.

Kellar-Guenther, Y., Rosenberg, S.A., Block, S.R. and Robinson, C.C. (2014) Parent involvement in early intervention: What role does setting play? *Early Years*, *34* (1): 81–93. DOI: 10.1080/09575146.2013.823382.

Kim, Y. (2009) Minority parental involvement and school barriers: Moving the focus away from deficiencies of parents. *Educational Research Review*, *4* (2): 80–102. DOI: 10.1016/j. edurev.2009.02.003.

Malin, J.L., Cabrera, N.J. and Rowe, M.L.(2014) Low-income minority mothers' and fathers' reading and children's interest: Longitudinal contributions to children's receptive vocabulary skills. *Early Childhood Research Quarterly*, *29* (4): 425–432. DOI: 10.1016/j.ecresq.2014.04.010.

Mass Observation Archive, University of Sussex, Directive: 'Mothers & Literacy in the early 1900s' (Autumn/Winter 1995).

Morgan, A., Nutbrown, C. and Hannon, P. (2009) Fathers' involvement in young children's literacy development: Implications for family literacy programmes. *British Educational Research Journal*, *35* (2): 167–185.

National Center for Education Statistics (1997) *Digest of Education Statistics: Fathers' Involvement in Their Children's Schools*. Washington, DC: U.S. Department of Education.

Nutbrown, C., Clough, P., Stammers, L., Emblin, N. and Aston-Smith, S. (2017) Family literacy in prisons: Fathers' engagement with their young children. *Research Papers in Education*. DOI: 10.1080/02671522.2017.1402085.

Nutbrown, C., Hannon, P. and Morgan, A. (2005) *Early Literacy Work with Families: Policy, Practice and Research*. London: Sage.

Ortiz, R.W. (2001) Pivotal parents: Emergent themes and implications on father involvement in children's early literacy experiences. *Reading Improvement, 38* (2): 132–144.

Roettger, M.E. and Swisher, R.R. (2013) Incarcerated fathers: Implications for father involvement. In J. Pattnaik (ed.), *Father Involvement in Young Children's Lives: A Global Analysis*. London: Springer, pp. 17–28.

Russell, F. (2007) Portage in the UK: Recent developments. *Child: Care, Health and Development, 33* (6): 677–683. DOI: 10.1111/j.1365-2214.2007.00759.x.

Sim, S.S.H., Berthelsen, D., Walker, S., Nicholson, J.M. and Fielding-Barnsley, R. (2014) A shared reading intervention with parents to enhance young children's early literacy skills. *Early Child Development and Care, 184* (11): 1531–1549. DOI: 10.1080/03004430.2013.862532.

Steinhoff, R. and Berman, A.H. (2012) Children's experiences of having a parent in prison: 'We look at the moon and then we feel close to each other'. *Scientific Annals of the 'Alexandru Ioan Cuza' University, Iaşi. Sociology and Social Work, 5* (2): 77–96.

Sylva, K. (2014) The role of families and pre-school in educational disadvantage. *Oxford Review of Education, 40* (6): 680–695. DOI:10.1080/03054985.2014.979581.

Sylva, K., Melhuish, E., Sammons, P., Siraj, I., Taggart, B., Smees, R., Toth, K., Welcomme, W. and Hollingworth, K. (2014) *Students' Educational and Developmental Outcomes at Age 16: Effective Pre-school, Primary and Secondary Education (EPPSE)*. DfE Research Brief RB354. ISBN 978-1-78105-403-1. DfE: London. www.ucl.ac.uk/ioe/research/pdf/RB354_-_Students__educational_and_developmental_outcomes_at_age_16_Brief.pdf (accessed 12 February 2018).

Thulstrup, S.H. and Karlsson, L.E. (2017) Children of imprisoned parents and their coping strategies: A systematic review. *Societies, 7* (15): 1–16. DOI: 10.3390/soc7020015.

Tizard, J., Schofield, W.N. and Hewison, J. (1982) Collaboration between teachers and parents in assisting children's reading. *British Journal of Educational Psychology, 52* (1): 1–15. DOI: 10.1111/j.2044-8279.1982.tb02498.x.

Topping, K. (1986) W.H.I.C.H. Parental Involvement in Reading Scheme? A guide for practitioners, *Literacy, 20* (30): 148–156. DOI: 10.1111/j.1467-9345.1986.tb00338.x.

UNICEF (2009) *Jordan's Early Childhood Development: Making Jordan Fit for Children*. UNICEF MENA-RO Learning Series, *Vol. 2*. www.unicef.org/jordan/jo_children_ecddocumentation2009en.pdf (accessed 12 February 2018).

Wang, Y., Deng, C. and Yang, X. (2016) Family economic status and parental involvement: Influences of parental expectation and perceived barriers. *School Psychology International, 37* (5): 536–553. DOI: 10.1177/0143034316667646.

8

INCLUSION AND DIVERSITY IN EARLY CHILDHOOD EDUCATION AND CARE

THIS CHAPTER WILL:

- reflect on recent research focusing on young children with identified special educational needs and learning difficulties
- highlight issues of 'race' and ECEC
- consider research on cultural diversity in ECEC settings
- suggest some research questions on the topic of inclusion and diversity in ECEC
- provide some recommended reading to follow up the issues discussed.

T his chapter focuses on research into aspects of inclusion in early childhood education and care. Whilst inclusive education was once the term by which the needs of young children with identified 'special educational needs' (SEN) were catered for in 'mainstream' education, the term has since broadened considerably to include many aspects of difference and learning difficulty. The 21st century has seen evolving and contested definitions of inclusion, and shifts in understanding, policy and practice of what inclusive practices actually mean, what inclusive settings might look like and whom they include.

Inclusion and exclusion reach into a whole host of factors including: 'race', disability, learning difficulty, gender, sexuality, poverty, migration, religion, languages and more. So much is changing in the world with regard to discrimination for reasons of difference, which means that there remains much work to do, both in terms of research, practice and changing negative perspectives and attitudes.

This chapter raises some of the complex issues around inclusive education in ECEC, touching on the themes of special educational needs and learning difficulties, 'race' and cultural diversity. These themes seem to the main foci of research in ECEC in this millennium and can be considered under the umbrella of inclusive education, which incorporates aspects of discriminative practices and policies. Several other chapters in this book also connect with aspects of inclusion and exclusion.

INTERNATIONAL CONTEXTS OF INCLUSION AND EXCLUSION

There has always been discrimination in the world; women in many countries have had to campaign and suffer to win their right to vote (some still do not have this right of citizenship); black people have lived with oppression throughout centuries; and struggles with health and well-being can exclude sufferers from their communities.

Mass migration in recent years, leading to more diverse populations, also brings challenges to communities as they adapt to the changes newcomers bring. Whilst the world over the centuries has always seen change, inequality and division, in recent years we have witnessed opposition (even hatred) of difference in many parts of the world, and just a few examples include the rise of the far right in different parts of the world, the racist divisions exposed by the UK referendum to leave the European Union, conflicts in the US over policies of the Trump administration, revision of benefit entitlement for families and for people with disabilities in England. The range of issues is wide, and reaches into any consideration of inclusion in ECEC, making the study of inclusion diverse and challenging. What unites the themes discussed in this chapter is that children who for some reason are different often suffer discrimination. Research into inclusion in ECEC still has a long way to go, but this chapter brings together some of the studies that inform our understanding.

As world changes have brought about considerable change to the populations in early childhood education and care settings, the demands and responsibilities on, and expectations of, early years practitioners are considerable. Many chapters in this book relate to inclusive practices and, perhaps more accurately, the impacts of exclusion and discrimination. This chapter focuses specifically on issues of what might be broadly defined as inclusive education, which is related to several other chapters in the book, because clearly almost every aspect of early childhood is, to a greater or lesser extent, a matter of belonging and inclusion or not belonging and exclusion. Chapter 2 has examined research related to children's rights. Chapter 6 highlighted the ways that childhood poverty can exclude young children from accessing educational opportunities in ways that would benefit them. Chapter 7 has, amongst other things, reflected on how parents are included in early years settings. And Chapter 15 will examine issues of linguistic diversity.

YOUNG CHILDREN WITH IDENTIFIED SPECIAL EDUCATIONAL NEEDS AND LEARNING DIFFICULTIES

So much has been written on young children with identified learning needs, over the decades, and in the past two decades there have been considerable policy shifts and some turmoil for parents. This section will not revisit policy changes, for good or bad, but rather will consider what recent research is telling us about 'special educational need', 'learning difficulty' and the early years of education and care. There has been a move away from thinking about SEN towards inclusive education, and as Hornby (2015) states, the two do not share the same philosophical roots. 'Special' education emanates from a diagnostic 'medical' model of disability, whereas inclusive education forms part of a more 'social model' of disability (Oliver, 1996). Hornby (2015: 234) argues that rather than being opposite and in opposition, 'inclusive special education' which 'comprises a synthesis of the philosophy, values and practices of inclusive education with the interventions, strategies and procedures of special education' could be a way forward to meet the needs of pupils with a wide range of learning difficulties and support needs. He summarises inclusive education as:

> generally considered to be a multi-dimensional concept that includes the celebration and valuing of difference and diversity, consideration of human rights, social justice and equity issues, as well as of a social model of disability and a socio-political model of education. (Hornby, 2015: 235)

One of the things that works against the inclusion of young children with formal assessment of learning needs is the difficulty some face in attending their local school. Nutbrown (1998) suggested that early years education 'at its best' *can be* inclusive education by default, yet whilst many young children begin their setting-based learning journeys in their local communities, those identified as in need of additional support may well not be able to continue into mainstream schooling with their peers from their nurseries and preschools. Rogers (2007) noted that:

> Young children can be very accommodating to the idiosyncrasies of others, and teachers tend on the whole to stay with their class, and thus get to know their pupils and be known by them. (2007: 55)

In her study involving 24 British parents of children identified with 'special education needs' within mainstream education, Rogers (2007) found that many children were 'included' in mainstream schools but some remained excluded in three ways: *practically* – when removed for individual teaching; *intellectually* – being unable to access the curriculum in the way that their classmates did; and *emotionally* – finding it difficult to form friendships and social interactions with their peers. Rogers points out that 'a testing and examination structure, cultural ignorance and misunderstandings about difference and difficulty' (2007: 63) created and compounded exclusionary practices. Rogers argues that holistic 'social inclusion' rather than 'inclusive education' should be the way forward for all children.

As Lundqvist et al. (2016) identified in their Swedish study, provision for young children varies, with some settings better able to meet the needs of young children with learning difficulties than others, and this in a country which values quality in ECEC highly and where children are legally entitled to a preschool place. The study found that resources and staffing were superior in specialist units, but that inclusive practice was not exclusive to specialist preschools. To some extent, inclusive educational practices are a matter of attitude. Clough and Nutbrown (2004) studied the perspectives of 94 preschool educators from a variety of settings in the four countries of the UK on issues related to working with young children with learning difficulties in specialist and 'mainstream' generic settings. They found five influencing factors: their personal experiences; their professional development; their views of childhood; their thoughts on inclusion and exclusion; and their beliefs and practices around the roles of parents. They concluded that different policies around the UK seek to achieve similar inclusion goals. More specifically they found that preschool educators were broadly supportive of inclusive early education and had strong views on inclusion of children with learning difficulties and were willing to share these views with openness and honesty. Finally they found that preschool educators' responses and emphases varied according to professional background and experience of systems and settings. In a similar study of 113 European preschool educators, Nutbrown and Clough (2004) highlighted the:

> importance of personal/professional experience in the development of individual educators' attitudes and practices; importance of properly resourced and critically informed continuing professional development at an advanced (and accredited)

higher education level; prevalence of 'hierarchies of tolerance' which reflect principled expressions of inclusive ideology in parallel with the maintenance of practices which effectively and selectively exclude; and the primacy of the role of the parent and home in children's early learning and development. (2004: 313)

Practice has been found to vary too. In another UK study, a survey of 380 families with children with SEN (Bajwa-Patel and Devecchi, 2014) found that parents had little real choice of school for their children but rather were confronted with either a special school or (if available) a mainstream school, neither of which could meet all their child's needs.

So much of successful inclusive practice for children with identified additional learning and support needs seems to depend on positive and reciprocal relationships. In an small-scale study, Parry (2015) found that young children 'labelled with SEN are active in contributing to the relationships they make with their peers' (2015: 361) and that 'practitioners should consider the value of stepping back to watch children engage in uninterrupted social exchanges and then pausing to reflect on what these mean' (2015: 362). Relationships between parents and practitioners are important too. Broomhead (2013), reporting on a study to develop student teachers' empathy towards parents of children with SEN, concluded that students needed to be prepared to form effective relationships with parents so as to better understand their needs as well as those of their children.

What is clear from recent studies is that children who have additional learning needs experience inequalities in education systems in many countries and, whilst research highlights the issues, it takes political will and commitment of resources to iron out inequalities.

FINDINGS ON 'RACIAL' BIAS IN ECEC RESEARCH

It has long been known that many children and their families suffer racial discrimination, and whilst studies have documented this over the years, and the issues around racial inequality are well rehearsed, still such inequalities and discrimination persist. New biases seem to be emerging as geopolitical events impact on countries and communities, bringing changes to local populations which have led to suspicion, fear and confrontation. In the days following the UK's vote to leave the European Union, for example, several families reported being asked, 'When are you leaving?' as they took their children to school. A considerable number of studies have evaluated the implications of racial bias settings on children's development, which indicate that some education professionals may respond to race when evaluating and interpreting children's behaviour (Chang and Demyan, 2007; McGrady and Reynolds, 2013) and imply that young children in early years settings may not always be treated equally.

Yates and Marcelo (2014) examined pretend play amongst 171 children identified as Hispanic, black, white, and bi/multiracial in the US, paying particular attention to imagination and affect across racial groups. Whilst researchers have shown that play is culturally influenced and embedded (Rogoff, 2003; Gaskins et al., 2007), complexity has been found to vary. Yates and Marcelo (2014: 2) use 'race' as an 'imperfect and socially constructed marker of culture, ethnicity and related constructs' in their study of racial differences in preschoolers' pretend play. They found that all children were similarly imaginative and expressive players and, importantly, in contrast to some earlier studies, the Yates and Marcelo study found that teachers rated play similarly across racial groups but differentiated according to race on some aspects. Specifically, black children were evaluated negatively, in comparison to non-black children with similar imaginative and expressive pretend play skills. However, adjustment to school was not explained by teachers according to race (as has been the case in an earlier study by Tenenbaum and Ruck, 2007). Yates and Morelo conclude that:

> Moreover, to the extent that these findings raise the possibility of teacher bias, and given its enduring negative effects we must take necessary steps to mitigate the expression of unconscious, socially structured beliefs and expectations in our classrooms. Amidst increasing emphasis on multicultural teacher training and education, these findings encourage educators and researchers to look beyond main effects and evaluate the potential for increasingly subtle, but equally silencing, ways that race may play out in early childhood education and development. (2014: 9)

There are implications here for professional development for those working with young children so that professionals are aware of what might be 'unconscious, socially structured beliefs and expectations'. Whilst this study was based in the US, there is every reason to suppose that similar biases creep into settings in the UK and elsewhere. Awareness, however provocative (as that which the Yates and Marcelo study gives rise to), is important so as to mitigate the damage that racially biased negative adult behaviour, however subtle, can do to children's self-esteem and development. A study involving Canadian kindergarteners, which attempted to use story books to confront and reduce racial bias (Johnson and Aboud, 2017), also concluded that professional development was important:

> Teachers may need training in how to engage children in these discussions and explicitly express their own attitudes of respect without sounding imposing or hypocritical. ... Adults who interact with children, specifically parents, teachers, religious educators and librarians, need guidance on what sort of commentary is required and how to engage children patiently in an open dialogue about friendship and diversity. They need guidance on how to address 'racist-sounding' comments from children. (2017: 121)

As cultural populations in ECEC settings change, it is important to remain aware of the circumstances of some families stigmatised by the media because of their asylum seeking status. Not only might families under these circumstances face racial bias, but they also face the prejudices that arise as a result of the circumstances of their arrival in their host country. Whitmarsh's (2011) study of parental partnership between a setting and six mothers from Afghanistan, Iran and Morocco, all asylum seekers in the UK, highlighted tensions in language learning, the lack of appropriate cultural resources, perceptions that the setting's teachers were the experts, and the values they desired for their children to hold. Though small in scale, this study contributes to the literature about asylum seeking families' views and expectations of ECEC and the mothers' accounts go some way to challenging stereotypical views about asylum seekers. The women are, of course, individuals who want to do the best for their children and apply themselves to understand what is expected of them by the preschool setting their children attend by engaging in events and practices offered to and expected of all parents. Whitmarsh identifies the need for tangible signs of the families' languages and cultures, to enable better inclusion. She also points to a possibly 'racialised discourse' which causes concern in the mothers about their children's ability to speak what they refer to as 'good English'. Whilst having a good standard of education (some with degrees in their home countries) they are now disadvantaged by circumstance, which may impact on how preschool educators perceive them. Whitmarsh concludes that:

 Acknowledging and valuing multiple perspectives of partnership, which may not necessarily conform to existing conceptual models of home–school partnership, may enable asylum-seeking mothers to engage further with their child's education and improve outcomes for the child, the family and the setting. (2011: 547)

This needs to be borne in mind when working with young children who will eventually, as Hernandez et al. (2009) show in a US study, contribute to the economy and civic society.

Those who work with young children bear the heavy burden of responsibility to maintain a vigilance around racial awareness and discrimination and to focus their attention on eliminating racial bias. Professional development needs to be thoughtfully delivered and appropriately funded for the benefit of individual children and to help to reduce racial discrimination and bias in communities and society.

STUDIES OF CULTURAL DIVERSITY IN ECEC SETTINGS

Global migration has, throughout history, brought shifts and changes in cultures, customs and practices. Over the centuries people have travelled, as individuals, tribes, peoples and nations to other places, sometimes peacefully, sometimes in acts of aggression, sometimes seeking safety. Whatever the reason, the movement of people between places and nations has always occurred. In the earliest days of travel, explorers and pioneer settlers did not know what they would find, and encountered what they considered to be 'strange' people, languages and customs. Discovery of 'the other' was often seen as exotic. Setting sail from Plymouth, England, in September 1620, to a 'new life', the 'Pilgrim Fathers' of the Mayflower eventually arrived and settled in what they named 'Plymouth' in Massachusetts, to become early European colonisers of what would eventually become known as the USA. They saw new things and brought new things (including their religion) to the place where they settled – often disregarding the indigenous peoples they found there. There are numerous other examples, including the transportation of convicted criminals from the UK to Australia, and the many colonised countries around the world, which are gradually returning to independence. But the point here is that people have always travelled and settled in places new to them (some in peace, some in desperation, some in acts of aggression and war).

Recent migration of people fleeing war, starvation and persecution has led to an upsurge in fear in some of the populations of host countries, with media reports that 'they' will use up existing resources of housing, education, welfare and health, that there is no room, and that 'they' will influence changes to established cultures and communities. Change through migration is inevitable, but that change is always negative is a misnomer.

One of the wonderful things about young children is their unfettered fascination with difference – they are able to investigate and embrace difference without prejudice, until they learn negative biases. Durand (2010) identifies the US as 'a nation of immigrants' and argues that in the US – as in many other countries – ECEC is 'pivotal' to the development of 'productive members of society'. She argues that :

> becoming cross-culturally competent does not require us to become an expert on every discernible category of diversity; in fact, this simply isn't possible. Rather, becoming comfortable and supportive of diversity requires a certain mindset, a certain point of view, a certain *process* of sensitivity that becomes almost automatic when we deal with children and families. (2010: 835)

This, Durand argues, requires educators to undertake a transformative journey, to de-centre from our own mindset and embrace difference as valuable. Children can do this when they are very young – some as they get older, lose that capacity and start to adopt prejudices that we experience around us.

Formosinho and Figueiredo (2014) report on a Portuguese study to examine how participatory pedagogy promotes the co-construction of learning (of children and adults in the setting), which includes a focus on rights, competencies, well-being and empowerment of all as underpinnings for learning in the context of social diversity. The study involved 220 children (aged four months to six years) and 60 adults (teachers, assistants, administrators, cleaning and maintenance staff), representing a range of socio-economic circumstances and diverse ethnic backgrounds. A starting point for this study was that:

> This social diversity encompasses an academic diversity since the newly arrived to compulsory schooling come from families not aware of the monolithic values, norms and motivations of formal education. This cultural diversity is often looked on by the school as a problematic academic heterogeneity since it breaks the traditional social homogeneity of the selective schools. (Formosinho and Figueiredo, 2014: 398)

The full study is deserving of a detailed read, but the authors conclude that disadvantaged groups can benefit from participatory educational teams and this needs investment to enhance staff capacity to work with a wider range of diversities and enables all to have their voice. With a similar focus on cultural diversity, Murray (2012) reports on a qualitative study in ten ECEC settings with practitioners and families from two urban settlements in two provinces of South Africa. Involving practitioners and families together was a prerequisite for exploring values and attitudes as a starting point in the development of 'an intercultural education programme that can contribute towards breaking down prejudice' (2012: 90). Murray concludes that successful intercultural education has to involve families, drawing parallels with initiatives in Northern Ireland and Israel (Bernard van Leer Foundation, 2007), and suggests that home visits by practitioners are one way of building personal relationships and partnerships which support each child's learning.

In the context of increasingly diverse populations in Canada, Perlman et al. (2010) examined the nature of 'diversity positive' approaches in 64 ECEC settings involving 103 preschool classrooms in Toronto. They found diversity-positive resources and practices, at a time in children's lives when they responded positively to difference, and concluded that:

> Counteracting the development of prejudicial attitudes in childhood can save many members of minority groups from the debilitating effects of discrimination in both childhood and adulthood. (2010: 763)

SOCIAL JUSTICE, INCLUSION AND DIVERSITY

As we have seen in this chapter, there has always been discrimination – usually rooted in inequalities and difference, and beliefs that one 'group' has superior status and value to another. We have also seen in studies carried out around the world, how attempts to highlight and address exclusionary and discriminatory practices can be successful. It is the case that young children are not born with prejudice, but that they quickly learn values and attitudes from those around them. Studies to confront discrimination and teach children to value and respect each other can help us to see how to enrich practice so that all can benefit.

Yet there remains much work to do to highlight discriminatory practices faced by young disabled children and their parents, which can exclude them from spaces and events enjoyed by their non-disabled peers. Issues of human rights and children's rights are centre stage when issues of inclusion and diversity are considered, and researchers confronting such issues in the pursuit of holistic 'social inclusion' pave the way for future practices where no one experiences exclusion.

Whilst issues of practice are vitally important, inclusive tendencies can be really very much a matter of attitude, of will, and of positive leadership, on the part of professionals and of policy-makers.

RESEARCH QUESTIONS ON INCLUSION AND DIVERSITY IN ECEC

The discussion in this chapter serves as an indication of how wide and diverse and complex the discussion of inclusion and early childhood education is. Continually evolving and contested definitions of inclusion shift our understanding and shape policy and practice around the development of inclusive societies and inclusive settings.

As we have seen from research discussed in this chapter, issues of 'race', disability, learning difficulty, gender, sexuality, poverty, migration, religion, languages and more are changing the world. Discrimination on the grounds of difference still needs considerable attention. Researching aspects of inclusion touches many lives and is an issue for everyone.

Some suggested research questions for early years practitioners and students include:

○ How do early years practitioners define 'inclusion' in their work?
   To address this question will mean talking with individuals, or if you are prepared to sacrifice 'depth' of response you could try using an online questionnaire. Small focus groups are also useful for gathering the perspectives of practitioners – some people prefer a group discussion to individual interviews because they can feel less pressured – others of course would prefer to be interviewed individuality because some issues could be sensitive.

○ How do young children understand and enact inclusion in their early years setting?
   Depending on the age of the children this is most likely to be a study where observations are key. Children around four and five years of age will be able

to engage in conversation about inclusion – in terms of 'belonging' and being different – but in the main children's play and behaviour will reveal a lot about their operational if not articulated understandings of inclusion and difference.

○ What are parents' expectations of inclusion in their children's early years setting?
This could involve talking with parents – either individually or in small groups. Questionnaires could be used to reach a larger number of parents, but breadth of research design is likely to mean sacrificing depth of detail that can be obtained by talking with people in more personal interview encounters.

○ How can aspects of inclusion be further developed in an early years setting?
This question is likely to involve a form of action research – designing and implementing a change to introduce more inclusive policies and practices. This will necessitate considerable discussion to reach agreement with colleagues and to implement and monitor the change.

A NOTE ON RESEARCH ETHICS AND INTEGRITY

Inclusion is a personal matter as well as a crucial focus for policy and practice. When researching questions of inclusion with individuals – practitioners, parents or children – it will be important to understand that everyone has their biases and there may well be some sensitivities around some topics of discussion born out of personal experience, and in some cases prejudice. Researchers will need to examine their own positionality in researching aspects of inclusion and exclusion and maintain their own integrity in the research process. This may include remaining 'neutral' in order that people express their own views without being influenced by the researchers' views. Conversely, and as has become more popular in recent times, researchers may choose to declare their own positionality around the issues being discussed so that the conversation takes place in a climate of openness and honesty rather than participants being 'distanced' from researcher views. Whatever stance a researcher takes, it is important always to remember that discussions of inclusion and exclusion are fundamental to lives, and to the political and cultural influences in those lives, and as such are intensely personal.

RECOMMENDED READING

Clough, P. and Nutbrown, C. (2004) Special educational needs and inclusion: Multiple perspectives of preschool educators in the UK. *Journal of Early Childhood Research*, 2 (2): 191–211. DOI: 10.1177/1476718X04043015.

This paper offers some insights into how practitioners think about inclusive issues.

Hernandez, D.J., Takanishi, R. and Marotz, K.G. (2009) Life circumstances and public policies for young children in immigrant families. *Early Childhood Research Quarterly*, 24 (4): 487–501. DOI: 10.1016/j.ecresq.2009.09.003.

This paper draws attention to issues of immigration, a topic which ECEC settings are increasingly developing their work on.

Murray, J. (2012) Learning to live together: An exploration and analysis of managing cultural diversity in centre-based early childhood development programmes. *Intercultural Education*, 23 (2): 89–103.

This paper focuses on inclusivity issues in relation to cultural diversity in ECEC settings.

Whitmarsh, J. (2011) Othered voices: Asylum-seeking mothers and early years education. *European Early Childhood Education Research Journal*, 19 (4): 535–551. DOI: 10. 1080/1350293X.2011.623540.

This paper highlights the experiences of exclusion of mothers who are settling as asylum seekers.

REFERENCES

Bajwa-Patel, M. and Devecchi, C. (2014) 'Nowhere that fits': The dilemmas of school choice for parents of children with statements of Special Educational Needs (SEN) in England. *Support for Learning, 29* (2): 117–135. DOI: 10.1111/1467-9604.12052.

Bernard van Leer Foundation (2007) Promoting social inclusion and respect for diversity in the early years. *Early Childhood Matters*, no. 108. The Hague: Bernard van Leer Foundation.

Broomhead, K.E. (2013) 'You cannot learn this from a book': Pre-service teachers developing empathy towards parents of children with Special Educational Needs (SEN) via parent stories. *European Journal of Special Needs Education*, 28 (2): 173–186. DOI: 10.1080/08856257.2013.778109.

Chang, D.F. and Demyan, A. (2007) Teachers' stereotypes of Asian, Black, and White students. *School Psychology Quarterly, 22* (2): 91–114. DOI: 10.1037/1045-3830.22.2.91.

Clough, P. and Nutbrown, C. (2004) Special educational needs and inclusion: Multiple perspectives of preschool educators in the UK. *Journal of Early Childhood Research, 2* (2): 191–211. DOI: 10.1177/1476718X04043015.

Durand, T.M. (2010) Celebrating diversity in early care and education settings: Moving beyond the margins. *Early Child Development and Care, 180* (7): 835–848. DOI: 10.1080/03004430802466226.

Formosinho, J. and Figueiredo, I. (2014) Promoting equity in an early years context: The role of participatory educational teams. *European Early Childhood Education Research Journal, 22* (3): 397–411. DOI: 10.1080/1350293X.2014.912902.

Gaskins, S., Haight, W. and Lancy, D.F. (2007) The cultural construction of play. In A. Göncü and S. Gaskins (eds), *Play and Development: Evolutionary, Sociocultural, and Functional Perspectives* (2nd edn). Mahwah, NJ: Erlbaum, pp. 179–202.

Hernandez, D.J., Takanishi, R. and Marotz, K.G. (2009) Life circumstances and public policies for young children in immigrant families. *Early Childhood Research Quarterly, 24* (4): 487–501. DOI: 10.1016/j.ecresq.2009.09.003.

Hornby, G. (2015) Inclusive special education: Development of a new theory for the education of children with special educational needs and disabilities. *British Journal of Special Education, 42* (3): 234–256. DOI: 10.1111/1467-8578.12101.

Johnson, P.J. and Aboud, F.E. (2017) Evaluation of an intervention using cross-race friend storybooks to reduce prejudice among majority race young children. *Early Childhood Research Quarterly*, 40: 110–122. DOI: 10.1016/j.ecresq.2017.02.003.

Lundqvist, J., Westling, M.A. and Siljehag, E. (2016) Characteristics of Swedish preschools that provide education and care to children with special educational needs. *European Journal of Special Needs Education, 31* (1): 124–139. DOI: 10.1080/08856257. 2015.1108041.

McGrady, P.B. and Reynolds, J.R. (2013) Racial mismatch in the class-room: Beyond black-white differences. *Sociology of Education, 8* (1): 3–17. DOI: 10.1177/ 0038040712444857.

Murray, J. (2012) Learning to live together: An exploration and analysis of managing cultural diversity in centre-based early childhood development programmes. *Intercultural Education, 23* (2): 89–103.

Nutbrown, C. (1998) Managing to include? Rights, responsibilities and respect. In P. Clough (ed.), *Managing Inclusive Education: From Policy to Experience*. London: Sage, pp. 167–176.

Nutbrown, C. and Clough, P. (2004) Inclusion and exclusion in the early years: Conversations with European educators. *European Journal of Special Needs Education, 19* (3): 301–315. DOI: 10.1080/0885625042000262479.

Oliver, M. (1996) *Understanding Disability: From Theory to Practice*. London: Macmillan Press.

Parry, J. (2015) Exploring the social connections in preschool settings between children labelled with special educational needs and their peers. *International Journal of Early Years Education, 23* (4): 352–364. DOI: 10.1080/09669760.2015.1046158.

Perlman, M., Kankesan, T. and Zhang, J. (2010) Promoting diversity in early child care education. *Early Child Development and Care, 180* (6): 753–766. DOI: 10. 1080/03004430802287606.

Rogers, C. (2007) Experiencing an 'inclusive' education: Parents and their children with special educational needs. *British Journal of Sociology of Education, 28* (1): 55–68. DOI: 10. 1080/01425690600996659.

Rogoff, B. (2003) *The Cultural Nature of Human Development.* London: Oxford University Press.

Tenenbaum, H.R. and Ruck, M.D. (2007) Are teachers' expectations different for racial minority than European American students? A meta-analysis. *Journal of Educational Psychology, 99* (2): 253–273. DOI: 10.1037/0022-0663.99. 2.253.

Whitmarsh, J. (2011) Othered voices: Asylum-seeking mothers and early years education. *European Early Childhood Education Research Journal, 19* (4): 535–551. DOI: 10. 1080/1350293X.2011.623540.

Yates, T.M. and Marcelo, A.K. (2014) Through race-colored glasses: Preschoolers' pretend play and teachers' ratings of preschooler adjustment. *Early Childhood Research Quarterly, 29*: 1–11.

9

MULTI-PROFESSIONAL AND INTER-DISCIPLINARY WORKING IN EARLY CHILDHOOD EDUCATION AND CARE

THIS CHAPTER WILL:

- briefly describe the recent international context of inter- and multi-disciplinary teams in early childhood education and care
- consider studies of initial training and multi-professionalism
- explore research which has focused on multi-disciplinarity: more than the sum of the parts
- suggest some research questions on the topic of multi-professional and inter-disciplinary working in ECEC
- provide some recommended reading to follow up the issues discussed.

This chapter focuses on research in the field of multi-professionalism and inter-disciplinary working and integrated provision in early childhood education and care. As work with young children has become more 'joined-up' there has been an increased emphasis on different professionals working collaboratively with and on provision for young children in their home and group settings. This chapter reviews some of the recent literature on the topic and suggests that lessons from international research identify five concerns. First, there is a need for *joined-up policies* – so that health, welfare, housing and education policies work in synergy and not in competition. Second, *shared professional development* is important for inter-disciplinary teams. Third, *resources* are essential for successful multi-disciplinary work. Fourth, *a shared language* – and understanding different professional meanings – is crucial. Fifth, *clarity of vision* is essential.

The chapter begins by briefly considering some origins and developments of cross-sector working with young children before reflecting on recent research on initial training of those working with young children and then considering how multi-professional working offers more than professionals working in isolation are able to provide.

ORIGINS AND DEVELOPMENTS OF CROSS-SECTOR WORKING WITH YOUNG CHILDREN

In a review of research in the UK from 2003–2017 (Payler and Wood, 2017) inter-professional practice and multi-agency working is identified as one for four key shifts in research in ECEC. Though the degree of success in terms of establishing modern day multi-disciplinary and inter-agency working is variable, it is clear that the UK has seen positive developments in multi-disciplinary working in the interests of young children (Cottle, 2011).

Developing inter-disciplinary initiatives to provide early childhood education and care provision for young children is not a new phenomenon. Famously, Margaret and Rachael McMillan pioneered the combination of health, education and social work in their work in London and Bradford – focusing on children's health and well-being to alleviate the effects of poverty and to support children's learning. In 1902, in London, because they believed that hungry children could not learn, Rachel and Margaret McMillan worked closely with James Keir Hardie and George Lansbury – leading campaigners for school meals to be provided for young children. That work was instrumental in the passing of the School Meals Act in 1906, an initiative that lasted for more than a century before being threatened by recent governments as a way of making cuts in education expenditure. It is a sobering observation that in the early part of 2018, food poverty gave rise, again, to the need for local authorities to face the fact that some children were going to school hungry.

In 1908 Rachel and Margaret McMillan opened the first school clinic and a 'Night Camp' where children living in the slums of London could wash, eat and get a clean set of clothing. Fuelled by her belief in social justice and her strong conviction that sick and hungry children could not learn, Margaret McMillan built medical and health support for children from the slums into her work. Struck by the poverty the children and their families lived in she wrote:

> The condition of the poorer children was worse than anything that was described or painted. It was a thing that this generation is glad to forget. The neglect of infants, the utter neglect almost of toddlers and older children, the blight of early labour, all combined to make of a once vigorous people a race of undergrown and spoiled adolescents; and just as people looked on at the torture two hundred years ago and less, without any great indignation, so in the 1890s people saw the misery of poor children without perturbation. (McMillan, 1925: 45)

This brings to mind the need for food banks in present time and, once again, charitable responses to alleviate the life threatening effects of poverty. In recent years, and following a small number of pioneering initiatives in the 1980s, to develop multi-professional and collaborative departmental working in parts of the UK (for example, Sheffield, Corby and Bradford), the bringing together of health, social services and education professionals in a single service was finally established in national policy under the Labour government of the late 1990s with Sure Start 'trail blazer' programmes in parts of the country deemed to need a new form of early intervention and support. In the UK, multi-agency working was established through Sure Start programmes where health, social services, education and other services came together to provide local services for young children and their families – departments of housing and children and family charities were also partners in some instances (Weinberger et al., 2005). The Department for Education and Skills established more Children's Centres (based on the original Sure Start centres but with less funding) in the early 2000s to provide joined up, integrated services (DfES, 2003). These, and the services they brought together, were later largely deconstructed (and some families might have said their services were destroyed entirely) when savage cuts to local authority budgets led to the withdrawal of necessary funding and vital services. Children's Centres, once neighbourhood 'hubs' for multi-agency professional learning and centres for improvement of quality early education for young children (Cotton, 2013), have been on the decline in England since 2010. In at least one local authority the number of centres was almost halved as the council sought to manage a radical reduction in budget. Parents whose children attended those centres were told that provision was not closing, but being relocated and there would always be a centre no more than a bus ride away. For parents living in poverty, if a return bus fare costs say £3, this amounts to £6 each day, and for a child attending every day this takes £30 from a weekly budget. Many parents simply do not have this money, and in addition for some parents the challenge of getting a baby, a toddler and a three-year-old on the bus at a given time every day is considerable. Policy changes and cuts to provision not only threaten children's opportunities but also add stress to families and are a drain on family finances, thus cuts in public expenditure and the reduction of neighbourhood provision mean that some families will not be able to access the inter-disciplinary 'one-stop' service that Sure Start Children's Centres in the UK once offered.

Paradoxically, as education and care provision has experienced increased demand over the past two decades, governments have initiated ambitious plans to realise the provision that is needed. In parallel with developments in the UK, for example, Australia saw the stated ambition that by '2020 all children have the best start in life to create a better future for themselves and for the nation' (Council of Australian Governments, 2009: 2). The review of ECEC carried out by the Organisation for Economic Co-operation and Development (OECD, 2017) has identified many examples of multi-professional working for young children and their families in many parts of the world.

Internationally, there is a general consensus that professionals in different disciplines can provide better services for families if they collaborate – with a more 'seamless' experience for families if these are joined up, and better still, under one roof. To achieve the positive benefits of inter-agency and multi-professional approaches a number of conditions need to exist. First, and crucially, national and international studies of the topic suggest that for inter-professional services to run smoothly there is a need for *joined-up policies* – where health, welfare, housing and education policies work in synergy and not in competition, and where local, regional and national policies need to fit together to form a coherent whole. Second, there is a burning need for *shared professional development* where people working with young children from a range of professions come together, to reach a better understanding of their respective roles, mutual concerns and specific contributions. This is not a substitute for discreet discipline-specific continuing professional development, which is necessary to maintain and enhance expertise in specific fields of work. Third, the necessary *resources* are needed to facilitate successful multi-disciplinary working. Co-ordination and collaboration across and within different disciplines takes additional effort, but yields important benefits, so must be adequately resourced. Fourth, *a shared language* is essential – around terms and terminology and the meanings attributed to professional terms and phrases. All professionals have different ways of expressing their work and use particular disciplinary terms. If reaching a shared language is not possible, then a way of understanding each other's professional language and meanings is important. Finally, and essential for any successful inter-disciplinary working, is a *clarity of vision*, where all involved agree on their mission for children and their families, from which ways of working to achieve that vision can flow.

RESEARCH INTO INITIAL TRAINING AND MULTI-PROFESSIONALISM

One of the difficulties in moving forward with integrated provision and multi-professional training for those beginning work in ECEC is how they are trained and what form multi-professional initial education for work with young children might take. Focusing on one multi-disciplinary course in one English university, Bath (2011) examined student and tutor perspectives on what such a course should address. Using participatory action research, findings suggest that students made connections between 'different disciplinary discourses' (2011: 187), yet those tutors teaching on the course suggested that such a course – which seeks to equip people for several different professions – undermined individual professional identity and that the course design constrained specific knowledge. Bath's evaluation involved 60 students enrolled on an Early Childhood Studies degree, which aimed to 'equip students for a future in a multi-professional early years workforce' (2011: 181), and six of their tutors. The evaluation highlighted issues of identity and 'communities of practice' (Wenger, 1998), where there were different degrees of alignment between conceptual understandings of different professional disciplines. Bath suggests that:

> even if it is difficult to prove that multi-professional approaches to practice directly lead to better outcomes for children, training professionals together and providing multidisciplinary courses for future early years professionals might be seen to have a positive impact on those outcomes. (2011: 190)

Thus multi-professional initial training and development and inter-agency working are seen generally to be 'a good thing' – even though there is insufficient evidence to be unequivocal about the benefits to children. Such training and opportunities to network and share concerns and practices can lead to enhanced professional confidence (Payler and Georgeson, 2013). It is clear that more studies on the effects of multi-professional training and working are needed in the UK and internationally.

A further example can be found in a US study where inter-disciplinary teacher education in ECE and early childhood special education (ECSE) has grown but research is limited. Miller and Losardo (2002) elicited the views of newly practising graduates of an ECE/ECSE inter-disciplinary teacher preparation course (birth to five/six years) through a postal survey. Graduates reported that they felt they were better prepared in areas of general child development than they were for working with children with special educational needs, and expressed a need for more content and opportunity to experience practice in working with families, behaviour analysis, and working with children who have moderate to severe disabilities. Miller and Losardo (2002) reiterated the need for more research in this aspect of initial preparation courses for early childhood practitioners.

The last two decades have witnessed an almost global focus on early childhood education and care and with that has come considerable attention being paid to who works with young children and how they are prepared for that work. Though some think that what has come to be known as the early childhood workforce is a relatively new phenomena, this is far from the case. Charlotte Mason, born in 1842, set up a training course for early childhood teachers in 1891 when she opened the House of Education, to train governesses and others working with young children. Since that time, others have emphasised the importance of good training on sound principles as crucial in establishing the best forms of early education and care for young children.

Focusing on first year students and graduates of the Department of Early Childhood Education of the Democritus University of Thrace, Greece, Rekalidou and Panitsides (2015) draw attention to the many factors – in addition to initial education and training – that impact on early career development. They say that:

> although universities' role in adequately preparing prospective early childhood teachers is undeniably critical, it is important to acknowledge the significance of environmental factors, such as the context the new teacher finds him or herself in and the support available, which might significantly improve teaching and limit attrition rates. (2015: 337)

Not all students in the study agreed on the contribution of their programme in preparing them for work with young children, pointing to issues around the programme curricula and the need for more research, the latter being a common concern in many countries.

STUDIES OF MULTI-DISCIPLINARITY: MORE THAN THE SUM OF THE PARTS

Concluding their review of research in ECEC in the UK from 2003–2017, Payler and Davis (2017) summarise thus:

> The professionalization of the workforce and ECEC as a career now face two competing issues. On one hand, research evidence has revealed the demanding nature and complexity of ECEC professional practice and the challenges of educating, training and continuously developing the workforce to work effectively with such complexity. But on the other hand, there are increasing political and economic demands for an 'affordable' childcare sector to provide greater capacity at lower costs. How can such competing drives be resolved to ensure a sustainable and transformative workforce? (2017: 21)

Following the policy line of recent UK governments, around collaboration between different professionals working with young children and their families, the effectiveness of collaborative work with young children remains 'patchy' in the UK, in particular where health teams are concerned (Bell et al., 2009). Bringing together different systems, approaches and values is not easy; it takes commitment and effort to break through disciplinary barriers, challenge long held perspectives and practices, and agree a shared vision and mission in work with young children. Research in the UK is mostly 'small-scale, draws on multi-disciplinary perspectives and incorporates a range of methodological approaches' (Payler and Wood, 2017: 113). This is a similar story internationally.

Duhn et al. (2016) focused on Edwards' (2005) work on an Australian Relational Agency Framework as a tool for what they refer to as 'horizontal' rather than top-down approaches to multi-disciplinary working. They concluded that:

> Developing common knowledge to 'think about one's own expertise and contribution in relation to what others with different disciplinary/community knowledges and practice bring' (Phase 6, RAF) generated new practices that aimed to create support for children and families by paying careful attention to fine-grained differences in professional practice and meaning making across sites. (Duhn et al., 2016: 387)

This approach focuses on building a sense and practice of 'belonging' between professionals with different practices, as Duhn et al. suggest:

> A critical sense of belonging would pay particular attention to the affective dimension to ask questions such as 'How can we build practices together in this place and with these people, and who else should be here to contribute, to listen or to speak?' (2016: 388)

This work brings us to the point where we can see that building of shared values and the development and adoption of a common language are crucial to successful and effective multi-disciplinary working in the interests of young children and their families. Where professionals with different roles and different and complementary skills work together with a shared vision, rather than working in opposition with limited common understanding, then multi-professional practice is more than the sum of its parts, and the value of investment in shared services is enhanced.

Of course, successful multi-professional practice demands good leadership, and leaders who understand the perspective of all involved in the work that a service or setting provides for young children and their families. This was apparent in the Sure Start programmes in the UK (Weinberger et al., 2005), where leadership of a multi-professional and inter-disciplinary team providing a range of health, social and education services was critical to the success of the programme. Such leadership requires considerable time and effort, and engagement of the will as well as the intellect.

With a focus on the needs of immigrant and refugee families in the US, Isik-Ercan et al. (2017) demonstrate the importance of linked services, working together to help meet families' specific needs, and conclude that:

> Schools, once at the centre of the community, may continue to serve an important role as hubs for linking families with consolidated and integrated services, such as applications for social services, educational career support, employment help, ESL classes, and marriage and family therapy. Some of these services may be provided in the school building, with the more experienced and visible parents meeting and mentoring the newer parents. Casual gatherings for families, such as coffee hours, cooking classes,

ADULTS

book club, and cultural events and fairs are examples that allow for more experienced
parental contributions to the schools. (2017: 1427)

This is an example of the range of services from different disciplines that can be provided,
en suite, for families and because they are part of one service and system, the likelihood
of take up is maximised.

In Germany, Schoyerer and van Santen (2016) focused on what they refer to as the
'interdisciplinary challenge' of early childhood education and care, arguing that:

ECEC needs to be more strongly viewed as an interdisciplinary challenge, and that
ways forward need to include a comprehensive professionalisation and workforce
development project: the aim must be to provide children and families with care and
support services tailored both quantitatively and qualitatively to their needs, thereby
offering not only support to facilitate the reconciliation of work and family obligations
and an alternative place of education for children, but also programmes of specific
support for disadvantaged and support-dependent children and families. (2016: 51)

This concept of bespoke provision to suit families' individual and specific needs is an
important one. Meeting the diverse needs of families cannot always be achieved by offering
a 'one size fits all' service. The German system of ECEC is diverse, with differing working
conditions depending on service providers, different structures and different systems and,
importantly, different working conditions for ECEC professionals depending on where they
work. Schoyerer and van Santen (2016) observe that families seem more ready in present
times to seek support, and out-of-home child care, than in previous decades, this being
largely due to changes in family structures and working practices. As the demand for provision for young children has increased, along with growing interest in enhancing the quality
of provision offered, so too has the investment needed to meet these needs and demands.
Seeing ECEC as an inter-disciplinary project, Schoyerer and van Santen (2016) suggest 'inte-
grative and cooperative approaches as the most promising ways forward' (2016: 60), but
this of course requires considerable investment to bring about the necessary developments
because 'what is needed is nothing less than the provision of a reliable, competent and professional support system in highly unstable and unpredictable circumstances' (2016: 60).

A MULTI-PROFESSIONAL AND INTER-DISCIPLINARY FUTURE FOR ECEC

Changes to the provision and the increasing demand for ECEC provision in many countries
in the world mean that the need for additional resources is a global issue. The bringing
together of services through multi-professional teams could mean that resources are

maximised to the benefit of families who then receive the provision they and their children wish for and need. This seems also to be the case in the Netherlands where there is considerable diversity of provision borne out of socio-political histories which run deep in the story of evolution of ECEC in the country. Van Oers (2013) argues that the way forward lies in a developmental education approach which is multi-disciplinary in nature and includes research collaboration involving ECEC practitioners in a community of practice.

In order that multi-professional and inter-disciplinary working amounts to more than the sum of the individual parts three things, at least, are essential: first, there must be real and deep understanding of what each professional and each discipline can offer families; second, those in positions of leadership need to understand the benefits and potential to be derived from multi-professionalism; and third, realistic and adequate investment must be made to build team understanding of the contributions of team members so that a deep understanding of the different roles represented in a team is achieved, in a fully integrated ECEC provision.

RESEARCH QUESTIONS ON MULTI-PROFESSIONAL AND INTER-DISCIPLINARY WORKING IN ECEC

Perhaps one of the greatest challenges of researching understandings and experiences of multi-professional and inter-disciplinary working in early childhood education and care is navigating the terrain of terminology and definitions, and reaching shared understandings of the terminology used. Clarity about roles, responsibilities, disciplines and expectations will be important if research studies, whatever their scale, are to be meaningful. Bringing together the international literature on any theme requires some dexterity in interpretation of terms, but on the topic of multi-professional and inter-disciplinary working in early childhood education and care, where the names of many disciplines vary with countries and even with local regions, makes the task even more complex. This needs to be remembered when developing research projects in this field of study.

Some suggested research questions for early years practitioners and students include:

- What forms of continuing professional development do multi-professional teams need?
  This question is best answered by asking the people involved. It might be worth consulting setting leaders as well. Sometimes the perceived needs of leaders and the practitioners themselves are not the same, so finding out the perspectives of both groups – through interview or questionnaire – is useful.

(Continued)

(Continued)

○ How does a Children's Centre bring together a multi-disciplinary team with a shared vision and values?

An ethnographic study which collects data over time, from the perspectives of all involved, and tells the story of an evolving multi-professional team would be a very useful contribution to our understandings of this question.

○ What are the advantages and challenges of working with professionals from different disciplines and how can advantages be maximised and challenges overcome?

One way to begin to answer this question would be to conduct some in-depth interviews with a small number of professionals from a range of disciplinary backgrounds. These would shed light on the varied perspectives of people who do a different job from themselves in working with and for young children and their families.

○ How are early childhood practitioners – in various roles – trained for inter-agency working?

This question could entail looking at various syllabi of courses that train ECE professionals and identifying relevant elements that are taught. It might also involve talking with ECE practitioners to find out, from their personal perspectives, what training they had for inter-agency working.

A NOTE ON RESEARCH ETHICS AND INTEGRITY

A key ethical issue when delving into the perspectives of professionals who work together is that no harm is done to the make-up of the team and the people who make up that team. If whole teams participate in the study, they will surely be identifiable to each other and participants need to be clear about that, so confidentiality may not be possible and it is likely that – even with pseudonyms – anonymity may be impossible to maintain. Another way to address these questions is to invite participants from a number of different teams – the bigger the sample, the less likely it is that people will be identifiable by their responses.

RECOMMENDED READING

Cottle, M. (2011) Understanding and achieving quality in Sure Start Children's Centres: Practitioners' perspectives. *International Journal of Early Years Education*, 19 (3–4): 249–265. DOI: 10.1080/09669760.2011.638859.

A useful and critical review of Sure Start from practitioners' perspectives.

Duhn, I., Fleer, M. and Harrison, L. (2016) Supporting multidisciplinary networks through relationality and a critical sense of belonging: Three 'gardening tools' and the Relational Agency Framework. *International Journal of Early Years Education*, 24 (3): 378–391. DOI: 10.1080/09669760.2016.1196578.

An important paper examining the creation of 'belonging' and usefulness of the Relational Agency Framework in Australian practice.

OECD (2017) *Starting Strong 2017: Key OECD Indicators on Early Childhood Education and Care*. Paris: OECD Publishing. DOI: 10.1787/9789264276116-en.

An important contextualisation of current concerns in ECEC internationally.

Weinberger, J., Pickstone, C. and Hannon, P. (eds) (2005) *Learning from Sure Start: Working with Young Children and Their Families*. Buckingham: Open University Press.

A fascinating and far-reaching account of the experiences of setting up one of the first Sure Start centres with community involvement and multi-agency services for families.

REFERENCES

Bath, C. (2011) Participatory concepts of multidisciplinary/professional working on an Early Childhood Studies degree course in the UK. *Early Years*, *31* (2): 181–192. DOI: 10. 1080/09575146.2011.561484.

Bell, A., Corfield, M., Davies, J. and Richardson, N. (2009) Collaborative transdisciplinary intervention in early years: Putting theory into practice. *Child: Care, Health and Development*, *36* (1): 142–148. DOI: 10.1111/j.1365-2214.2009.01027.x.

Cottle, M. (2011) Understanding and achieving quality in Sure Start Children's Centres: Practitioners' perspectives. *International Journal of Early Years Education*, *19* (3–4): 249–265. DOI: 10.1080/09669760.2011.638859.

Cotton, L. (2013) 'It's just more in the real world really': How can a local project support early years practitioners from different settings in working and learning together? *Early Years: An International Research Journal*, *33* (1): 18–32. DOI: 10.1080/09575146.2011.642850.

Council of Australian Governments (2009) *Protecting Children Is Everyone's Business: National Framework for Protecting Australia's Children 2009–2020*. Canberra: Commonwealth of Australia. www.dss.gov.au/sites/default/files/documents/child_protection_framework. pdf (accessed 12 February 2018).

DfES (Department for Education and Skills) (2003) *Every Child Matters* (Green Paper). London: HMSO. www.gov.uk/government/uploads/system/uploads/attachment_data/ file/272064/5860.pdf (accessed 29 January 2018).

Duhn, I., Fleer, M. and Harrison, L. (2016) Supporting multidisciplinary networks through relationality and a critical sense of belonging: Three 'gardening tools' and the Relational Agency Framework. *International Journal of Early Years Education, 24* (3): 378–391. DOI: 10.1080/09669760.2016.1196578.

Edwards, A. (2005) Relational Agency: Learning to be a resourceful practitioner. *International Journal of Educational Research, 43*: 168–182.

Isik-Ercan, Z., Demir-Dagdas, T., Cakmakci, H., Cava-Tadik, Y. and Intepe-Tingir, S. (2017) Multidisciplinary perspectives towards the education of young low-income immigrant children. *Early Child Development and Care, 187* (9): 1413–1432. DOI: 10. 1080/03004430.2016.1173037.

McMillan, M. (1925) *Children, Culture and Class in Britain*. London: George Allen and Unwin.

Miller, P.S. and Losardo, A. (2002) Graduates' perceptions of strengths and needs in interdisciplinary teacher preparation for early childhood education: A state study. *Teacher Education and Special Education, 25* (3): 309–319.

OECD (2017) *Starting Strong 2017: Key OECD Indicators on Early Childhood Education and Care*. Paris: OECD Publishing. DOI: 10.1787/9789264276116-en.

Payler, J. and Davis, G. (2017) Professionalism: Early years as a career. In J. Payler and E. Wood (eds), *BERA-TACTYC Early Childhood Research Review 2003–2017*. London: British Educational Research Association. www.bera.ac.uk/wp-content/uploads/2017/05/BERA-TACTYC-Full-Report.pdf?noredirect=1 (accessed 29 January 2018).

Payler, J. and Georgeson, J. (2013) Multiagency working in the early years: Confidence, competence and context. *Early Years: An International Research Journal, 33* (4): 380–397. DOI: 10.1080/09575146.2013.841130.

Payler, J. and Wood, E. (eds) (2017) *BERA-TACTYC Early Childhood Research Review 2003–2017*. London: British Educational Research Association. www.bera.ac.uk/wp-content/uploads/2017/05/BERA-TACTYC-Full-Report.pdf?noredirect=1 (accessed 29 January 2018).

Rekalidou, G. and Panitsides, E.A. (2015) What does it take to be a 'successful teacher'? Universities' role in preparing the future early-years workforce. *Early Years, 35* (4): 333–350. DOI: 10.1080/09575146.2015.1080231.

Schoyerer, G. and van Santen, E. (2016) Early childhood education and care in a context of social heterogeneity and inequality: Empirical notes on an interdisciplinary challenge. *Early Years, 36* (1): 51–65. DOI: 10.1080/09575146.2015.1075966.

van Oers, B. (2013) Educational innovation between freedom and fixation: The cultural-political construction of innovations in early childhood education in the Netherlands. *International Journal of Early Years Education, 21* (2–3): 178–191. DOI: 10.1080/09669760.2013.832949.

Weinberger, J., Pickstone, C. and Hannon, P. (eds) (2005) *Learning from Sure Start: Working with Young Children and Their Families*. Buckingham: Open University Press.

Wenger, E. (1998) *Communities of Practice: Learning, Meaning and Identity*. Cambridge: Cambridge University Press.

10

PROFESSIONALISM, QUALIFICATIONS AND STATUS

THIS CHAPTER WILL:

- describe the international ECE workforce
- consider what 'being professional' means
- discuss the qualifications of those working in ECEC
- discuss workforce status
- highlight the importance of a stable workforce for sustained relationships with young children
- suggest some research questions on the topic of professionalism, qualifications and status
- provide some recommended reading to follow up the issues discussed.

The ECEC workforce varies greatly from setting to setting, and from country to country. It has no shared nomenclature and few 'core' conceptualisations. This chapter considers some international research into the ECEC workforce, focusing particularly on professionalism, qualifications and status. Drawing on studies from some 25 countries, this chapter highlights shared international concerns about the quality of the ECEC workforce, and identifies a need for deeper, more substantial studies along with longer-term investment and political will to foster sustained retention and improvement.

THE INTERNATIONAL ECEC WORKFORCE

Internationally, research on the early childhood education and care workforce is patchy and variable and participant samples vary greatly, with the majority of studies having between one and 25 participants. The small number of studies conducted with larger samples tend to be online surveys (for example, Dalli, 2008). This chapter draws on the existing international research published since the year 2000 to first describe the international ECEC workforce. This is followed by a consideration of 'professionalism' and emerging typologies of ECEC 'professionalism' in different geo-political contexts. Qualifications and 'status' in the ECEC workforce, in particular 1) identity, 2) pay and conditions of service, and 3) recognition and respect, are discussed. The chapter concludes with a consideration of the contribution of research to understanding international ECEC workforces, in particular the importance of relationships with young children (see also Chapters 4, 5 and 12). In a globalised context, despite recent political moves to strengthen borders rather than make them more permeable, we must still anticipate the need for international exchange within a sustainable ECEC workforce of the future.

WHO ARE THE ECEC WORKFORCE?

Internationally, 21st century research around the ECEC workforce has highlighted policy confusion and the need for action. With no universally and often no nationally agreed nomenclature, it is difficult to find a single meaningful term to refer to all who work in ECEC (Andrew, 2015) and in many instances, the same job title is used to cover many different roles and responsibilities, and remuneration varies greatly.

In any profession, job titles carry connotations of role, status and value, and the labels given to particular ECEC roles can denote the philosophies connected with those roles and reflect understandings and beliefs about the work involved. Titles are helpful in understanding priorities, however disparate job titles can work against coherence and communities of practice (Cameron et al. 2002; Banković, 2014), especially when the same word, 'teacher' for example, is used to describe many different roles.

ECEC settings also have many different generic names, and perhaps with the notable exceptions of Steiner Waldorf kindergartens and Montessori nursery schools many UK provisions have changed identities on a regular basis – often when new governments undertake a sort of 'rebranding' exercise, seemingly to demonstrate what new policies have been introduced.

What we call the jobs people do and the ECEC settings they work in is important – they place those roles within a profession (Adams, 2008), and this has the effect of uniting the people who perform similar roles, which in turn brings strength of identity and awareness of practices, rights, responsibilities and conditions.

WHAT IS PROFESSIONALISM IN ECEC?

Constructions of 'professionalism' can be 'fluid, contentious and constantly under re-construction' (Dalli and Urban, 2008: 151) and are often dependent on terminology and socio-cultural contexts, which vary from country to country (Karila, 2008). Thus, defining *what* an ECEC professional *is* can be a challenge. The nature of professional identities is often contested in the literature, offering no easy fixes for policy-makers seeking to address ECEC workforce issues. In England, various recent government attentions have impacted on the roles, status and multiple definitions of members of the ECEC workforce (Moss, 2006; Osgood, 2006; 2010). In 2006 a new accredited status was introduced with some graduate-educated practitioners gaining Early Years Professional Status (EYPS); many who first earned the status were already teachers with QTS (Qualified Teacher Status – the recognised status of teachers required in UK state schools). This policy was seen as an attempt to 'professionalise' what had been hitherto a largely non-graduate workforce (Miller, 2008; Lloyd and Hallet, 2010; Simpson, 2010a, 2010b), so the policy decision to attract graduates and introduce the term 'professional' into the job titles and to recognise the status of some ECEC workers thrust the notion of professionalism to the fore. This change of nomenclature underscored a policy decision to enhance the status of the workforce which, for Osgood (2009: 744) 'represents government constructions of professionalism'. Gewirtz et al. (2009) urge us not to consider:

> professionalism as *either* a genuine concern about standards and ethics and 'doing one's job well' *or* as a legitimating discourse that reproduces particular forms of (classed, 'raced' and gendered) identity, power and in/exclusion, but as simultaneously both of these things. (2009: 4)

Many political and cultural perspectives influence what constitutes 'professionalism' (Oberhuemer, 2000; Rosenthal, 2003) and the literature tends to consider professionalism as a socially constructed concept. As Musgrave has it: 'a better educated workforce can help to develop their own construction of professionalism' (2010: 440). The form of professionalism envisioned with the introduction of EYPS was likely one of 'toeing the line' and following 'company' policy; thus potentially 'constrained' in its definition and expectation (Vincent and Braun 2011; Campbell-Barr, 2014). Certainly those gaining EYPS were expected to implement and lead settings in their use of the required curriculum framework (the Early Years Foundation Stage) and to help their provisions do well in quality control OFSTED inspections. However, 'professionalism' can also be practised when issues are contested and the height of professionalism can include challenging perceived 'wrongs' and questioning flawed and restrictive policies.

TYPOLOGIES OF PROFESSIONALISM

Three distinct typologies of professionalism in ECEC have emerged recently, developed in collaboration with those who consider themselves to be ECEC professionals. This roots-up rather than policy-imposed approach to defining ECEC professionalism was first adopted by Dalli (2008) in New Zealand, who considered 'the evolving characteristics of early childhood professional practice' (2008: 174). Early childhood teachers in New Zealand were invited to participate in a national survey, which led to a collective reflection of teachers' professional experiences. Dalli identified three main themes: 'a) pedagogical style, b) specialist professional knowledge, c) practices and collaborative relations' (2008: 175). Using a similar approach, Rose and Rogers (2012) put forward the notion of the 'plural practitioner' whose role is conceptualised in 'Seven Selves': Critical Reflector, Carer, Communicator, Facilitator, Observer, Assessor and Creator. Brock's (2012) seven elements typology is based on her study with 12 practitioners and focuses on: 1) knowledge, 2) qualifications, training and professional development, 3) skills, 4) autonomy, 5) values, 6) ethics, and 7) rewards.

These widely differing typologies seek to conceptualise ECEC professionalism yet comparison reveals some quite distinct positions on what is important. Dalli emphasises pedagogy, yet Rose and Rogers, along with Brock, do not. Rose and Rogers appear to foreground 'care' whilst Brock places some emphasis on training and qualifications as conditions of professionalism. However, in the latter two typologies the number of participants involved in contributing to them was very small and this perhaps explains their lack of synergy.

DO QUALIFICATIONS MATTER?

For several decades the need for appropriate qualifications has been taken as a 'given' for a professional workforce (Katz, 1985) and well-qualified staff have been shown to help to improve the outcomes of the children (Barnett, 2003; Sylva et al., 2003; 2004;

Oberhuemer et al., 2010; Cameron and Harding, 2017). Reporting on a multi-state study in the US, Early et al. (2006) make a clear connection between high-level qualifications with professionalism: 'Requiring a degree and compensating the teachers accordingly professionalizes the early childhood workforce. More can be expected of professional teachers who are credentialed' (2006: 192). However, qualifications alone are not enough – because it is not possible to teach every 'quality' that is needed and because 'the narrow focus of these measures may mean they will have limited success' (Cumming, 2015: 54). Early et al. (2006), following Pianta et al. (2005), argued that having a degree is not sufficient to improve quality and child outcomes:

> It may be that having a Bachelor's degree will prove to be a necessary condition for attaining high quality, but education and credentials by themselves are not sufficient. Instead, program administrators must institute measures to track quality in terms of what happens to children in the classrooms on a daily basis to ensure that these programs meet their goals of improving outcomes for all children. (2005: 193)

Gomez et al. (2015) also argue that because the quality of ECEC provision in the US is considered to be generally poor, the status of its ECEC workforce needs to be enhanced. This necessitates sustained investment in ECEC professional training, for long enough to achieve positive change. Fresh calls for new professional development strategies (Kagan et al., 2014) have been made alongside a shared, international understanding of the workforce and the issues it faces (Oberhuemer, 2011; 2015).

Qualifications are seen as essential to a high quality workforce which leads to good experiences and outcomes for young children (DfE, 2012; Ejuu, 2012; SCSEEC, 2012; Department of Education: Australia, 2014; Siraj and Kingston, 2015). Dalli (2011) comments on the push forward for qualifications in New Zealand, considering that:

> Policies within the strategic plan to progressively upgrade staff qualifications across all teacher-led early childhood services to a benchmark level of a three-year diploma or degree marked out New Zealand as a leader in professionalising its early years workforce. (2011: 229)

In a review of qualifications for England and Wales, Nutbrown (2012) recommended a mix of qualifications including qualified teachers – with a career progression route to ensure enhanced status. In this way qualifications were seen as signifiers of knowledge, skills and understanding, which came together in a set of attributes by which people could work well with young children and their families. Nutbrown's recommended progression route (Figure 10.1) made room for the 16-year-old apprentice and the graduate entrant whilst seeking to address concerns about poor quality qualifications and workforce status.

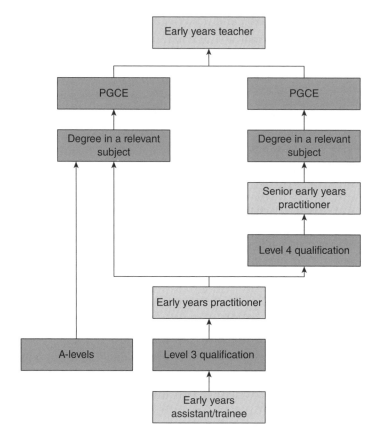

Figure 10.1 Nutbrown's proposed typical routes through a career working in the early years

Source: Nutbrown, 2012: 47, para 4.12

What Nutbrown was putting forward was an argument for levels of quality in qualifications, which enabled people to become fitted for their job, and here the place of teachers with QTS, in this multi-qualified team, was important. This new career structure was designed to fit with varying levels of qualifications and consistent job titles as set out in Table 10.1, and progression and promotion were important to the status of the workforce. The model was designed to make it possible for ECEC workers to advance in their career whilst continuing to work with children in a multi-qualified team, and to break out of the existing system which appeared to be keeping lower qualified members of the workforce in the same position with little prospect of advancement. In a workforce where some 98 per cent were women, this opportunity was important.

Approaches to training ECEC staff in different countries vary as do the contexts and values of those societies (Moss, 2000), and as international interest in ECEC grows, and

Table 10.1 Nutbrown's proposals for consistent job titles and roles

Job title	Level of full and relevant early years qualification	Included in rations for EYFS?	Role includes
Early Years Assistant/Trainee	Unqualified, level 2, perhaps on a training route to level 3	No	Supervised support work within a setting, learning on the job
Early Years Apprentice	Unqualified, level 2, on an Apprenticeship route	No	Supervised support work within a setting, learning on the job
Early Years Practitioner	Level 3	Yes	Leading practice within a room, working directly with children and families, could be a manager in a small setting
Senior Early Years Practitioner	Level 4 and above	Yes	Leading practice across a number of rooms, working directly with children and families, could be a manager
Early Years Professional	Graduate, with EYPS	Yes	Leading practice across a setting, working directly with children and families, could be a manager
Early Years Teacher	Graduate, with QTS	Yes	Providing overall pedagogical leadership for a setting, working directly with children and families, and supporting staff with lower levels of qualifications

Source: Nutbrown, 2012: 46, para 4.9

national policies have become interested in the workforce, there has tended to be an initial injection of funding for the particular qualifications that a country needs to sustain the workforce. Though such funding is often insufficient and short-lived it has the effect of bringing yet more state regulation of qualifications. Funding to support workforce training and qualifications is rarely maintained for long enough to bring about real workforce enhancement and expansion of provision is not always supported by the expansion of a high calibre workforce (Cameron and Harding, 2017). In Scotland, it has been suggested that a focus on qualifications has led to a new professional workforce for children and young people (Davis et al., 2014), yet the impact on outcomes for children could not be determined at the time (Dunlop, 2015). The positive relationship between the education of educators and the outcomes of the children they work with has been highlighted in several studies (Loeb et al., 2004; Early et al., 2006; 2007) and is, after all, a central purpose of establishing a well-educated workforce.

ISSUES OF STATUS IN THE ECEC WORKFORCE

Recent international ECEC workforce research highlights concerns around three key issues: 1) identity, 2) pay and conditions of service, and 3) recognition and respect.

IDENTITY

In a review of workforce qualifications in England and Wales, Nutbrown's (2012) vision for early childhood education and care was stated as one where the professional identities of early years practitioners were bound together with the quality of the experiences they offered young children and their families, and:

> every child is able to experience high quality care and education whatever type of home or group setting they attend; early years staff have a strong professional identity, take pride in their work, and are recognised and valued by parents, other professionals and society as a whole; high quality early education and care is led by well qualified early years practitioners; and the importance of childhood is understood, respected and valued. (2012: 10)

However, multiple job titles for broadly similar roles and many different roles and qualifications lead to varied perceptions (and often realities) of the status of ECEC practitioners in society (Gibson, 2013). This seems to be an international problem where the lack of coherence contributes to low status.

An interpretive meta-analysis of 38 empirical studies from nine countries identified an interest in the UK in the introduction of EYPS and conflict between personal and professional values (Cumming et al., 2013). However, a government-funded review of the perspectives of UK practitioners with EYP status concluded that the award gave them 'professional confidence and agency to lead and inspire others in pedagogy, provision and practice' (Hallet, 2013: 320). We do not know if it was the experience, new learning or the enhanced status that came with the title EPYS that led to these changes. In parallel to Hallet's UK study, Harwood and Tukonic (2016: 489) investigated the perspectives of 54 practitioners in Ontario, who reported the importance of particular qualities (e.g. good listener, patient and understanding), but they gave little attention to more complex theoretical concerns around professionalism.

Langford's (2008) Canadian study of women early childhood educators led to a call for a discourse of criticality as a way of changing ECEC graduate identity:

> Criticality encourages early childhood educators to look outward as a social and political subject and worker rather than just inward as a psychological subject with gendered qualities and feelings, and to explore issues of dilemma, ideology, social position, contradictory values, and competing sources of discourse. (2008: 98.)

Similarly, the participants in an English study of career development decision-making, particularly in relation to progression to higher education, 'did not express a strong sense of their professional identity or particularly see themselves as part of a professional community beyond their own setting' (Kendall et al., 2012: 556). They were reported to show little awareness of national policy moves to 'professionalise' the workforce, with some describing themselves as 'second class' to school teachers and accepting, rather than challenging, that view. Further, Kendall et al. conclude that 'some "barriers" to progression manifest as intrinsic and are bound to core understandings of self and identity' (2012: 557) and McGillivray (2008) too discusses issues of identity amongst a range of ECEC practitioners.

The hierarchy of status is a factor in many countries, including Italy where different qualifications and conditions of service have resulted in a 'significant gap' in the status perceived by ECEC practitioners. This 'is increasingly affecting the professional relationships between *educatori* (workers with the under threes) and *insegnanti* (teachers)' (Lazzari et al., 2013: 135). Further, Lazzari et al. (2015: 284) identify 'increasing discontinuity, characterising professionalisation initiatives across the 0–3 and 3–6 sectors [which] might lead to widening the gap among professionals working across these services'. And of course, the gap is further widened by disparities in pay and conditions of service across and within ECEC sectors of provision.

PAY AND CONDITIONS OF SERVICE

Higher (degree level) qualifications generally mean higher pay, and in the US Huss-Keeler et al. (2013) found greater motivation in younger entrants than in workers who were established in their ECEC roles. ECEC workers, mainly women, are amongst the lowest paid in the US (Boyd, 2013: 3), and several US studies concur that low rates of pay and poor professional status bring difficulties in recruitment and retention (Lifton, 2001; Holochwost et al., 2009; Barford and Whelton, 2010; Bessie Tartt Wilson Initiative for Children, 2010; Vance, 2010). Many argue that low rates of pay in ECEC work are perpetuated because the workforce is mainly female (most countries having just 2% of men in the ECEC workforce).

Most of the 32 early years teacher-participants in Boyd's (2013) study commented on long hours and no additional pay for extra hours. Pay was generally low with some workers on poverty-level rates, prompting many teachers to move on to teach older children where pay and conditions (including job security) were better. This trend is also found in the UK (Skeggs, 2001; Kendall et al.. 2012) and Australia (Warrilow and Fisher, 2003; Gibson, 2013). Whilst there is a difficulty in the international literature because there are different statuses to a 'teacher' and with those differences, pay and conditions vary, the need for investment to address workforce issues, in particular pay and conditions, is clear and consistent (Whitebook and Sakai, 2003; Fenech et al., 2009; Nutbrown, 2012).

In Finland expansion of provision has been brought about by a shift in priorities in terms of professional qualifications, reducing the number of teachers with degrees in favour of a larger number of less well-qualified staff who receive lower pay (Karila, 2008). As Karila notes, a wider understanding is needed of the nature of provision for children and the responsibilities of those who work with them. A greater understanding of workforce *identity* may help address problems of sustainability brought about by low and unequal pay, a lack of professional status, workplace stress and professional development opportunities, thus addressing problems of workforce recruitment and retention (Cumming et al., 2013: 223).

Good conditions of service with improved health and well-being of the workforce impact positively on children because the whole environment is lifted to a different level (Whitebook and Ryan, 2011). As such this could be considered the right of the young children, and this of course leads to consideration of how work with young children is recognised and respected. Several studies have highlighted the importance of strong, high quality relationships for young children that develop over time (Crockenberg, 1987; Farver and Branstetter, 1994; Denham, 1998; Hamre and Pianta, 2005). Where low pay and poor conditions lead to high staff turnover, the opportunity for children to enjoy sustained and positive relationships with adults is threatened. In their California-based study, Bridges et al. (2011) explored the effects of an incentive programme on workforce retention and found that those holding entry level roles were more transient. Because young children need sustained engagement with known adults it is important that pay and working conditions are sufficient to retain staff in settings for sufficient time for children to know them and rely on their presence. Constant changes of staffing, and consequent variations in the quality of the provision, are detrimental to young children's well-being and development.

RECOGNITION AND RESPECT

In 2003, the UK government acknowledged a need to enhance the performance and status of the ECEC workforce in England (DfES, 2003: 22) yet in 2016 the many attempts to reform, rejuvenate and give due recognition to the workforce were continuing, with limited success (Boyd, 2013). Despite a lack of public appreciation of their role, the educators in Boyd's sample valued their work, and this is the case in many countries, where ECEC practitioners report that although they are underpaid they still feel that what they do is important. However, this is not always the case, as Goouch and Powell (2012) reported:

> One of the challenges of any work with practitioners from baby rooms in nurseries is in overcoming their perceptions of being 'the lowest of the low' in terms of practitioners' status. (2012: 87)

The introduction in England of a new job title and status (the EYPS) is an example of Gewirtz et al.'s (2009) multiple definition, a political attempt to both highlight a 'job well done' suggesting 'status' whilst simultaneously confining and defining the level and expectations of that 'job'. Karp (2005) argued strongly that early childhood teachers in the US should be respected and respect themselves for their work, yet acknowledged that self-respect is difficult when pay and conditions are poor. Similar feelings have been expressed in the UK (Hargreaves, and Hopper 2006), and ECEC assistants in 15 European countries reported care/education hierarchies with related perceptions of value and respect (van Laere et al., 2012). Hierarchies, by virtue of professional status, and conditions can bring division unless everyone sees value in their specific roles. The privileging of acts of pedagogy over acts of care can perpetuate such divisions and without appreciation of the plaited nature of education and care, and until there is greater recognition and respect for those who carry out these sometimes diverse roles (Langford, 2007), such divisions will continue.

A SUSTAINABLE AND RESPECTED ECEC WORKFORCE

Identity, conditions of service and recognition of the contribution of ECEC workforces dominate recent international research and there remains international concern about the quality of the early childhood workforce. Ryan and Whitebook (2012) describe research on the US ECEC workforce as 'piecemeal' (2012: 105) and call for attention to be paid to 'three critical ingredients – compensation, preparation and professional development and work environments that support adult learning' (2012: 106).

In 1999, putting forward an alternative paradigm and professionalising ECEC in the US, Morgaine (1999) anticipated how the professionalisation of ECEC workers could be realised and supported. She argued that professionalism, salaries and status were interconnected and linked with further professional development and training. Similarly, in the UK, the government was warned that 'Longer term commitment will be needed to arrest a decline in the standards of qualifications and enhance their quality for the future' (Nutbrown 2012: 3). The world is still waiting for Morgaine's paradigm to be realised, and the sustained investment for enhanced quality that Nutbrown called for has yet to be seen.

Whilst research into ECEC workforce issues continues, the apparent lack of sufficient political will and absence of long-term investment remain an international concern and so research can only paddle in the shallow water. The cost of providing high quality experiences for young children with well-qualified and well-paid professionals is high, but the cost of not doing so is higher – for the children, their families and our wider societies and economies.

It is clear that political will to recruit, educate and reward people who create quality early years environments for young children is essential. Some of the arguments put forward in this chapter echo those of early pioneers including Charlotte Mason, Susan Isaacs and Rachael and Margaret McMillan, yet concerns about the ECEC workforce in many countries persist more than 100 years later. Such perpetual concerns, including a lack of sufficient investment, are a reflection of how young children themselves are viewed and valued by governments and societies. International concern about the quality of the workforce remains, and deeper, more substantial studies are needed, along with longer-term investment and political will to foster a sustained and improved ECEC workforce.

RESEARCH QUESTIONS ON PROFESSIONALISM, QUALIFICATIONS AND STATUS

As this chapter has shown, there is great diversity across the ECEC workforce, from setting to setting, and country to country. With no shared nomenclature international research into the ECEC workforce needs some careful examination and interpretation when comparing professionalism, qualifications and status across countries. However, we can see that there are many shared international concerns about the quality of the ECEC workforce, and a need for deeper, more substantial studies along with longer-term investment and the political will to foster sustained retention and improvement.

Some suggested research questions for early years practitioners and students include:

⟳ What is the motivation for early years practitioners to work with young children? Why did they choose to do the job they do?
   This question is probably best answered by using a life historical approach with a relatively small sample of practitioners at various points in their careers.

⟳ How has the training of early years practitioners changed in the last century?
   This question will require some investigation of historical archives. It could include investigating the approach to teacher training established by Charlotte

Mason, by the McMillan sisters in the 1920s, and the Montessori approach. This could be compared with the requirements now for working with young children in terms of length of training and course content.

○ How does the nomenclature of early years practitioners 'define' their identities?

In recent years many different terms have been used to refer to the people who work with young children in early education and care settings. Investigating this question in the UK for example, would entail finding out from practitioners who have a number of job titles and roles, how they feel their particular 'label' defines them in their role. It will also be worth including some parents in this study – to find out what they understand by the different roles.

○ Considering the status of ECEC practitioners, Goouch and Powell (2012: 87) write that 'One of the challenges of any work with practitioners from baby rooms in nurseries is in overcoming their perceptions of being 'the lowest of the low' in terms of practitioners' status'. How can practitioners in a particular setting respond to this notion?

Goouch and Powell are not the first to highlight this issue. Talking with ECE practitioners about their views of their own status can shed light on the circumstances that perpetuate this view and their aspirations for their future career in ECEC.

A NOTE ON ETHICS AND INTEGRITY

Whilst researching the issues discussed in this chapter, and focusing on the research questions suggested, it will be important to remember not only issues of anonymity and confidentiality, but also that issues such as qualifications, status and professionalism are intensely personal for practitioners who work in ECEC. The focus on their fitness to practice, their levels of qualification and their career prospects and remuneration have drawn attention to them in recent years in ways that have never been the case before. Any study will need to develop sensitivity to the personal nature of the study and consider how the questions reach into lives as well as professional identities and careers.

RECOMMENDED READING

Bridges, M., Fuller, B., Huang, D.S. and Hamre, B.K. (2011) Strengthening the early childhood workforce: How wage incentives may boost training and job stability. *Early Education and Development*, 22 (6): 1009–1029. DOI: 10.1080/10409289.2010.514537.

This paper focuses on the important issue of remuneration of the ECEC workforce.

Brock, A. (2012) Building a model of early years professionalism from practitioners' perspectives. *Journal of Early Childhood Research*, 11 (1): 27–44. DOI: 10.1177/14767 18X12456003.

This paper is one of several mentioned in this chapter which offers a typology of professionalism.

Dalli, C. (2011) A curriculum of open possibilities: A New Zealand kindergarten teacher's view of professional practice. *Early Years*, 31 (3): 229–243. DOI: 10.1080/09575146.2011.604841.

This is an influential paper which focuses on New Zealand practitioners' own constructions and practice of professionalism.

Fenech, M., Waniganayake, M. and Fleet, A. (2009) More than a shortage of early childhood teachers: Looking beyond the recruitment of university qualified teachers to promote quality early childhood education and care. *Asia-Pacific Journal of Teacher Education*, 37 (2): 199–213. DOI: 10.1080/13598660902804022.

This paper draws attention to the relationship of workforce shortage to qualifications and quality of ECEC teachers and provision.

REFERENCES

Adams, K. (2008) What's in a name? Seeking professional status through degree studies within the Scottish early years context. *European Early Childhood Education Research Journal, 16* (2): 196–209. DOI: 10.1080/13502930802141626.

Andrew, Y. (2015) Beyond professionalism: Classed and gendered capital in childcare work. *Contemporary Issues in Early Childhood, 16* (4): 305–321. DOI: 10.1177/1463949115616322.

Banković, I. (2014) Early childhood professionalism in Serbia: Current issues and developments. *International Journal of Early Years Education, 22* (3): 251–262. DOI: 10.1080/09669760.2014.944885.

Barford, S. and Whelton, W. (2010) Understanding burnout in child and youth care workers. *Child & Youth Care Forum*, 39 (4): 271–287.

Barnett, W.S. (2003) Better teachers, better preschools: Student achievement linked to teacher qualifications. *Preschool Policy Matters*, 2. New Brunswick, NJ: National Institute for Early Education Research.

Bessie Tartt Wilson Initiative for Children (2010) *Blueprint for early education compensation reform*. www.btwic.org/wp-content/uploads/2010/01/Blueprint-for-Early-Ed-Compensation-Reform1.pdf (accessed 15 December 2017).

Boyd, M. (2013) 'I love my work but …': The professionalization of early childhood education. *The Qualitative Report, 18* (36): 1–20. http://nsuworks.nova.edu/tqr/vol18/iss36/1 (accessed 12 February 2018).

Bridges, M., Fuller, B., Huang, D.S. and Hamre, B.K. (2011) Strengthening the early childhood workforce: How wage incentives may boost training and job stability. *Early Education and Development, 22* (6): 1009–1029. DOI: 10.1080/10409 289.2010.514537.

Brock, A. (2012) Building a model of early years professionalism from practitioners' perspectives, *Journal of Early Childhood Research, 11* (1): 27–44. DOI: 10.1177/1476718X12456003.

Cameron, C., Mooney, A. and Moss, P. (2002) The child care workforce: Current conditions and future directions. *Critical Social Policy, 22* (4): 572–595.

Cameron, G. and Harding, C. (2017) *No Shortcuts: Quality and the Free Childcare Extension*. London: Family and Childcare Trust.

Campbell-Barr, V. (2014) Constructions of early childhood education and care provision: Negotiating discourses. *Contemporary Issues in Early Childhood, 15* (1): 5–17.

Crockenberg, S. (1987) Predictors and correlates of anger toward and punitive control of toddlers by adolescent mothers. *Child Development, 58*: 964–975.

Cumming, T. (2015) Early childhood educators' experiences in their work environments: Shaping (im)possible ways of being an educator? *Complicity: An International Journal of Complexity and Education, 12* (1): 52–66.

Cumming, T., Sumsion, J. and Wong, S. (2013) Reading between the lines: An interpretative meta-analysis of ways early childhood educators negotiate discourses and subjectivities informing practice. *Contemporary Issues in Early Childhood, 14* (3): 223–240. DOI: 10.2304/ciec.2013.14.3.223.

Cumming, T., Sumsion, J. and Wong, S. (2015) Rethinking early childhood workforce sustainability in the context of Australia's early childhood education and care reforms. *International Journal of Child Care and Education Policy, 9* (2). DOI 10.1007/s40723-015-0005-z.

Dalli, C. (2008) Pedagogy, knowledge and collaboration: Towards a ground-up perspective on professionalism. *European Early Childhood Education Research Journal, 16* (2): 171–185. DOI: 10.1080/13502930802141600.

Dalli, C. (2011) A curriculum of open possibilities: A New Zealand kindergarten teacher's view of professional practice. *Early Years, 31* (3): 229–243. DOI: 10.1080/09575146.2011.604841.

Dalli, C. and Urban, M. (2008) Towards new understandings of the early years profession: The need for a critical ecology. *European Early Childhood Education Research Journal*, 16 (2): 150–155. DOI: 10.1080/13502930802141600.

Davis, J.M., Bell, A. and Pearce, M. (2014) *Taking the First Steps: Is Childhood Practice Working? Report*. Edinburgh: University of Edinburgh.

Denham, S.A. (1998) *Emotional Development in Young Children*. New York: Guilford Press.

Department of Education: Australia (2014) *2013 Early Childhood Education and Care Workforce Review: Workforce Review Report*. Melbourne: Department for Education

DfE (Department for Education) (2012) *Statutory Framework for the Early Years Foundation Stage*. http://webarchive.nationalarchives.gov.uk/20130404110654/https://www.education.gov.uk/publications/standard/AllPublications/Page1/DFE-00023-2012 (accessed 28 February 2018).

DfES (Department for Education and Skills) (2003) *National Standards for the Under 8s: Day Care and Childminding*. Nottingham: DfES.

Dunlop, A. (2015) Aspirations and actions: Early childhood from policy to practice in Scotland. *International Journal of Early Years Education*, 23 (3): 258–273. DOI: 10.1080/09669760.2015.1074559.

Early, D.M., Bryant, D.M., Pianta, R.C., Clifford, R.M. Burchinal, M.R., Ritchie, S., Howes, C. and Barbarin, O. (2006) Are teachers' education, major, and credentials related to classroom quality and children's academic gains in pre-kindergarten? *Early Childhood Research Quarterly*, 21 (2): 174–195. DOI: 10.1016/j.ecresq.2006.04.004.

Early, D.M., Maxwell, K.L. and Burchinal, M. (2007) Teachers' education, classroom quality, and young children's academic skills: Results from seven studies of preschool programs. *Child Development*, 78 (2): 558–580.

Ejuu, G. (2012) Implementing the early childhood development teacher training framework in Uganda: Gainsand challenges. *Journal of Early Childhood Research*, 10 (3): 282–293. DOI: 10.1177/1476718X12437114.

Farver, J. and Branstetter, W. (1994) Preschoolers' prosocial responses to their peers' distress. *Developmental Psychology*, 30 (3): 334–341.

Fenech, M., Waniganayake, M. and Fleet, A. (2009) More than a shortage of early childhood teachers: Looking beyond the recruitment of university qualified teachers to promote quality early childhood education and care. *Asia-Pacific Journal of Teacher Education*, 37 (2): 199–213. DOI: 10.1080/13598660902804022.

Gewirtz, S., Mahony, P., Hextall, I. and Cribb, A. (2009) *Changing Teacher Professionalism: International Trends, Challenges and Ways Forward*. London: Routledge.

Gibson, M. (2013) 'I want to educate school-age children':Producing early childhood teacher professional identities. *Contemporary Issues in Early Childhood*, 14 (2): 127–137. DOI: 10.2304/ciec.2013.14.2.127.

Gomez, R.E., Kagan, S.L. and Fox, E.A. (2015) Professional development of the early child-hood education teaching workforce in the United States: An overview. *Professional Development in Education, 41* (2): 169–186. DOI: 10.1080/19415257.2014.986820.

Goouch, K. and Powell, S. (2012) Orchestrating professional development for baby room practitioners: Raising the stakes in new dialogic encounters. *Journal of Early Childhood Research, 11* (1): 78–92. DOI: 10.1177/1476718X12448374.

Hallet, E. (2013) 'We all share a common vision and passion': Early years professionals reflect upon their leadership of practice role. *Journal of Early Childhood Research, 11* (3): 312–325. DOI: 10.1177/1476718X13490889.

Hamre, B.K. and Pianta, R.C. (2005) Can instructional and emotional support in the first-grade classroom make a difference for children? *Child Development, 76*: 949–967.

Hargreaves, L. and Hopper, B. (2006) Early years, low status? Early years teachers' per-ceptions of their occupational status. *Early Years, 26* (2): 171–186. DOI: 10.1080/09575140600759971.

Harwood, D. and Tukonic, S. (2016) Babysitter or professional? Perceptions of profession-alism narrated by Ontario early childhood educators. *International Electronic Journal of Elementary Education, 8* (4): 589–600.

Holochwost, S., DeMott, K., Buell, M., Yannetta, K. and Amsden, D. (2009) Retention of staff in the early childhood education workforce. *Child & Youth Care Forum, 38*: 227–237.

Huss-Keeler, R., Peters, M. and Moss, J.M. (2013) Motivation for attending higher edu-cation from the perspective of early care and education professionals. *Journal of Early Childhood Teacher Education, 34* (2): 121–139. DOI: 10.1080/10901027.2013.787475.

Kagan, S.L., Gomez, R.E. and Friedlander, J. (2014) The status of early care and education: Teacher preparation in the United States. In W.E. Fthenakis (ed.), *Naturwissen Schaffen.* Bremen: University of Bremen, pp. 1–44.

Karila, K. (2008) A Finnish viewpoint on professionalism in early childhood educa-tion. *European Early Childhood Education Research Journal, 16* (2): 210–223. DOI: 10.1080/13502930802141634.

Karp, N. (2005) Building a new early childhood professional development system based on the 3 Rs: Research, Rigor, and Respect. *Journal of Early Childhood Teacher Education, 26* (2): 171–178. DOI: 10.1080/10901020590955798.

Katz, L.G. (1985) Research currents: Teachers as learners. *Language Arts, 62* (7): 778–782.

Kendall, A., Carey, D., Cramp, A. and Perkins, H. (2012) Barriers and solutions to HE pro-gression for early years' practitioners. *Journal of Vocational Education & Training, 64* (4): 543–560. DOI: 10.1080/13636820.2012.727858.

Langford, R. (2007) Who is a good early childhood educator? A critical study of dif-ferences within a universal professional identity in early childhood education preparation programs. *Journal of Early Childhood Teacher Education, 28* (4): 333–352. DOI: 10.1080/10901020701686609.

Langford, R. (2008) Making a difference in the lives of young children: A critical analysis of a pedagogical discourse for motivating young women to become early childhood educators. *Canadian Journal of Education, 31* (1): 78–101.

Lazzari, A., Picchio, M. and Balduzzi, L. (2015) Professionalisation policies in the ECEC field: Trends and tensions in the Italian context. *International Journal of Early Years Education, 23* (3): 274–287. DOI: 10.1080/09669760.2015.1078725.

Lazzari, A., Picchio, M. and Musatti, T. (2013) Sustaining ECEC quality through continuing professional development: Systemic approaches to practitioners' professionalisation in the Italian context. *Early Years, 33* (2): 133–145. DOI: 10.1080/09575146.2012.758087.

Lifton, N. (2001) Child care is a labor issue. *Social Policy, 31* (1): 4–10.

Lloyd, E. and Hallet, E. (2010) Professionalising the early childhood workforce in England: Work in progress or missed opportunity? *Contemporary Issues in Early Childhood, 11* (1): 75–88. DOI: 10.2304/ciec.2010.11.1.75.

Loeb, S., Fuller, B., Kagan, S.L. and Bidema, C. (2004) Child care in poor communities: Early learning effects of type, quality, and stability. *Child Development, 75* (1): 47–65.

MacDonald, C.L. and Merrill, D. (2002) 'It shouldn't have to be a trade': Recognition and redistribution in care work advocacy. *Hypatia, 17* (2): 67–83.

McGillivray, G. (2008) Nannies, nursery nurses and early years professionals: Constructions of professional identity in the early years workforce in England. *European Early Childhood Education Research Journal, 16* (2): 242–254. DOI: 10.1080/13502930802141659.

Miller, L. (2008) Developing professionalism within a regulatory framework in England: Challenges and possibilities. *European Early Childhood Research Journal, 16* (2): 255–268. DOI: 10.1080/13502930802141667.

Morgaine, C. (1999) Alternative paradigm and professionalizing childhood care and education: The Oregon example. *Child & Youth Care Forum, 38* (1): 5–19.

Moss, P. (2000) Training of early childhood education and care staff. *International Journal of Educational Research, 33*: 31–53.

Moss, P. (2006) Structures, understandings and discourses: Possibilities for re-envisioning the early childhood worker. *Contemporary Issues in Early Childhood, 7* (1): 30–41. http://journals.sagepub.com/doi/pdf/10.2304/ciec.2006.7.1.30.

Moss, P. (2010) We cannot continue as we are: The educator in a struggle for survival. *Contemporary Issues in Early Childhood, 11* (1): 8–19. DOU: 10.2304/ciec.2010.11.1.8.

Musgrave, J. (2010) Educating the future educators: The quest for professionalism in early childhood education. *Contemporary Issues in Early Childhood, 11* (4): 435–442. http://journals.sagepub.com/doi/pdf/10.2304/ciec.2010.11.4.435.

Nutbrown, C. (2012) *Foundations for Quality: The Independent Review of Early Education and Childcare Qualifications, Final Report.* Cheshire: Department for Education. www.gov.uk/government/uploads/system/uploads/attachment_data/file/175463/Nutbrown-Review.pdf (accessed 12 January 2018).

Oberhuemer, P. (2000) Conceptualizing the professional role in early childhood centers: Emerging profiles in four European countries. *Early Childhood Research and Practice*, 2 (2). http://ecrp.uiuc.edu/v2n2/oberhuemer.html.

Oberhuemer, P. (2011) The early childhood education workforce in Europe between divergencies and emergencies. *International Journal of Child Care and Education Policy*, 5 (1): 55–63.

Oberhuemer, P. (2015) Parallel discourses with unparalleled effects: Early years workforce development and professionalisation initiativesin Germany. *International Journal of Early Years Education*, 23 (3): 303–312. DOI: 10.1080/09669760.2015.1074560.

Oberhuemer, P., Schreyer, I. and Neuman, M.J. (2010) *Professionals in Early Childhood Education and Care Systems: European Profiles and Perspectives*. Opladen & Farmington Hills, MI: Barbara Budrich.

Osgood, J. (2006) Deconstructing professionalism in early childhood education: Resisting the regulatory gaze. *Contemporary Issues in Early Childhood*, 7 (1): 5–14. DOI: 10.2304/ciec.2006.7.1.5.

Osgood, J. (2009) Childcare workforce reform in England and 'the early years professional': A critical discourse analysis. *Journal of Education Policy*, 24 (6): 733–751. DOI: 10.1080/02680930903244557.

Pianta, R., Howes, C., Burchinal, M., Bryant, D., Clifford, R.M., Early, D. M. and Barbarin, O. (2005) Features of pre-kindergarten programs, classrooms, and teachers: Prediction of observed classroom quality and teacher–child interactions. *Applied Developmental Science*, 9 (3): 144–159.

Rose, S. and Rogers, J. (2012) *The Role of the Adult in Early Years Settings*. Buckingham: Open University Press.

Rosenthal, M.K. (2003) Quality in early childhood education and care: A cultural context. *European Early Childhood Education Research Journal*, 11 (2): 101–116. DOI: 10.1080/13502930385209191.

Ryan, S. and Whitebook, M. (2012) More than teachers: The early care and education workforce. In R.C. Pianta, L.M. Justice and S.M. Sheridan (eds), *Handbook of Early Childhood Education*. New York: Guilford Press, pp. 92–110.

SCSEEC (Standing Council on School Education and Early Childhood) (2012) *National Early Childhood Development Strategy 2010–11 and 2011–2012 Progress Report*. Carlton: South Victoria.

Simpson, D. (2010a) Becoming professional? Exploring early years professional status and its implications for workforce reform in England. *Journal of Early Childhood Research*, 8 (3): 269–281. DOI: 10.1177/1476718X10362505.

Simpson, D. (2010b) Being professional? Conceptualising early years professionalism in England. *European Early Childhood Research Journal*, 18 (1): 5–14. DOI: 10.1080/13502930903520009.

Siraj, I. and Kingston, D. (2015) *An Independent Review of the Scottish Early Learning and Childcare (ELC) Workforce and Out of School Care (OSC) Workforce*. London: UCL www.gov.scot/Resource/0047/00477419.pdf (accessed 12 February 2018).

Skeggs, B. (2001) Gender reproduction and further education: Domestic apprenticeships. *British Journal of Sociology of Education*, 9 (2): 131–149.

Sylva, K., Melhuish, E., Sammons, P., Siraj-Blatchford, I. and Taggart, B. (2003) *The Effective Provision of Preschool Education Project: Findings from the Preschool Period*. Research Brief RBX15-03. London: Institute of Education.

Sylva, K., Siraj-Blatchford, I., Taggart, B., Melhuish, E. and Sammons, P. (2004) *The Effective Provision of Pre-school Education (EPPE) Project: Findings from the Early Primary Years*. London: Institute of Education.

Vance, F. (2010) A comparative analysis of competency frameworks for youth workers in the out-of-school time field. *Child & Youth Care Forum*, 39 (6): 421–441.

van Laere, K., Peeters, J. and Vandenbroeck, M. (2012) The education and care divide: The role of the early childhood workforce in 15 European countries. *European Journal of Education*, 47 (4): 527–541.

Vincent, C. and Braun, A. (2011) 'I think a lot of it is common sense. …' Early years students, professionalism and the development of a 'vocational habitus'. *Journal of Education Policy*, 26 (6): 771–785. DOI: 10.1080/02680939.2010.551143.

Warrilow, P. and Fisher, K. (2003) Early childhood teachers and qualified staff shortage. Paper presented at the 8th Australian Institute of Family Studies Conference. February, Melbourne, Australia.

Whitebook, M. and Ryan, S. (2011) *Degrees in Context: Asking the Right Questions About Preparing Skilled and Effective Teachers of Young Children*. New Brunswick, NJ: National Institute for Early Education Research.

Whitebook, M. and Sakai, L. (2003) Turnover begets turnover: An examination of job and occupational instability among child care center staff. *Early Childhood Research Quarterly*, 18 (3): 273–293. DOI: 10.1016/S0885-2006(03)00040-1.

11

LEADERSHIP IN EARLY CHILDHOOD EDUCATION AND CARE

THIS CHAPTER WILL:

- consider how research studies define leadership in ECEC settings
- describe the findings of selected studies of pedagogical leadership
- highlight concerns around leadership and quality
- provide some recommended reading to follow up the issues discussed.
- suggest some research questions on the topic of leadership in ECEC
- provide some recommended reading to follow up the issues discussed.

This chapter focuses on research in the field of leadership in early childhood education and care. With the increase in provision for young children outside the home in the past two decades, there is an increasing need for leadership of settings, of policy developments and practice initiatives. Key issues in leadership include: the need for leadership of teaching and learning, good role models which promote equity, equality and social justice, leaders of service quality at all levels – to promote high quality experiences for young children and their families.

Whilst some of the relatively sparse studies of leadership in ECEC relate to particular leadership models, this chapter focuses not so much on models of leadership or management, but on *who* these leaders are, what ECEC leaders *do*, and *how* they work to create high quality in ECEC settings.

The emphasis here is on leadership in the interests of young children and their families, specifically how leadership in ECEC settings can foster the kinds of experiences and opportunities that promote optimum benefits for learning and development.

WHAT IS LEADERSHIP IN EARLY CHILDHOOD EDUCATION AND CARE?

Most studies of leadership in ECEC in the last two decades have been relatively small in scale, tending to focus on a small number of schools or settings and low numbers of participants. The picture of leadership in ECEC is not clear, but the issues that are emerging from small-scale studies in various parts of the world are good indicators of the issues that need to be addressed.

The Nutbrown Review (2012) of workforce qualifications in England and Wales highlighted the need for excellence in pedagogical leadership where all early years practitioners should have progression opportunities to become pedagogical leaders, this being especially important for black and minority ethnic groups to ensure that they were properly represented in and not excluded from senior roles in pedagogical leadership. The Review highlighted the importance of graduate qualifications in developing leadership roles and the need for teachers to be formally qualified to Qualified Teacher Status (a recommendation later rejected by the English government). Nutbrown (2012) found that:

> The evidence also suggests that those with higher levels of qualification – degree level specialism in early childhood – have the greatest impact. Research has shown the benefits that graduate leaders and, in particular, qualified teachers bring to early years settings. They have positive impacts both in terms of curriculum and pedagogical leadership, and in terms of measurable improvement in children's outcomes in early literacy, social development, mathematics and science. There are many examples, too, of teachers working with other professionals in the arts to provide children with rich arts-based learning experiences, thus fostering children's creativity and imagination.(2012: 15, para 1.10)

Pointing to the importance of good pedagogical leadership Nutbrown stated that:

> In my vision for the early years sector, pedagogical leaders are those practitioners who have extensive knowledge and understanding of child development, of play, of individual needs of children and their families and how to support them all. They are experts in their field. They know how to develop children's interests and plan to extend their learning and apply this expertise to everyday practice. They share it with the other practitioners to ensure every child is receiving care that is warm and welcoming and supports their physical, cognitive, social and emotional development and learning. (2012: 56, para 5.6)

There needs to be a clear distinction in ECEC provision between management of settings and services – including administration of budgets and deployment of staff – and leadership of the work that is done day to day with and for young children and their families; what we might in brief refer to as teaching and caring. Heikka and Hujala (2013: 568) talk of 'enactments of leadership'. Their Finnish study of distributed leadership identified a number of different approaches to leadership and found that extended models of distributed leadership between ECE municipal leaders, centre directors and teachers were rare, but that interdependencies in leadership led to enhanced quality. Heikka and Hujala suggest that:

> Interdependence between people and their enactments of leadership is a core element of implementing distributed leadership … [and] … Interdependence of leadership practice exists when the implementation of leadership tasks involves interactions between multiple persons. (2013: 571)

Larger than most recent qualitative studies on ECEC leadership, their study involved 21 focus groups made up of the three groups of leaders across 7 municipalities in Finland with a total of 164 participants (46 ECE leaders, 61 centre directors and 57 teachers). Key concerns for the Finnish participants were 'quality improvement, pedagogical leadership, daily management, human resources management, external relations and advocating for ECE within the municipality' (2013: 573) but the two biggest issues were 'quality improvement and pedagogical leadership' (2013: 574). Heikka and Hujala conclude that there is space for development of distributed leadership in the interests of enhancing pedagogical leadership and providing more support for teachers in their pedagogical role.

Issues of equity and social justice form another important leadership responsibility; in a study of 16 school leaders in England, Mistry and Sood (2015) found that, in a sample of multi- and mono-cultural schools:

' the ideology of social justice, equality and equity was interpreted differently in each Early Years setting. The multi-cultural schools used a variety of activities to embed social justice principles that involved their diverse communities more to enrich the curriculum in contrast to the mono-cultural schools. (2015: 548). '

They concluded that because many schools were occupied with the implementation of many policy changes in early years settings, time and space for implementing their aspired vision for a more equitable and socially just curriculum were limited. Findings indicated that whilst the participant schools were trying to provide a high quality curriculum underpinned by principles of social justice, equity and equality their aspirations did not always match their practice.

In many parts of the world, early years services have developed as inter-agency in nature, with multi-professional teams offering 'one stop shops' where parents can draw on the advice and services of health professionals, educators, and social workers. Focusing on the Australian context, Cartmel et al. (2013) considered how pedagogical leadership might be strengthened in multi-agency provision. Highlighting the complexity of the organisation of inter-agency teams and the need for transdisciplinarity amongst mixed discipline teams, Cartmel et al. demonstrate the particular challenges of researching and developing practice in these emerging contexts. They highlight the need for sharing of theory, values and vision in the development of services for children and their families, which in turn point to the importance of transdisciplinary professional development.

Clearly, leadership in the early years is an under-researched topic (Mistry and Sood, 2012) and one area where this might be addressed is in initial teacher education, where new early years practitioners can be better prepared for leadership through their training. Professional development in relation to leadership of early childhood education is another important aspect of leadership research, which is still lacking. The remainder of this chapter will focus on studies of pedagogical leadership, role models, gender and leadership, and finally, issues of leadership and quality in ECEC.

STUDIES OF PEDAGOGICAL LEADERSHIP

As the need for skilled people to lead change in early years settings has grown, so the need for pedagogical leadership has developed (Andrews, 2009). The need for confidence in pedagogical leadership is perhaps parallelled in the need for more and better research, and this is a global concern.

In the Australian context Cheeseman (2007) calls for the need for early childhood experts in pedagogy to speak up about important national policy developments in a call 'for pedagogical leadership to influence and shape early childhood policy agendas'

(2007: 244). In a study of ECE teacher leaders in Norway, Bøe and Hognestad (2017) suggest that thought needs to be given to 'leading knowledge development' where, as a pedagogical leader, they assume responsibility not only for practice but for promoting the learning of others working with young children. Their participants expressed the importance of good communication with all members of their team whatever (and sometimes according to) their experience and level of qualification. They found that the teacher leaders in the Norwegian settings that participated in their study had considerable freedom in terms of choices and decision-making and this led to increased responsibility to be 'strong leaders'.

In England, early years practitioners with a specified Early Years Professional Status are often required to lead pedagogical practice and raise standards. In a study of graduate leaders from one local authority in England, six volunteers were chosen as case study participants to examine their leadership of quality practice with children under five in voluntary, independent and private early years group settings (Hallet, 2013). The study found that these six EYP status practitioners believed themselves to be a specialised group, passionate about working with young children. They also identified as leaders of other practitioners with lesser qualifications, leaders of change in pedagogy and practice, reflective on their work with children and their families and a learning community themselves. Whilst the participants in these case studies identified their role strongly with leadership, there was a concern about where their own professional development might be obtained and how they were supported in their leadership. This EYP status was replaced in 2013 by the Cameron Coalition government.

Perhaps the requirement of English EYP status practitioners to provide pedagogical leadership was troubled because, as Heikka and Waniganayake (2011: 499) suggest, 'pedagogical leadership cannot be considered on its own'. They argue that:

 If early childhood leaders attempt to practise pedagogical leadership by itself, and as a traditional leader working alone, it will not be effective (Heikka et al., 2012). It has to be considered within the full extent of leadership roles and responsibilities expected of today's early childhood leaders. This is not possible without an adequate understanding and theorizing of the foundational concepts of leadership and pedagogy. (2011: 499)

Heikka and Waniganayake discuss 'pedagogical leadership' as a concept and explore what it *actually* means in practice and in relation to holistic leadership of services, settings and practices, where research too is lacking. They argue that the growing interest in pedagogy and pedagogical leadership requires much more clarity and understanding:

 notions of pedagogical leadership can engender vociferous dialogue by both the informed and the uninformed. This is partly a reflection of the lack of conceptual

> clarity and consensus about the foundational concepts of pedagogy and leadership. It may also be that in countries such as Australia and Finland, while the vocabulary of pedagogy is being used extensively within the education academy, pedagogy is a relatively new concept for many early childhood educators. (Heikka and Waniganayake, 2011: 502)

So, it seems that whilst the term 'pedagogical leadership' is gaining currency in terms of usage, there is still much to do in understanding and articulating quite what is understood, and by whom. The separating off of pedagogy from other aspects of leadership (and management) can cause a disjuncture, and the impacts have been made clear (Robertson and Hill, 2014), thus a more holistic approach may be better for early years settings – many of which are small and with limited resources.

The Effective Leadership in the Early Years Sector (ELEYS) Study (Siraj-Blatchford and Manni, 2007), which investigated early years sector leadership in England, identified three fundamental requirements for leadership which supported learning: contextual literacy, commitment to collaboration, and improvement of children's learning outcomes. Coupled with these they suggested ten practices for effective leaders: identifying and articulating a collective vision; ensuring shared understandings; effective communication; encouraging reflection; monitoring and assessing practice; commitment to ongoing, professional development; distributed leadership; building a learning community and a team culture; encouraging and facilitating parent and community partnerships; and leading and managing – striking a balance (Siraj-Blatchford and Manni, 2007: 28). This paints a much broader role of leadership than the distinct, singular responsibility for leading teaching and learning. Siraj-Blatchford (2008) suggests it requires a blend of science and art, seeing pedagogy as 'the science and the art of teaching' where teachers are 'practicing artists' (2008: 2). But we could equally refer to them as 'designers', 'architects' or 'weavers' of learning.

In their insightful international overview of what might constitute pedagogical leadership, Heikka and Waniganayake (2011) offer suggestions as to what pedagogical leadership might be considered to be, and its reach into ECEC work:

> pedagogical leadership is connected with not only children's learning, but also the capacity building of the early childhood profession, and values and beliefs about education held by the wider society or community. In early childhood settings, pedagogical leadership means taking responsibility for the shared understanding of the aims and methods of learning and teaching of young children from birth to 8 years. (2011: 510).

It is such 'shared understanding, together with informed articulation, that ultimately will really take forward pedagogical practices that enhance children's learning and improve their education and developmental outcomes.

ECEC LEADERSHIP AND QUALITY

Ho (2011) examined leadership roles in two Hong Kong schools with 'excellent' quality assurance ratings. Qualitative interviews were conducted with participants holding different roles in the schools (school governors, principals, teachers, support staff and parents) to explore effective leadership. The study showed that it was often the case that teachers, support staff and parents regarded themselves as 'followers' of the head teachers who, in their views, held three roles: role model, manager and mentor of curriculum and pedagogy. These are characterised by Ho as 'moral, managerial and instructional leadership' (2011: 47), which she identified as dominant in western literature. Further, Ho argues that there are implications for promoting moral leadership and for the further development of leadership in teachers.

Parental choice in Hong Kong has led to competition for enrolment amongst many preschools trying to attract parents to choose their school for their child. In this 'marketplace' context, parents can influence the decisions the school makes and the qualities it emphasises (albeit indirectly). Ho highlights the importance of moral leadership for programme quality, which she suggests is an:

> enormous challenge for principals in the preschool marketplace to act as a moral leader to maintain a good balance between professional values and parental preferences while ensuring that the provision of care and education is truly relevant and of a high quality. (2011: 57)

As ECEC provision becomes commercial in many parts of the world, and market-driven forces turn parents into paying customers, attention needs to be paid to how parents receive information about what constitutes good quality provision for young children and how ECEC leaders take on a moral role in their leadership to ensure principles and values are not compromised in the interests of 'selling' preschool places. As Ho puts it:

> moral leadership should be grounded in the valuation process that captures the full range of human actions, in addition to showing the relationship with social ethics. (2011: 58)

Studies in the UK have indicated links between the quality of leadership in settings and the provision for young children (Muijs et al., 2004; Siraj-Blatchford and Manni, 2007). UK studies have shown the importance of quality provision in terms of young children's learning outcomes and developmental progress (Siraj-Blatchford et al., 2008; Sylva et al., 2011).

This includes maintaining stable staffing, which has been identified as a perpetual problem in ECEC provision (Nutbrown, 2012), partly due to pay and conditions of service

(Ang, 2012), which in turn impacts on the quality of children's experiences, but good leadership and strong ECEC leaders have been shown to reduce staff turnover and create settings where staff grow together and share their vision, values and practice.

GROWING LEADERSHIP FOR THE FUTURE QUALITY OF ECEC

It is clear that, as the need for services for young children and places in ECEC settings grows, so the need for leadership of settings and services will grow too. Research needs to keep pace with this – and this is an international need. What is interesting though, is the way in which important roles in pedagogical leadership need better definition. There appears to be insufficient support for those leading practice in individual settings to access their own professional development and to support others in the setting team. To lead teaching and learning all practitioners need to develop confidence in their work with children and have time to reflect together on their observations of and interactions with young children on a day to day basis. Talking about what they do, the decisions they take, and why they take them is a key element of leading work to promote young children's learning. This is probably why there is so much interest internationally in the Reggio Emilia approach, which can be interpreted as one where pedagogical leadership – of a variety of forms – is undertaken by all involved with young children.

What is clear is that studies of ECEC leaders and leadership are limited and there is a great need for more work focusing on a range of countries and cultures, so that influences of context, culture, geography and history can be appreciated and approaches to leadership can evolve to the benefit of young children, while – as Hard and Jónsdóttir (2013) identify – avoiding dominant western stereotypes of hierarchy.

RESEARCH QUESTIONS ON LEADERSHIP IN ECEC

Research into leadership in early childhood education and care shows that there is a need for improved leadership, in settings, in terms of policy development and in leading practice. Leadership of teaching and learning is a clear priority, and we still need to know much more about *who* the ECEC leaders are, what they *do*, and *how* they work to create high quality in ECEC settings and services for young children and their families.

Some suggested research questions for early years practitioners and students include:

○ What do early years practitioners expect from those in leadership roles in their settings?

  This question can be explored by interviewing a number of early years practitioners. Inviting participants who work in a range of setting type and size would add richness to the study.

○ How does leadership in ECE settings impact and influence the quality of children's experiences?

  This question might be investigated by making some video observations of practice in the setting and then asking setting leaders to view the footage and what their role is in bringing about such practice.

○ What does 'pedagogical leadership' look like in an ECE setting? Do all practitioners feel that they have a role in taking a lead in practice?

  This question would be one to investigate through group discussion – informal discussion may help less experienced and less confident practitioners to participate and make suggestions about how they see their role – to draw out examples of instances where they have taken a lead, and understand something of their expectations of those who they see as having responsibility for leading practice.

○ How are leadership roles shared and enacted in ECEC settings?

  This question might focus on one or more settings, but the point here is to examine who does what in taking the lead on different aspects of leading the work of a setting or settings. Participants could include all who work in a setting or representatives of particular staff and 'user' groups.

A NOTE ON RESEARCH ETHICS AND INTEGRITY

It will be important to conduct any study that interrogates qualities of leadership in settings in a way which does not confront or specifically aim to be critical of specific individuals. However, what studies so far have shown is the need to understand more fully what leadership in ECEC is, how it is manifest in practice and how those in leadership positions or roles enact their leadership behaviour for the benefit of the children in their settings. Processes of anonymity and confidentiality will be essential, as will research methods that open up dialogue rather than criticise individuals. Careful selection and sampling of participants will also be important.

RECOMMENDED READING

Bøe, M. and Hognestad, K. (2017) Directing and facilitating distributed pedagogical leadership: Best practices in early childhood education. *International Journal of Leadership in Education*, 20 (2): 133–148. DOI: 10.1080/13603124.2015.1059488.

This study focusing on ECE teacher leaders in Norway suggests that a focus on 'leading knowledge development' is needed, by which is meant the responsibility pedagogical leaders assume for promoting the learning of others working with young children as well as leading practice. The participants highlighted the importance of good communication within a team at all levels of experience and qualification. The study found that the Norwegian teacher leaders who participated had considerable freedom in terms of choices and decision-making, which in turn led to an increased responsibility to be 'strong leaders'.

Mistry, M. and Sood, K. (2015) Permeating the social justice ideals of equality and equity within the context of early years: Challenges for leadership in multi-cultural and mono-cultural primary schools. *Education 3–13*, 43 (5): 548–564. DOI: 10. 1080/03004279.2013.837944.

This study of 16 school leaders in England focused on equity and social justice as aspects of leadership responsibility. The study concluded that time and space for implementing leaders' expressed vision for a more equitable and socially just curriculum were limited because their schools were occupied with the implementation of many policy changes in early years settings.

Siraj-Blatchford, I. and Manni, L. (2007) *Effective Leadership in the Early Years Sector: The ELEYS Study*. London: University of London, Institute of Education.

This paper reports on the Effective Leadership in the Early Years Sector (ELEYS) Study, which investigated early years sector leadership in England. The study identified three fundamental requirements for leadership which supported learning – contextual literacy, commitment to collaboration, and improvement of children's learning outcomes – and suggested ten practices for effective leaders.

REFERENCES

Andrews, M. (2009) Managing change and pedagogical leadership. In A. Robins and S. Callan (eds), *Managing Early Years Settings: Supporting and Leading Teams*. London: Sage, pp. 45–64.

Ang, L. (2012) Leading and managing in the early years: A study of the impact of a NCSL Programme on Children's Centre leaders' perceptions of leadership and practice.

Educational Management Administration and Leadership, 40 (3): 289–304. http://ema. sagepub.com/cgi/doi/10.1177/1741143212436960.

Bøe, M. and Hognestad, K. (2017) Directing and facilitating distributed pedagogical leadership: Best practices in early childhood education. *International Journal of Leadership in Education, 20* (2): 133–148. DOI: 10.1080/13603124.2015.1059488.

Cartmel, J., Macfarlane, K. and Nolan, A. (2013) Looking to the future: Producing transdisciplinary professionals for leadership in early childhood settings. *Early Years, 33* (4): 398–412. DOI: 10.1080/09575146.2013.852522.

Cheeseman, S. (2007) Pedagogical silences in Australian early childhood social policy. *Contemporary Issues in Early Childhood, 8* (3): 244–254.

Hallet, E. (2013) 'We all share a common vision and passion': Early years professionals reflect upon their leadership of practice role. *Journal of Early Childhood Research, 11* (3): 312–325. DOI: 10.1177/1476718X13490889.

Hard, L. and Jónsdóttir, A.H. (2013) Leadership is not a dirty word: Exploring and embracing leadership in ECEC. *European Early Childhood Education Research Journal, 21* (3): 311–325. DOI: 10.1080/1350293X.2013.814355.

Heikka, J. and Hujala, E. (2013) Early childhood leadership through the lens of distributed leadership. *European Early Childhood Education Research Journal, 21* (4): 568–580. DOI: 10. 1080/1350293X.2013.845444.

Heikka, J. and Waniganayake, M. (2011) Pedagogical leadership from a distributed perspective within the context of early childhood education. *International Journal of Leadership in Education, 14* (4): 499–512. DOI: 10.1080/13603124.2011.577909.

Heikka, J., Waniganayake, M. and Hujala, E. (2012) Contextualizing distributed leadership within early childhood education: Current understandings, research evidence and future challenges. *Educational Management Administration and Leadership, 41* (1): 30–44. DOI: 10.1177/1741143212462700.

Ho, D.C.W. (2011) Identifying leadership roles for quality in early childhood education programmes. *International Journal of Leadership in Education Theory and Practice, 14* (1): 47–59. DOI: 10.1080/13603120903387561.

Mistry, M. and Sood, K. (2012) Challenges of early years leadership preparation: A comparison between early and experienced early years practitioners in England. *Management in Education, 26* (1): 28–37. DOI: 10.1177/0892020611427068 mie.sagepub.com.

Mistry, M. and Sood, K. (2015) Permeating the social justice ideals of equality and equity within the context of early years: Challenges for leadership in multi-cultural and mono-cultural primary schools. *Education 3–13, 43* (5): 548–564. DOI: 10. 1080/03004279.2013.837944.

Muijs, D., Aubrey, C., Harris, A. and Briggs, M. (2004) How do they manage? A review of the research on leadership in early childhood. *Journal of Early Childhood Research, 2* (2): 157–169.

Nutbrown, C. (2012) *Foundations for Quality: The Independent Review of Early Education and Childcare Qualifications, Final Report*. Department for Education. www.gov.uk/govern ment/uploads/system/uploads/attachment_data/file/175463/Nutbrown-Review.pdf (accessed 12 January 2018).

Robertson, L.H. and Hill, D. (2014) Policy and ideologies in schooling and early years education in England: Implications for and impacts on leadership, management and equality. *Management in Education, 28* (4): 167–174. DOI: 10.1177/0892020614550468.

Siraj-Blatchford, I. (2008) Understanding the relationship between curriculum, pedagogy and progression in learning in early childhood. *Hong Kong Journal of Early Childhood, 7* (2): 6–13.

Siraj-Blatchford, I. and Manni, L. (2007) *Effective Leadership in the Early Years Sector: The ELEYS Study*. London: University of London, Institute of Education.

Siraj-Blatchford, I., Taggart, B., Sylva, K., Sammons, P. and Melhuish, E. (2008) Towards the transformation of practice in early childhood education: The effective provision of pre-school education (EPPE) project. *Cambridge Journal of Education, 38* (1): 23–36.

Sylva, K., Melhuish, E., Sammons, P., Siraj-Blatchford, I. and Taggart, B. (2011) Pre-school quality and educational outcomes at age 11: Low quality has little benefit. *Journal of Early Childhood Research, 9* (2): 109–124.

12

ETHICS OF WORK WITH YOUNG CHILDREN IN EARLY CHILDHOOD EDUCATION AND CARE

THIS CHAPTER WILL:

- consider key concerns around ethical work and research with young children
- discuss an ethic of care
- consider ethical practices in supporting children's learning
- examine research into ethics of professionalism
- explore ethics and integrity in researching with young children
- suggest some research questions on the topic of ethical practices with young children
- provide some recommended reading to follow up the issues discussed.

This chapter discusses research focusing on the ethics of working with young children in early childhood education and care. As early childhood professionals become more conscious of their responsibilities to and for the children they work with, and of the complexities of their roles, the ethical and moral issues and tensions are increasingly highlighted. This chapter discusses the contribution of research to understanding ethical practices in work with young children and considers key concerns around ethical work and research with young children. It discusses an ethic of care in ECEC, considers ethical practices in supporting children's learning, examines research into ethics of professionalism. Finally the chapter explores ethics and integrity in researching with young children.

ETHICAL WORK AND RESEARCH WITH YOUNG CHILDREN

'Ethics is about how we inhabit uncertainty together' (Massumi, 2003: 217) and whilst policy around early childhood education and care seeks to portray certainty about outcomes from prescribed foci, the interactions of sensitive adults with young children are often characterised by uncertainty. The kind of trusting uncertainty that tuned-in ECEC professionals experience leads to dynamic learning encounters, based on reciprocal pedagogy, which informs practice and research.

ETHICAL WORKING WITH YOUNG CHILDREN

There are many views on what might constitute ethical practice in working with young children and indeed, many of the issues discussed in this book come together under an umbrella of moral and ethical responses to young children and provision made for them and their learning and care. This section of the book has focused variously on a range of issues that adults must consider in relation to their roles in ECEC. How adults work with young children, how they come to 'be' with them, and how they support children's participation in their own learning, are matters of concern for most who work with young children, though in many countries, these matters are not given prominence in national policy documents.

ETHICS AND INTEGRITY OF RESEARCH INVOLVING YOUNG CHILDREN

As well as ethical practice in working with young children, it is crucial to think about the ethics and integrity of research involving young children. Ethical issues and practices pervade every aspect and process of researching in early childhood education and care from research design through to research dissemination. The overarching code is that a researcher should do no harm, to themselves or their participants, and further to the wider field of research in ECEC. Many guidelines for research conduct and codes of practice exist (for example, AARE, 1993; BERA, 2011; EECERA, 2015), but whatever guidelines are followed, it is the additional responsibility of the researcher to develop his or her own set of moral principles that they apply to their work. Universities in the UK and elsewhere require researchers to gain ethical approval for all studies involving human beings, though gaining institutional approval is only the start of the process of ethical research. Conducting ethical research means much more than rigidly adhering to a set of predetermined principles. Every research situation is different, all participants are different, and all researchers are different. Researchers, especially those researching with children and with families, must be continually attentive and reflective. Researching with young children brings additional responsibilities due to their vulnerability – by virtue of their young age amongst other things – and builds on expected ethical practices where children are participants (Landown, 2004).

AN ETHIC OF CARE

In the last two decades, perhaps prompted by heightened accountability around the UN Convention on the Rights of the Child, there has been an increased emphasis on listening to young children, on gaining their perspectives, and on 'giving voice' to their views (Dahlberg and Moss, 2005; Landown, 2005; Rinaldi, 2006). And in this context, 'listening' is not confined to the auditory and 'voice' is not limited to the spoken word. In the sense of Reggio Emilia's 'hundred languages of children' (Rinaldi, 2006: 65), 'listening' and 'voice' refer to all the modes in which children choose to communicate:

 Sensitivity to the patterns that connect, to that which connects us to others; abandoning ourselves to the conviction that our understanding and our own being are but small parts of a broader integrated knowledge that holds the universe together. (2006: 65)

We can consider listening to children as a fundamental, basic building block in an ethic of care for them, where Foucauldian notions of power are constantly challenged and opposed and where adults (who hold 'power') use it lovingly and in children's best interests. Much has been written about an ethic of care, particularly in relation to children and those who are deemed to be 'vulnerable' in one way of another. And 'care' is seen by many as a feminine pursuit, the responsibility of women, but building on Foucault's (1988) notion of an ethic of care, Noddings (2002: 13) offers us the concept of 'receptive attention' where vulnerability is set aside and the carer and the cared-for enter into a reciprocal (but unequal) relationship where both gain from the encounter. Feminist perspectives on care and caring challenge traditional views of 'women's work'.

A small-scale study of 25 Canadian, Nigerian and South African early childhood educators' views of their work, the roles they carry out, the responsibilities they shoulder and their perspectives on professionalism (Harwood et al., 2013) showed that an 'ethic of care' was identified as intrinsic to teaching and the practitioners' ideas of professionalism, and an earlier review of literature on the topic concluded similarly (Owens and Ennis, 2005). The place of an ethic of care in ECEC professionalism is complex, and contested, as Osgood (2006) puts it:

> In the pursuit of professionalism through development activities and reflexivity, space to retain integrity, an ethic of care and 'feminine' attributes offer an alternative to the technical performance of competencies as embodied within the new managerialist version of 'professionalism'. (2006: 195)

ETHICAL PRACTICE IN CHILDREN'S LEARNING

Moving from a needs-based through a rights-based approach to ECEC, researchers are turning their thoughts now to developing moral and ethical practices to support young children's learning. And this is taking many forms and being expressed in different ways in many countries. Focusing on child participation, Ghirotto and Mazzoni (2013) consider these issues in the context of a Reggio-Emilia infant-toddler centre. Taking a position where adult power can be seen as positive in supporting children's developing ideas, they argue this to be an important resource, and that asymmetrical practice is important in this process:

> The role of adults in terms of interdependence with children seems to be pivotal in designing educative experiences; education starts with the potentiality of the child, but the flourishing of these capabilities depends on the adult's abilities to be active listeners. The project we have presented shows the richness of asymmetry, while the rights-based approach risks overlooking it. Indeed, asymmetry is an integral and positive part of education rather than a negative feature of the adult–child relationship.
>
> What is essential in education is asymmetry, not as an end in itself nor a function of the adult's power over children. Asymmetry is a condition that creates a mutual and interdependent relationship when it works from a positive perspective.
>
> The capability of adults to perceive their power from the care/educative perspective allows this power to be considered and designed for learning that involves children's participation. In conclusion, from our point of view, coping with power becomes a fundamental criterion for defining the quality of the care/educative relationship – especially in the construction of shared knowledge. (2013: 307)

Deep thinking about the ways in which professionals in ECEC work with young children is necessary and part of the moral and ethical response to the adult role.

Another example of ethical practice in working with young children is to be found in the Lisbon-based 'School-as-a-Tree' project (Vasconcelos, 2006) where the space is the 'locus for ethical practices' around decision-making. The core achievement of the project is summarised thus:

> Transforming children's spaces into sites for ethical practices means educating the whole child and looking at the child as a young citizen, with rights and duties and his/her own ideas about the world. It involves seeking to understand the child's innermost needs and desires. But it also means educating the whole child in collective environments where, according to Fendler, 'no aspect of the child must be left uneducated: education touches the spirit, the soul, motivation, wishes, desires, dispositions and attitudes of the child to be educated' (Fendler, 2001, p. 121). (Vasconcelos, 2006: 180)

When work with young children is considered in the light of thinking around that work being 'ethical practice', different values surface which in turn inform the moral core of what happens and the learning relationships that are formed. As Vasconcelos concludes:

> We need utopia in order to continue with our daily struggles and cope with injustices; we frequently see our work as early childhood professionals under-valued. Aware that we are beings born for emancipation, for fullness and for a 'good life', we try to create small 'utopias' in our close surroundings, like the 'School-as-a-Tree', so that we may believe that the world has many possibilities. (2006: 180)

So, there are times when an ethical uncertainty (Massumi, 2003) is necessary to open up, rather than close down, children's processes of learning and discovery, and when trusting uncertainty can lead to dynamic learning exchanges. Allowing and nurturing uncertainty in ethical pedagogy leads Maier-Höfer (2015) to argue for:

> The *virtualisation* of knowledge, abilities and competencies for the training of teaching staff ... I am no longer that which I know, because I am able to question (my) knowledge. What does this virtualisation involve? – through their research on the theory and practice of ECEC, researchers, teachers and artists create a self-sufficient system of uttering without systematisation in the manner of modern totalitarian assumptions. That which combines 'attitude' and 'posture' in this transformational pedagogy is the capacity for learning and innovation which is continually maintained and improved. It can only be actualised in an unpredictable way within changing contexts, which reoccur structurally, locally and historically. In this consideration, traditional learning environments in universities as well as in preschools would need to be replaced by the *knowledge of becoming*. (2015: 378)

And this argument, for profound change in pedagogy at all levels of education, moves us from ethical practice to consideration of the ethics of professionalism.

ETHICS OF PROFESSIONALISM

The notion of 'being professional' and professionalism was discussed in Chapter 7, which noted that whilst policy may construct professionalism in ECEC to mean 'toeing the line' and following 'company policy', it can and should include challenging perceived 'wrongs' and questioning flawed and restrictive policies.

To this end, and in the context of increased government intervention in ECEC, and faced with ECEC professionals who see challenging policy to be against their professionalism, Fenech and Lotz (2016) suggest that ethically grounded professionalism means getting involved in the 'political sphere'. Their study involving four Australian early childhood teachers examined how they engaged in advocacy as part of their professional practice, spurred on by their own ethical codes. They suggest that teacher professionalism should include support for systems advocacy, and argue that:

> programs could alert pre-service teachers to issues of injustice/inequity faced by children, families with young children, and early childhood teachers and educators; instill critical literacy skills to build students' capacity to critique early childhood policies and practices from a social justice perspective; and scaffold the building of advocacy-related virtues. (2016: 13)

Focusing specifically on the training of ECEC professionals, Taggart (2016) argues for an ethical approach which is not merely functional, or based on the traditional perspective that working with young children was women's work. He proposes a feminist approach to ethics, which is 'socially critical and psychologically affective or flexible', as particularly appropriate to the professional identities of early childhood education and care professionals. Central to Taggart's argument is that the concept of 'compassion' 'foregrounds the ethical dimension of the work whilst overcoming false dichotomies between discourses of "children's rights" and "care"' (2016: 173). He argues that:

> Human activities which would be described as compassionate are those which seek to alleviate suffering, vulnerability or inequality in a public sphere whilst also calling upon distinct personal emotions for their motivation. ... I am making my case that professional work in ECEC is a compassionate practice and, as such, accommodates both the discourses of care and of rights, since compassion 'involves all our faculties and facilities comprising mind-body-heart-spirit (and whatever else is part of this ontological package called human being)' (Bai, 2014: 4). (Taggart, 2016: 176)

The implications for training and professional development are interesting. Such a model would, as Taggart puts forward, necessitate an examination of what constitutes compassionate pedagogy, and what traits and characteristics a 'compassionate' ECEC professional would possess and cultivate. Putting forward a compassionate paradigm for ECEC, Taggart notes that:

 As it becomes increasingly clear that the modernist mindset no longer serves us, compassionate pedagogy allows us to draw upon this new paradigm in training future practitioners without falling into pity and sentimentality. For example, when a graduate from a programme in compassionate pedagogy acknowledges her own nervousness in meeting a new parent, she does not need sentimentality or pity, only understanding. In a nursery serving an area of deprivation, she warmly welcomes the mother and child into a side room. She is not thinking of the training on 'customer care' demanded by the nursery chain. She simply responds with smiles and animated interest to the child's questions whilst appreciating the courage of the mother to enter somewhere unfamiliar and strange. An open discussion can then start. In such critical pedagogy, this emotion of compassion is key to ethical practice. (2016: 181–182).

ETHICS AND INTEGRITY IN RESEARCHING WITH YOUNG CHILDREN

Researching with young children is shot through with issues of power, and researchers take on a heavy responsibility when they decide to invite young children as research participants. Cameron (2005: 609) sets out her consideration of basic skills for engaging children as interviewees, in a spirit of 'gentle cooperation between interviewer and child', but what is most important in engaging children in the research process is a respect for them and for their ideas. We ask children to help us with our research because we believe them to be the experts in the topic we are focusing on. Our research protocols need to take this thesis as a starting point and flow from there. This section sets out some key and core ethical considerations when research participants are young children.

INFORMED CONSENT

The ethical practice of ensuring that research participants understand what they are agreeing to do in the research process is important. Where young children are concerned it is particularly important to do all we can to ensure children understand what they are involved in and to show due regard for their right to withdraw (or not participate at all). This is important for their parents too, not all of whom will be fully aware of their right to decline or withdraw from participation, and it is our responsibility to tell them

(Nutbrown, 2011). As Dockett et al. (2012) point out, children's decisions to dissent from research receive much less attention in the research literature than does discussion of techniques to gain their assent.

It is not uncommon for adults (usually parents) to make decisions about whether or not children can participate in research studies, and whilst that is appropriate due to children's age and the need for guardianship, it is possible to inform some young children about the research process in ways that they can understand. This is desirable practice which can be carried out in a number of ways: through pictures, telling a story, making a special book about the research study, a group conversation, the opportunity to ask questions. And just as researchers must find appropriate ways to obtain children's agreement to participate, so must they develop research methods that fit with young children's understanding and ways of being, including approaches such as the now popular Mosaic Approach developed by Clark and Moss (2001).

Consent, and particularly *informed* consent, is a complex terrain where young children are concerned. Parental consent is also important, and this too must be sought in ways that are sensitive to parents' understanding and their linguistic and literacy abilities. Where parents give consent to their children being involved in a research study, children still need an opportunity (indeed multiple opportunities) to understand what is being required of them in the research process. They may well agree to being involved through body language or drawings rather than the signed documents often required from adults. Children may walk away from a research situation – effectively withdrawing, for that point in time – their agreement to being part of the data collection that day. It should be easy for children to withdraw from the research process at any point and do something that they prefer to do.

CHILDREN AS RESEARCH PARTICIPANTS

Children have rights as social agents in the research process and so must be regarded as participants and not 'subjects' to be observed, questioned and tested. Researchers must respect young children as the individuals they are, paying attention to their individual needs, interests and wishes (including the right to withdraw from the research process at any point). Researching with young children requires researchers to engage in a continual process of 'reflexive engagement' (Powell et al., 2016).

CONFIDENTIALITY AND ANONYMITY

Confidentiality and anonymity are key issues for ethical research, but like most elements of ethical research there is nothing straightforward about them. Research participants may be willing to talk about their thoughts and feelings if they know that they will not be identified in any way in the final report. Some children may want their names and pictures of themselves to be included in a research report (Nutbrown, and Clough, 2009), and so researchers must decide if confidentiality can and should be promised and how to deal with participant requests *not* to remain anonymous. There is often a 'taken-for-granted' assumption that all research with children should promise anonymity – including the changing of children's names, settings, local authorities and so on. This goes so far as the pixilation of images of children, and the fictionalisation of some information about children's circumstances (Henderson, 2018). These strategies may be correct, however it is important to consider the default position and to be critically aware of the decisions that are made and why.

Nutbrown (2011) suggests that research with young children as participants raises new metho-ethical challenges, which must be kept to the fore. She questions the way in which photographs of children are used in research studies. With the protection of children uppermost, Nutbrown argues against the routine pixilation of photographic images of children included in research reports, claiming that such an approach distorts the image of the child, thus:

> When we involve young children in our research, there are the usual things we well know that we must attend to – issues of access, informed consent, anonymity, confidentiality, protection, safety, and well-being. I fully acknowledge the importance of these broadly discussed concerns that do not need further rehearsal here. Discussions of these themes are well served in the literature (Cocks, 2006; Danby & Farrell, 2004; Dockett & Perry, 2007; Heath et al., 2007) and the arguments are not only well known but (quite rightly) continually troubled over in the forefront of debate. Indeed they must form part of the moral fabric of anyone working with young participants in research. (2011: 10)

Further, Nutbrown points to more complex issues which are more difficult to resolve: the need for 'guardians' of young research participants – not 'gatekeepers'; the place of 'care' in research practices where researchers and early years practitioners are not 'over protective' but *are* 'deeply caring'; and finally, taking a view of children, not as 'othered' and done to, in research but as 'Other-wise' – 'having a different way of knowing' – and research can hope to learn something of 'what that wisdom might be' (2011: 11).

This way of thinking about research with young children raises many important issues: is it ethical to include photographs of babies and very young children in research reports? Should images of young children be pixilated in research reports? Should we consider the notion of 'research guardians' as opposed to 'gatekeepers'?

RESEARCH QUESTIONS ON ETHICAL PRACTICES WITH YOUNG CHILDREN

This chapter has explored some of the ethical issues around working and researching with young children. The usual ethical issues and matters of research integrity, which apply generally in all social sciences research, are magnified where young children are concerned. Every turn in the research process needs to be examined, and examined again to ensure there is no intentional exploitation or manipulation of young research participants and their families. It is crucial that researchers do not waste children's time – and that they focus on issues that are meaningful to their young participants.

Some suggested research questions for early years practitioners and students include:

○ What do ECEC practitioners consider to be the key ethical concerns in working with young children? How do they define 'ethical practices'?

Getting under the surface of practice and finding out what the people who do the job really think is important, and so a series of in-depth interviews with ECEC practitioners in different roles would go some way to answering this question. Open questions, stimulated by extracts from papers on the topic, might help to elicit a range of perspectives.

○ How do ECEC practitioners understand and define an 'ethic of care'?

The notion of an 'ethic of care' is used by several researchers to think about the role of care in reciprocal relationships. Focus groups or interviews will provide useful insights into ECEC practitioners' thinking.

○ What might an 'ethic of uncertainty' look like when supporting young children's learning?

Policy in many countries is written in a language of certainty, to produce predicable outcomes in children's learning. Observations of practitioners who are willing to work with uncertainties might uncover narratives of pedagogical uncertainties where children are trusted in their explorations, supported by knowledgeable adults who are prepared to be patient in children's learning encounters with them.

○ How do ECEC practitioners think about ethics of professionalism?

Several recent studies have focused on professionalism and professional identity, but few have considered the 'ethics' of professionalism, which requires the willingness to challenge what is wrong. Interviews, focus groups or questionnaires are all ways of finding out from ECEC professionals what they think are the ethical underpinnings of their job and whether this means 'toeing the line' or standing up and 'speaking truth to power' even if those truths are unpopular or run counter to policy.

A NOTE ON RESEARCH ETHICS AND INTEGRITY

Taking aspects of professional and research ethics as the focus of a research project still requires considerable attention to be given to the protocols of ethical approval and integrity that other projects demand. What is crucial is clarity of expression and meaning so that all concerned have an understanding of what is expected of them and how the study will progress.

RECOMMENDED READING

Cohen, L., Manion, L. and Morrison, K. (2018) The ethics of educational and social research. In L. Cohen, L. Manion and K. Morrison (eds), *Research Methods in Education* (8th edn). London: Routledge, pp. 111–143.

This chapter is a fully comprehensive overview of the main issues underpinning ethical research in the social sciences.

Ghirotto, L. and Mazzoni, V. (2013) Being part, being involved: The adult's role and child participation in an early childhood learning context. *International Journal of Early Years Education*, 21 (4): 300–308. DOI: 10.1080/09669760.2013.867166.

This is an account of work in a Reggio Emilia infant-toddler centre focusing on child participation and arguing for the positive use of adult 'power' as an important resource for children.

Nutbrown, C. (2011) Naked by the pool? Blurring the image? Ethical issues in the portrayal of young children in arts-based educational research. *Qualitative Inquiry*, 17 (1): 3–14. DOI: 10.1177/1077800410389437.

This paper questions the way in which photographs of children are used in research studies. With the protection of children uppermost Nutbrown argues against the pixilation of photographic images of children included in research reports, claiming that such an approach distorts the image of the child. This paper raises many important issues, which are worth considering as you think about your own project.

Williamson, E., Goodenough, T., Kent, J. and Ashcroft, R. (2005) Conducting research with children: The limits of confidentiality and child protection protocols. *Children and Society*, 19 (5): 397–409.

This paper raises the important issue of when researchers, in the interests of safeguarding children, limit undertakings of confidentiality.

Yee, W.C. and Andrews, J. (2006) Professional researcher or a 'good guest'? Ethical dilemmas involved in researching children and families in the home setting. *Educational Review*, 58 (4): 397–413.

This paper stresses the notion of children as individuals who have specific rights in the research process, emphasising the need during the research process to address ethical concerns particularly when conducting research with children in their own homes.

REFERENCES

AARE (Australian Association for Research in Education) (1993) *Code of Ethics*. www.aare.edu.au/pages/aare-code-of-ethics.html (accessed 19 February 2018).

BERA (British Educational Research Association) (2011) *Ethical Guidelines for Educational Research*. www.bera.ac.uk/wp-content/uploads/2014/02/BERA-Ethical-Guidelines-2011.pdf (accessed 19 February 2018).

Cameron, H. (2005) Asking the tough questions: A guide to ethical practices in interviewing young children. *Early Child Development and Care, 175* (6): 597–610. DOI: 10.1080/03004430500131387.

Clark, A. and Moss, P. (2001) *Listening to Young Children: The Mosaic Approach*. London: National Children's Bureau.

Cocks, A.C. (2006). The ethical maze: Finding an inclusive path towards gaining children's agreement to research participation. *Childhood, 13*: 247–266.

Dahlberg, G. and Moss, P. (2005) *Ethics and Politics in Early Childhood Education*. London: Routledge.

Danby, S. and Farrell, A. (2004) Accounting for young children's competence in educational research: New perspectives on research ethics. *Australian Educational Researcher, 31* (3): 35–50.

Dockett, S., Einarsdóttir, J. and Perry, B. (2012) Young children's decisions about research participation: Opting out. *International Journal of Early Years Education, 20* (3): 244–256. DOI: 10.1080/09669760.2012.715405.

Dockett, S. and Perry, B. (2007) Trusting children's accounts in research. *Journal of Early Childhood Research, 5* (1): 47–63.

EECERA (European Early Childhood Education Research Association) (2015) *Ethical Code* www.eecera.org/wp-content/uploads/2016/07/EECERA-Ethical-Code.pdf (accessed 19 February 2018)

Fendler, L. (2001) Educating flexible souls: The construction of subjectivity through developmentality and interaction. In K. Hultqvist and G. Dahlberg (eds), *Governing the Child in the New Millennium*. New York: RoutledgeFalmer, pp. 119–142.

Fenech, M. and Lotz, M. (2016) Systems advocacy in the professional practice of early childhood teachers: From the antithetical to the ethical. *Early Years, 38* (1): 19–34. DOI: 10.1080/09575146.2016.1209739.

Foucault, M. (1988) The ethic of care for the self as a practice of freedom (trans. J.D. Gauthier). In J. Bernauer and D. Rasmussen (eds), *The Final Foucault*. Cambridge, MA: MIT Press, pp. 1–20.

Ghirotto, L. and Mazzoni, V. (2013) Being part, being involved: The adult's role and child participation in an early childhood learning context. *International Journal of Early Years Education, 21* (4): 300–308. DOI: 10.1080/09669760.2013.867166.

Harwood, D., Klopper, A., Osanyin, A. and Vanderlee, M. (2013) 'It's more than care': Early childhood educators' concepts of professionalism. *Early Years, 33* (1): 4–17. DOI: 10. 1080/09575146.2012.667394.

Heath, S., Charles, V., Crow, G. and Wiles, R. (2007) Informed consent, gatekeepers and go-betweens: Negotiating consent in child and youth-orientated institutions. *British Educational Research Journal, 33*: 403–417.

Henderson, E. (2018) *Autoethnography in Early Childhood Education and Care: Narrating the Heart of Practice.* London: Routledge.

Landown, G. (2004) Participation and young children. *Early Childhood Matters, 103*: 4–14.

Landown, G. (2005) *Can Anybody Hear Me? The Rights of Young Children to Participate in Decisions Affecting Them.* Working Papers, No 36. The Hague: Bernard Van Leer Foundation.

Maier-Höfer, C. (2015) Attitude and passion: Becoming a teacher in early childhood education and care. *Early Years, 35* (4): 366–380. DOI: 10.1080/09575146.2015.1104651.

Massumi, B. (2003) Navigating movements (interview). In M. Zournazi (ed.), *Hope: New Philosophies of Changes.* London: Routledge, pp. 210–242.

Noddings, N. (2002) *Starting at Home: Caring and Social Policy.* Berkeley: University of California Press.

Nutbrown, C. (2011) Naked by the pool? Blurring the image? ethical issues in the portrayal of young children in arts-based educational research. *Qualitative Inquiry, 17* (1): 3–14. DOI: 10.1177/1077800410389437.

Nutbrown, C. and Clough, P. (2009) Citizenship and inclusion in the early years: Understanding and responding to children's perspectives on 'Belonging'. *International Journal of Early Years Education, 17* (3): 191–206.

Osgood, J. (2006) Professionalism and performativity: The feminist challenge facing early years practitioners. *Early Years, 26* (2): 187–199. DOI: 10.1080/09575140600759997.

Owens, L.M. and Ennis, C.D. (2005) The ethic of care in teaching: An overview of supportive literature. *Quest, 57* (4): 392–425. DOI: 10.1080/00336297.2005.10491864.

Powell, M.A., Graham, A. and Truscott, J. (2016) Ethical research involving children: Facilitating reflexive engagement. *Qualitative Research Journal, 16* (2): 197–208. DOI: 10.1108/QRJ-07-2015-0056.

Rinaldi, C. (2006) *In Dialogue with Reggio Emilia.* London: Routledge.

Taggart, G. (2016) Compassionate pedagogy: The ethics of care in early childhood professionalism. *European Early Childhood Education Research Journal, 24* (2): 173–185. DOI: 10.1080/1350293X.2014.970847.

Vasconcelos, T. (2006) Children's spaces as sites for ethical practices: A 'School-as-a-Tree' in an economically impoverished neighbourhood. *International Journal of Early Years Education, 14* (2): 169–182. DOI: 10.1080/09669760600661690.

REFLECTION ON PART II
RESEARCH FOCUSING ON ADULTS

This part (of six chapters) has reviewed ECE research since 2000 organised around the broad theme of *Adults*. In this reflection I have identified what stands out for me.

ON PARENTS AND EARLY CHILDHOOD EDUCATION

It has long been the case that mothers have been the main focus of parental involvement in early childhood education, and even though programmes over the decades have referred to 'parental involvement', in reality they have been 'mother involvement' programmes. Because of growing emphasis on the importance of involving fathers in their children's early learning, a number of programmes and initiatives have been developed in recent years aimed at the specific involvement of fathers. It is particularly good to see these programmes being evaluated so that successful features of these initiatives can be adopted and developed and the less successful elements are not repeated in future work.

NEXT STEPS

We can see from studies in various countries how effective home visiting can be in helping parents support their children, and this approach to working with families is most often welcomed by parents. Programmes need to be tailored to the needs of families and meaningfully engage with their interests. Starting points need to be those things that families already do. The small but growing number of programmes designed to increase the involvement of fathers is important. Future research needs to consider tailored programmes which are not gendered or exclusive, but which are meaningful to mothers and fathers. Not all engagement is visible, but tangible signs of involvement can be found, if the opportunities to engage are fitted to families, and if researchers ask the right questions about who is getting involved, at home, with young children's learning.

ON INCLUSION AND DIVERSITY

Mass migration in recent years, leading to more diverse populations, also brings challenges to communities as they adapt to the changes newcomers bring. Whilst the world over the centuries has always seen change, inequality and division, in recent years we have witnessed opposition (even hatred) of difference in many parts of the world, and just a few examples include the rise of the far right in different parts of the world, the racist divisions exposed by the UK referendum to leave the European Union, conflicts in the US over policies of the Trump administration, revision of benefit entitlement for families and for people with disabilities in England. The range of issues is wide, and reaches into any consideration of inclusion in ECEC, making the study of inclusion diverse and challenging.

NEXT STEPS

There are many inclusion and exclusion issues that are 'of the moment'. Building on studies undertaken with communities and individual families, it seems important now to develop projects which, whilst researching the issues, also begin to build bridges and create inclusive solutions. It feels as if the political upheavals that create divisions must be challenged by collaborative, co-produced studies that are created with the people who are currently excluded. There are many studies *of* minority communities, for example. So what is needed now are more studies *with* communities, with families, with disabled and with otherwise excluded people. The definition of inclusion is now very broad, and researchers are focusing on particular issues, such as gender, 'race' and refugees, as well as the more traditional issues that attract attention in relation to inclusion, which are learning difficulties and special educational needs. The phenomena of inclusion and exclusion have long been studied, what is needed now is evidence of effective inclusion in action to help build more inclusive societies where young children flourish.

ON MULTI-PROFESSIONALISM AND INTER-DISCIPLINARITY

Internationally, there is a general consensus that professionals in different disciplines can provide better services for families if they collaborate, and even better services – with a more 'seamless' experience for families if these are joined up – and better still, under one roof. To achieve the positive benefits of inter-agency and multi-professional approaches a number of conditions need to exist. First, and crucially, national and international studies of the topic suggest that conditions for inter-professional services to run smoothly need *joined-up policies* – so that health, welfare, housing and education policies work in synergy and not in competition. Both local, regional and national policies need to fit together to form a coherent whole. Second, there is a burning need for *shared professional development* where people working with young children from a range of professions come together, to reach a better understanding of their respective roles, mutual concerns and specific contributions. This is not a substitute for discreet discipline-specific continuing professional development, which is necessary to maintain and enhance expertise in specific fields of work. Third, the necessary *resources* are needed to facilitate successful multi-disciplinary working. Co-ordination and collaboration across and within different disciplines takes additional effort, but yields important benefits, so must be adequately resourced. Fourth, *a shared language* is needed – around terms and terminology and the meanings attributed to professional terms and phrases. All professionals have different ways of expressing their work and particular disciplinary terms. If reaching a shared language is not possible, then a way of understanding each other's professional language and meanings is important. Finally, and essential for any successful inter-disciplinary working, is a *clarity of vision*, where all involved agree on their mission for children and their families, from which ways of working to achieve that vision can flow.

NEXT STEPS

There are accounts describing successful multi- and inter-disciplinary working in ECEC, and these are useful in building multi-professional teams. Perhaps what is missing – or at least less frequent – are studies of the professionals themselves. Do we know what it is like to work as a professional in a team of people from different disciplines? How do people negotiate their own distinct professional identity in a context of difference? Research focusing on the life stories of people who identify as part of a multi-professional group would be interesting, and would help to move forward understanding of how to build multi-professionalism, what makes it successful, what is difficult, and how individuals maintain their own professional identity within the team and create additional multi-professional identities.

ON PROFESSIONALISM, QUALIFICATIONS AND STATUS

It is clear that political will to recruit, educate and reward people who create quality early years environments for young children is essential. Some of the arguments put forward in this chapter echo those of early pioneers including Charlotte Mason, Susan Isaacs and Rachel and Margaret McMillan, yet concerns about the ECEC workforce in many countries persist more than 100 years later. Such perpetual concerns, including a lack of sufficient investment, are a reflection of how young children themselves are viewed and valued by governments and societies. International concern about the quality of the workforce remains, and deeper, more substantial studies are needed along with longer-term investment and the political will to foster a sustained and improved ECEC workforce.

NEXT STEPS

The studies drawn upon in this book to discuss professionalism, qualifications and status indicate a lack of resources for researching the topic. Many are small-scale and short-term studies; a single, small cohort of completing students, for example. What is needed here is a long, hard look at who the 'professionals' are, whether their qualifications fit them for practice, how they are supported, and how their qualifications equip them for their respective roles. Research into this theme needs to be rigorously planned, and should reflect on how the qualifications undertaken work for the individuals who study for them and, importantly, how they ultimately work for children and their families. Perhaps the question to be answered is this: How/do current ECEC qualifications help to build a profession in early childhood education and care?

ON LEADERSHIP

As ECEC provision becomes commercial in many parts of the world, and market-driven forces turn parents into paying customers, attention needs to be paid to how parents receive information about what constitutes good quality provision for young children and how ECEC leaders take on a moral role in their leadership to ensure principles and values are not compromised in the interests of 'selling' preschool places.

NEXT STEPS

Leadership in ECEC is another area of study where more can be done. There is a place for research here in understanding and providing new perspectives on the multiple facets of leadership. Leadership and management need to be untangled, and it will be important in the future to be clear about the differences in leadership depending on the type of setting and how it is funded. 'For profit' ECEC settings will present different leadership challenges and responsibilities than those which are state funded. Leadership of practice and pedagogy is a further dimension and this requires people who are deeply aware of children and their learning, experienced and resourced to support others in developing their confidence and enquiry around pedagogy.

ON ETHICS OF WORKING AND RESEARCH WITH YOUNG CHILDREN

'Ethics is about how we inhabit uncertainty together' (Massumi, 2003: 217) and whilst policy around early childhood education and care seeks to portray certainty about outcomes from prescribed *foci*, the interactions of sensitive adults with young children are often characterised by uncertainty. The kind of trusting uncertainty that tuned-in ECEC professionals experience leads to dynamic learning encounters, based on reciprocal pedagogies that inform practice and research.

NEXT STEPS

Research has contributed considerably to the development of ethical practices in pedagogy and in research with young children. Alongside views that children are capable learners with perspectives of their own, and with contributions to make to research, it is important to remember that young children are also vulnerable and that they need researchers to ensure there is guardianship in place. As researchers have shown creativity and flexibility in developing new ethical practices when working with young research participants, so the research process can take longer and become much more involved. Gaining assent from the youngest children takes time and the examples we have of this are a marker for work going forward. Future studies involving young children and their families need to continue to give us rich stories of their lives and learning so that policy impacts are evaluated from this human perspective. Ethical practices and research integrity must continue to be demonstrated and in the future studies can build on some of the exemplary work – ethical approaches cannot be skimped, they take time and resources and experienced researchers.

PERSONAL REFLECTION AND PLANNING

I have, above, identified some of the striking features from the second part of the book. But these are personal identifications, and you may well have found other things in these chapters that are more pertinent for you in terms of research focusing on *adults* in early childhood education. I have included the questions below to suggest a way of thinking about these issues and you may wish to make some notes and/or discuss in groups.

- What stands out for you? Which piece of research would you award a prize to? What gave you the biggest surprise? And what may be particularly useful to you as a practitioner? Did anything made you feel, 'Yes, but ... so what?'
- Are there any research findings here that you suspect or doubt? Or that you strongly disagree with? Is this 'just a hunch' or do you have evidence – from your own life- and practice-experience, or from other reading – to support that view?
- Is there something (that you've come across) missing from this account?
- Which of the researchers reported would you like most to meet, and what would you want to ask them?

In the next five years ...

- What do *you* think are the most important topics for future research around adults and early childhood education research?
- What does your experience and reading of the literature suggest are likely to be the barriers to the development of work with and for young children's ECE in these years?

PART III
LEARNING AND TEACHING

The first two parts of this book dealt in turn with 'Children' and with 'Adults' – a rather artificial way, I admitted, of sorting the phenomena of education and care associated primarily with one or other of them. It is an unreal separation because in the lived-world reality of childhood settings they are fundamentally related on pain of ceasing to be: the adult constructs and mediates the child no less than the child constructs and mediates the environment which the adult (at least partly) provides. In this final part I focus on the means and the media which – formally at least – they use to reach each other.

The first chapter in this part comprises a broad look at what I think of as the *virtual furniture* of the setting: the decisions about what, where and how learning shall be realised, often starting in central governments, but changing shape – however subtly – as those decisions are mediated by local constitution: the local authority, the school or setting itself, the governors, parent groups, local communities, and, of course, practitioners themselves, for it is they who finally interpret and realise that cascade of formulation. (And, again of course, irradiating all those processes at each stage and seldom fully explicit are the philosophies that give them breath.)

Traces of those philosophies may be more visible in the underpinning theories which are adduced to justify and promote what we do with children; and their effects are seen in the Chapters 14 and 15, dealing with literacy and with languages; and of course since the very concept of literacy has been both amplified and contested by the rapacious explosion of information technologies, I then focus more specifically in Chapter 16 on how digital technologies themselves are expanding the *quanta* of learning and teaching, and how, in many countries, digital literacies are becoming an important research focus in the early years.

All consideration of learning and teaching is necessarily and inescapably bound in a triangle with forms of assessment, and the penultimate chapter in this part addresses the perpetual crisis in the profound if deceptively simple question: *To what end shall we assess young children's learning?* I believe that the *How ...?* question – the practices and tools of assessment – comes after this most regressed enquiry: What shall we do with the knowledge that we create with our measurements? What will it really tell us *about the child* and *of formative educational use*? My own experience with challenging Baseline Assessment over the years does not escape inclusion, and the search for respectful assessment is so often distorted by flawed policy.

13

CURRICULAR APPROACHES: PEDAGOGY AND PRACTICE IN EARLY CHILDHOOD EDUCATION AND CARE

THIS CHAPTER WILL:

- describe the main themes of international research in curriculum and pedagogy in ECEC
- consider studies of curricular approaches based on socio-cultural perspectives and children's working theories
- review research focusing on play and play pedagogies
- suggest some research questions on the topic of curriculum and pedagogy in ECEC
- provide some recommended reading to follow up the issues discussed.

This chapter builds on Chapter 4, studies of play, and considers research internationally into approaches to creating learning opportunities for young children, and the forms and approaches to curricula. With increased policy intervention in the role of ECEC in children's future learning, and the increasing rigidity and prescription of curricula in many countries, this chapter examines research which sheds light on the forms of curricula that support children's learning opportunities. Rather than offer a repetition of the many accessible explanations and descriptions of curriculum approaches, which include widely known and celebrated work including Te Whāriki in New Zealand and the Reggio Emilia approach, the chapter explores some of the lesser known studies in order to complement those established and more commonly examined phenomena. The chapter considers research into curricular approaches which include a socio-cultural view of learning and children's working theories, studies of the place of play in curricula, and the contribution research can make to critiquing national policies on ECEC curricula.

OVERARCHING THEMES OF INTERNATIONAL RESEARCH IN CURRICULUM AND PEDAGOGY IN ECEC

In a review of recent UK research focusing on learning, development and curriculum, Rose and Gilbert (2017) discussed research trends in nine main themes: personal, social and emotional development; communication, language and literacy; mathematics; expressive arts and design; physical development; outdoor learning; scientific enquiry and understanding the world; learning and development in a digital world; curricular tensions. They concluded that much more research is needed on the early years curriculum in the UK, and that:

> For the most part, traditional insights have been restated, such as the significance of active engagement with the sociocultural context and how nurturing and contingent relationships mediate much of young children's learning. Young children need diverse, multi-sensory experiences to help them develop self-reflective and self-regulatory skills to foster their own learning. The importance and nature of dialogic encounters continue to receive attention and well-rehearsed debates regarding literacy development remain unresolved beyond a reiteration of how literacy and numeracy are collaborative and collective acts facilitated through cultural experiences and identities. (2017: 75)

These themes and sentiments are echoed in the international literature on the topic of curriculum and pedagogy but, perhaps because socio-cultural contexts vary so much around the globe, there are different emphases in different continents. One of the key tensions in the UK review was the increasing pressure from national policy on formalisation of learning in the earliest years and the sometimes prescriptive role of the adult who is seen as the controller of what is learned – running counter to much of the published studies in and beyond the UK. The overarching international concerns in this chapter are: curricular approaches, quality, policy, play and play pedagogies, and this chapter draws on examples of the international literature in these areas of research. The relatively small number of studies focusing on specific curricular areas (including mathematics, science, the environment and digital learning) are not included here because specific subject learning was not a dominant theme in international research.

STUDIES OF CURRICULAR APPROACHES

Reflecting on three approaches to curricula – the English Foundation Stage, the New Zealand Te Whāriki, and the Italian Reggio Emilia approach, Soler and Miller (2003: 57) argue that curricula can be what they call 'sites of struggle'. Comparing different visions, beliefs and values, and their embeddedness in specific curricula approaches, they depict different curricular approaches on a continuum:

> At one end are the progressive views of the curriculum which emphasise the individual child and the decentring of adult authority. At the other end of the continuum are the vocational and instrumental views of education, which stress the authority of the adult over the child, and the needs of society rather than the individual. (Soler and Miller, 2003: 58)

It is possible to plot various approaches along such a continuum, which demonstrates how children are constructed by policy and by provisions, and what early years curricula are intended *for*. At one end, children are valued as active, constructive learners with rights as equal members of society and community; at the other, a curriculum is designed to bring about changes in the passive learner to fit them to be the kind of citizen that policy-makers want them to be. In one approach knowledge is constructed and immediately meaningful to the learner, in the other information is transmitted and often has little meaning for the learner.

In many contexts, developmental and educational psychology dominate national curricula in early childhood education leading, as Wood and Hedges (2016) argue, to a focus on child development theory where curricula can be controlled and outcomes are more predictable. They conclude that:

> curriculum in theory and in practice remains contentious in ECE, because clarity and coherence within policy documents are problematic; guidance about developmental goals and the content of children's learning is, at best, inconsistent. Nevertheless, policy faith in control must be maintained in order to justify economic investment ... Curriculum should be seen as incorporating dynamic working practices, specifically what children choose to do and talk about with each other, and what practitioners enact with children to support their learning and development in a variety of ways

> through play-based provision, through reciprocal relationships, as well as through intentional and responsive teaching. (2016: 401)

Such an approach would go some way to challenge the perpetuation of what Ang (2007: 183) warns is the 'cultural hegemony [which] continue[s] to powerfully inform the curriculum, and work to sustain pedagogical practices of monoculturalism and monolingualism'.

Writing from a New Zealand context and the Te Whāriki approach (NZ Ministry of Education, [1996] 2017) to ECE, Hedges and Cooper (2014) consider the early childhood education curriculum which emphasises 'social-pedagogic' as well as academic outcomes in an holistic approach that considers learning 'dispositions' and 'working theories'. Reporting on a two-year qualitative study exploring children's interests, inquiries and working theories, Hedges and Cooper expose the 'knowledge, skills and strategies, and attitudes and expectations' as integrated elements within working theories, and highlight children's identity development as 21st century learners. They define 'dispositions' and 'working theories' thus:

> holistic curricular learning aspirations enhanced within participatory approaches to learning that highlight the content (knowledge) and process (skills and attitudes) of children's learning ... (2014: 397)

Importantly, working theories are set out in *Te Whāriki* (NZ Ministry of Education, [1996] 2017), which states that:

> In early childhood, children are developing more elaborate and useful working theories about themselves and the people, places, and things in their lives. These working theories contain a combination of knowledge about the world, skills and strategies, attitudes, and expectations. Children develop working theories through observing, listening, doing, participating, discussing, and representing within the topics and activities provided in the programme. As children gain greater experience, knowledge, and skills, the theories they develop will become more widely applicable and have more connecting links between them. ([1996] 2017: 44)

One working theory told to me by a young child in England was that the sea in the seaside town where she lived had to go a long way out each day so that she could play in the wet sand and that children in Australia got their turn to swim in the sea. As a working theory about the globe and tidal patterns, and about fairness, she made a pretty good effort at developing a rational explanation for the sea leaving the harbour. Hedges and Cooper's (2014) detailed observations, captured on video, give rich detail of the evolution of children's working theories and their dispositions for learning supported by 'tuned in' adults. Yan (2005) considers naive theory in practice as applied by four women teachers in Chengdu, China, and does not critique the theory, but rather seeks in a mixed method study to identify how children's theories could be made more explicit, and how exposing children's thinking as posed in their questions – such as a question 'What is life?' – puts curriculum control in the hands of the teacher, whereas the development of working theories builds from children's responses to their environments and learning collaborations.

Continuing with children's perspectives, Rosen's (2010) study of curriculum influences with 34 children and three teachers in the British Columbian preschool in Canada where she worked, examined a children's rights approach to consulting children on the curriculum. The findings indicate that whilst it is possible for children to feel that they have agency in curriculum development and implementation, what is clear is that teachers are the final arbiters and their preferences about what is included in the curriculum prevail. Whilst the children reported that they would like to have their views included in what is learned, structures and systems often prevented this. Rosen concludes that broader societal disparities and inequalities by virtue of their age prevailed against real child participation beyond their offering of ideas:

> A most notable obstacle is the issue of intergenerational inequality. While some of the children interviewed articulated the differential status accorded to children and adults, it is not clear if they were aware of how their participation may be constrained by this inequality.
> Respecting children's participation rights and implementing democratic practice in preschool is, therefore, not merely a matter of asking children for their ideas and opinions. (2010: 105)

There appears to be considerable need and space for more studies where children's own expertise is sought and exploited in curriculum development, alongside the pedagogic knowledge of tuned-in early years practitioners.

As we saw earlier, the focus in *Te Whāriki* (NZ Ministry of Education, [1996] 2017: 47) is on children's working theories where the emphasis is on 'a combination of knowledge about the world, skills and strategies, attitudes, and expectations'. Working theories in the ECE curriculum were first defined as:

> a unique system of ideas that is based on a person's experience and provides them with a hypothesis for understanding their world, interpreting their experience, and deciding what to think and how to behave. This system is in a constant state of development and change. (NZ Ministry of Education, [1996] 2017: 95).

Building an ECEC curriculum around this starting point places children centrally in their learning, and as active decision-makers in their settings and communities. Writing from an international perspective, Wood and Hedges note that:

> Working theories offer a way to incorporate social pedagogic and academic goals within the context of valuing children's play alongside the conversations, inquiries, and debates that occur within participatory learning experiences. (2016: 398)

For national governments where the emphasis is on controlling what is taught, and therefore what is learned, this approach does not sit well, because it situates control with the child, rather than the teacher or policy-maker. Curriculum, understood narrowly as subject matter and syllabi, seems still to dominate policy, and there is far more control over what is taught than *how* it is taught.

Interestingly, Stephen (2010) suggests that Piagetian ideas still influence pedagogy, with curriculum 'opportunities' for children which do not necessarily lead to 'sustained and purposeful encounters'. Putting forward a socio-cultural approach to pedagogy, Stephen suggests an enhanced role for the adult leading to more agency, through interaction, for children in their own learning:

> Adopting a sociocultural perspective on learning means being concerned with the influence of the contexts in which children learn, how learning varies with social and cultural experiences and the ways in which adults, other children, tools and resources support and shape learning. For those who adopt the sociocultural approach acting and thinking with others drives learning and at the heart of that process is dialogue and interaction. (2010: 21)

RESEARCH FOCUSING ON PLAY AND PLAY PEDAGOGIES

A recent review of research in the UK highlights play as an overarching theme in the UK research literature:

> Play is a golden thread that runs through much of the literature related to learning and development. The early years curriculum continues to be hindered by controversies related to increasing formalisation of content delivery and the didactic role of adults. Further research is needed to show how practitioners in the four UK contexts are responding to these challenges. (Wood et al., 2017: 116)

A Scottish study (Martlew et al., 2011) affirms this concern, with the finding that teachers are restricted in how they can provide for and give time to children's open-ended play:

> teachers possibly held different conceptions of active learning, and found it difficult to reconcile the idea of active learning with the practical pedagogical realities such as

large numbers of children in the primary classroom compared with the much higher child/adult ratio in the nursery setting. (2011: 81)

This highlights two needs, one for the curtailment of inhibitive policies which impose increased formalisation on early years teachers, and one for the enhanced training of teachers to support their engagement in play pedagogies. As Wood and Chesworth (2017) emphasise:

> Although this review focuses on the UK, the themes resonate with much international research, not least because the instrumental use of educational play is now a global phenomenon. The research evidence paints a complex picture of irreconcilable tensions, pragmatic accommodations, and a continuing endeavor to understand the complexities of what existential and educational forms of play mean to children. (2017: 57)

Focusing on child-initiated pedagogies in Finland, Estonia and England, Robertson et al. (2015) carried out an ethnographic study with three- to six-year-olds in 14 settings, examining children's perspectives on their own and adult's views around learning. They conclude that:

> Despite the meaning-making initially constructed independently in each culture and setting, the data do suggest coherence in child-initiated pedagogies as perceived by children. This includes acknowledging and taking control of the boundaries within which to collaborate and share decisions, as well with adults as with peers. Overall, the sense of control was perceived valuable and enjoyable. (2015: 1824)

In these ways socio-cultural approaches to pedagogy can be seen to evolve with relevance in culturally specific contexts which, though they vary greatly, share critical commonalities of children's agency and control.

A Swedish study of preschool teachers' perspectives of children's learning in relation to their national curriculum showed that teachers in the study held different views, some seeing:

> social knowledge as fundamental to children's learning. Others have a broader learning-oriented approach, which is grounded in the Swedish preschool curriculum and in modern theories of learning. This is an integrated learning approach, which is assumed to promote children's learning and development in a long-term perspective. (Williams et al., 2014: 227)

With a strong emphasis on child-led and play-based learning, Swedish preschool teachers tend to stress experiential learning over imposed targets and prescription. Bringing together ecological and socio-cultural theories, culture and the broader environment is central to Swedish children's preschool experiences and the 30 preschool teachers (from the 30 participating preschools) who were interviewed in the Williams et al. (2014) study emphasised the importance of teacher–child and group collaboration in promoting social and cognitive knowledge, but (according to the teachers) not all such collaborations were dependent upon the teachers:

> Children's collaboration appears as something that often happens by itself in encounters between children. It also appears to be situation dependent and irrespective of whether the teacher is an active constructor of the situation or not. While the teachers say that they are active in the sense that they challenge children's thinking by posing questions, it seems that it is the children's own actions within the situation, which are crucial for collaborative learning. Children's collaboration is thus largely left to the children themselves. To stimulate children's peer learning, the teachers say that they make use of organizational competence in arranging situations where children can play and be challenged through tasks and materials that contribute to collaboration, reflection and problem-solving. (2014: 236)

For the teachers in the study, it seemed that social knowledge was core to the children's learning, perhaps indicative or reflective of values permeating Swedish society. This contrasts with Payler's (2007) study of 10 four-year-old children in two early years settings in England, where pedagogies featured 'open or closed interactive spaces, inviting, building on, or limiting children's contributions' (2007: 237). The study indicated how restrictive and controlling pedagogic styles can limit children's possibilities, and close down spaces for learning:

> Children in the study who were the youngest in their cohorts had far less opportunity for participating in such open interactive spaces. These children entered school reception when just four years old and, for those such as Paul who were seen as of below-average levels of achievement on entry, their participation was much more controlled and limited. The control and focus on vertical discourse led to some measurable progress in learning outcomes (though considerably less than their 'high achieving' peers, widening the gap between them). However, it contributed to a growing identity of being 'less capable', dependent learners, exhibiting distinct, visible relief when teaching and learning episodes ended. (2007: 251)

Payler concludes that the 'tiny nuances' of children's interactions with others are of crucial importance in shaping their learning, and in a similar vein Fleer (2015) discusses teachers' positioning 'inside' and 'outside' of children's play; crucially, this is something that curricula and curriculum guidance that are outcomes driven can overlook.

RESEARCH QUESTIONS ON CURRICULUM AND PEDAGOGY IN ECEC

There are so many issues at work in ECEC curricula at present, and research is not, it seems, keeping pace with developments in practice. Nor is there sufficient policy critique from an empirical base. Many studies are small scale, probably reflecting the limited funding now available for qualitative studies of children's learning and the building of curricula to support them. Where policy imposes outcomes-driven curricula, the job of research is to monitor the impact on learning, and identify where children's learning may be inhibited by predetermined outcomes which, in turn, inevitably lead to pre-planned rather than responsive and reciprocal practice and pedagogies.

Some suggested research questions for early years practitioners and students include:

○ What do children know about play?

 This question would require asking children what they think play is; when they play, what they play, how they organise themselves; and the cusp of what's 'real' and what's 'pretend'. Watching film with children and talking about what they do when they are playing is a good stimulus to discussion with them.

○ What do ECE professionals understand by the term 'working theories' as applied to young children's learning and how do they use children's working theories in practice?

 There are several ways to investigate this question. It could be a case of informal discussion or unstructured interviews, and observation. Talking with professionals about particular learning episodes and if and how they supported learning through adopting a 'working theories' approach to pedagogy could be very insightful.

○ What does a socio-cultural view of young children's learning look like?

 In a similar way to the studies mentioned in this chapter that focus on a socio-cultural view of children's learning, this question is best investigated by watching the learning interactions between children and between children and adults to uncover some of the rich accounts of children's learning. Deep and specific observations of children, analysed in ways which do justice to those data, will be a good way to study this topic.

○ How can ECEC practitioners build curricula based on children's play interests?

 A study on this topic would necessitate detailed observations of practitioners working with young children and developing their 'tuned-in' responses to children's play in ways which open up possibilities for new learning – in the way Payler describes – to expose the possibilities and impact of such an approach to curriculum.

A NOTE ON RESEARCH ETHICS AND INTEGRITY

Studies of curriculum and pedagogy involve children and their practitioners. Where fine-grained studies are called for, ethical issues of safeguarding, of protection of identity, and of alertness to children's discomfort and their privacy are important. It is also vital that children's time is not wasted by ill-conceived studies or data collection methods that are intrusive and which inhibit their play and learning. It is important when designing research studies which involve looking at the variably subtle interactions between children, and between them and their early childhood educators, that researchers do not destroy the very thing they are looking at.

RECOMMENDED READING

Robertson, L.H., Kinos, J., Barbour, N., Pukk, M. and Rosqvist, L. (2015) Child-initiated pedagogies in Finland, Estonia and England: Exploring young children's views on decisions. *Early Child Development and Care*, 185 (11–12): 1815–1827. DOI: 10. 1080/03004430.2015.1028392.

A useful tri-country perspective on children's contributions to curriculum decisions, from a UN Convention on the Rights of the Child perspective.

Rose, J. and Gilbert, L. (2017) Learning, development and curriculum. In J. Payler and E. Wood (eds), *BERA-TACTYC Early Childhood Research Review 2003–2017*. London: British Educational Research Association. www.bera.ac.uk/wp-content/uploads/2017/05/BERA-TACTYC-Full-Report.pdf?noredirect=1 (accessed 29 January 2018).

This chapter provides an overview of recent UK research on learning, development and curriculum.

Soler, J. and Miller, L. (2003) The struggle for early childhood curricula: A comparison of the English Foundation Stage Curriculum, Te Whāriki and Reggio Emilia. *International Journal of Early Years Education*, 11 (1): 57–68. DOI: 10.1080/0966976032000066091.

This compares three distinct examples of curricula to demonstrate how 'vocational and instrumental' curriculum influences can pressurise 'progressive and socio-culturally inspired' early years curricula approaches.

Wood, E. and Hedges, H. (2016) Curriculum in early childhood education: Critical questions about content, coherence, and control. *The Curriculum Journal*, 27 (3): 387–405. DOI: 10.1080/09585176.2015.1129981.

This is an important discussion of curriculum which critiques outcomes-driven curricula

REFERENCES

Ang, L. (2007) Cultural diversity and the curriculum guidance for the Foundation Stage in England. *European Early Childhood Education Research Journal*, *15* (2): 183–195. DOI: 10.1080/13502930701321428.

Fleer, M. (2015) Pedagogical positioning in play – teachers being inside and outside of children's imaginary play. *Early Child Development and Care*, *185* (11–12): 1801–1814. DOI: 10.1080/03004430.2015.1028393.

Hedges, H. and Cooper, M. (2014) Engaging with holistic curriculum outcomes: Deconstructing 'working theories'. *International Journal of Early Years Education*, *22* (4): 395–408. DOI: 10.1080/09669760.2014.968531.

Martlew, J., Stephen, C. and Ellis, J. (2011) Play in the primary school classroom? The experience of teachers supporting children's learning through a new pedagogy. *Early Years*, *31* (1): 71–83. DOI: 10.1080/09575146.2010.529425.

NZ Ministry of Education ([1996] 2017) *Te Whāriki: He Whāriki Mātauranga mā ngāMokopuna o Aotearoa. Early Childhood Curriculum.* https://education.govt.nz/assets/Documents/Early-Childhood/ELS-Te-Whariki-Early-Childhood-Curriculum-ENG-Web.pdf (accessed 20 February 2018).

Payler, J. (2007) Opening and closing interactive spaces: Shaping four-year-old children's participation in two English settings. *Early Years*, *27* (3): 237–254. DOI: 10.1080/09575140701594392.

Robertson, L.H., Kinos, J., Barbour, N., Pukk, M. and Rosqvist, L. (2015) Child-initiated pedagogies in Finland, Estonia and England: Exploring young children's views on decisions. *Early Child Development and Care*, *185* (11–12): 1815–1827. DOI: 10.1080/03004430.2015.1028392.

Rose, J. and Gilbert, L. (2017) Learning, development and curriculum. In J. Payler and E. Wood (eds), *BERA-TACTYC Early Childhood Research Review 2003–2017*. London: British Educational Research Association. www.bera.ac.uk/wp-content/uploads/2017/05/BERA-TACTYC-Full-Report.pdf?noredirect=1 (accessed 29 January 2018).

Rosen, R. (2010) 'We got our heads together and came up with a plan': Young children's perceptions of curriculum development in one Canadian preschool. *Journal of Early Childhood Research*, *8* (1): 89–108. DOI: 10.1177/1476718X09345517.

Soler, J. and Miller, L. (2003) The struggle for early childhood curricula: A comparison of the English Foundation Stage Curriculum, Te Whāriki and Reggio Emilia. *International Journal of Early Years Education*, *11* (1): 57–68. DOI: 10.1080/0966976032000066091.

Stephen, C. (2010) Pedagogy: The silent partner in early years learning. *Early Years*, *30* (1): 15–28. DOI: 10.1080/09575140903402881.

Williams, P., Sheridan, S. and Sandberg, A. (2014) Preschool – an arena for children's learning of social and cognitive knowledge. *Early Years*, *34* (3): 226–240. DOI: 10.1080/09575146.2013.872605.

Wood, E. and Chesworth, L. (2017) Play and pedagogy. In J. Payler and E. Wood (eds), *BERA-TACTYC Early Childhood Research Review 2003–2017*. London: British Educational Research Association. www.bera.ac.uk/wp-content/uploads/2017/05/BERA-TACTYC-Full-Report.pdf?noredirect=1 (accessed 29 January 2018).

Wood, E. and Hedges, H. (2016) Curriculum in early childhood education: Critical questions about content, coherence, and control. *The Curriculum Journal, 27* (3): 387–405. DOI: 10.1080/09585176.2015.1129981.

Wood, E., Payler, J. and Georgeson, J. (2017) Conclusion: Key messages. In J. Payler and E. Wood (eds), *BERA-TACTYC Early Childhood Research Review 2003–2017*. London: British Educational Research Association. www.bera.ac.uk/wp-content/uploads/2017/05/BERA-TACTYC-Full-Report.pdf?noredirect=1 (accessed 29 January 2018).

Yan, C. (2005) Developing a kindergarten curriculum based on children's 'naive theory'. *International Journal of Early Years Education, 13* (2): 145–156. DOI: 10.1080/09669760500171162.

14

EARLY LITERACY DEVELOPMENT AND LEARNING

THIS CHAPTER WILL:

- give a brief overview of research that led to our present understanding of emergent literacy
- discuss research which illustrates various 'strands' of early literacy
- discuss studies which enhance our understanding of digital technologies and multi-modal literacies
- discuss some studies of the role of parents in children's early literacy development
- suggest some research questions on the topic of early literacy development and learning
- provide some recommended reading to follow up the issues discussed.

This chapter focuses on research in the field of early literacy development and learning. As a crucial key to education and participation in society, growing up literate is widely regarded as essential. The 21st century inherited a rich seam of research from the last two decades of the 20th century, unlocking a whole new understanding of how young children's literacy 'emerged' in print-rich environments. With the increased emphasis on literacy skills taking and increasing hold in the earliest years, this chapter considers the contribution of research to understanding how best to support young children as they take their place in the world as confident and competent readers and writers. This chapter first gives a brief overview of research that led to our present understanding of emergent literacy. This is important because studies at that time changed, in fundamental ways, understanding, attitudes and practices towards the place of literacy in early years pedagogy. The chapter then goes on to consider research which illustrates various 'strands' of early literacy. Moving into new areas of study the next section focuses on research to enhance our understanding of digital technologies and multi-modal literacies. The chapter concludes with research into the role of parents in children's early literacy development.

A BRIEF OVERVIEW OF RESEARCH UNDERPINNING PRESENT UNDERSTANDINGS OF EMERGENT LITERACY

> As young literacy learners transact with written texts during reading and composing, the same dynamic tension exists between their personal constructions of literacy knowledge (invention) and society's construction of agreed upon social uses of literacy (conventions). (Whitmore, 2004: 291)

Since the 1980s, research has stimulated interested in the literacy development of children under five, opening up a world of enquiry that until that time had been virtually ignored. This chapter considers the contribution of research to our understanding of the development of young children's literacy from birth to five years.

It was Yetta Goodman (1980; 1986) in the US, who wrote about the 'roots' of literacy developing in the preschool period; these 'roots' included: print awareness in situational contexts (Hassett, 2006); awareness of connected discourse in written language; meta-cognitive and meta-linguistic awareness about written language; using oral language about written language; functions and forms of writing. Goodman's work in the 1980s shed new light on how young children come to writing, leading to the valuing of what might earlier have been called 'scribble' as early, 'emergent' or 'developmental' writing. Nursery and kindergarten teachers – particularly in the US, UK and Australia – began to get excited at the literacy that young children displayed, having watched those children close to them using literacy in everyday contexts, and imitating adults' literacy practices.

These teachers moved from trying to protect young children from the worries generated by learning to read and write too early, to nurturing the emergent elements of literacy that young children seemed spontaneously to exhibit, and encouraging parents to do the same, with a new confidence that they were supporting early literacy development.

Studies of individual children's early literacy achievements were carried out by researchers who mainly studied their own children over a number of years (Bagdahn, 1984; Payton, 1984; Bissex, 1985; Schickedanz, 1994). This led to the development of an 'emergent' perspective on early literacy that showed how much very young children knew about reading and writing. Emergent literacy pointed to several underpinning aspects which needed due attention: links between reading and writing; the importance of the home and parents in early literacy development; the importance of play to literacy; the importance of context and meaning to the development of writing and reading. In short, an emergent or developmental literacy perspective supposes that young children are active in developing literacy skills, knowledge and understanding, long before they go to school or have formal teaching of these things; and because their literacy seems spontaneous, we can assume that this is something they enjoy doing. In this sense children's literacy development *emerges* in cognate *socio-cultural* contexts.

Ferreiro and Teberosky (1982) put forward a notion of children's self-generated hypotheses about writing rules. They found that many children expected written strings of letters for people's names to be proportional to the size (or age) of the person rather than the actual length of their name:

> David thinks that the written representation 'papa' is longer than the one for 'David Bernardo Mendez' (his own complete name) ... a girl who has just turned five ... says 'Write my name. But you have to make it longer because yesterday was my birthday.' (1982: 180–184)

The example by Gregg (Figure 14.1) – age four years and one month – illustrates Ferreiro and Teberosky's research into this hypothesis. Whilst the strings for 'my dad' and 'my mum' both contain nine characters, Gregg has made the first look much bigger.

Ferreiro and Teberosky (1982) summarise children's writing activity in relation to the hypothesis that a bigger object must have a big word:

> They ... use greater numbers of graphic characters, larger characters, or longer graphic stories if the object is bigger, longer, older, or if a great number of objects are referred to. (1982: 184)

Ferreiro and Teberosky argued that literacy comes about through a long developmental process during the preschool years, from initial conceptions about print to the final sophistications and understandings about function, form and convention.

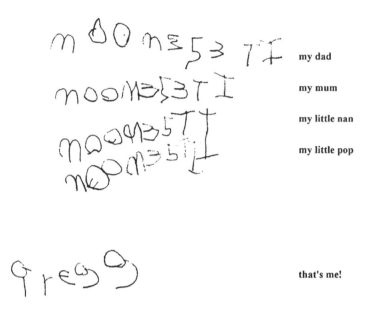

my dad

my mum

my little nan

my little pop

that's me!

Figure 14.1 Gregg's writing

> To understand print, pre-school children have reasoned intelligently, elaborated good hypotheses about writing systems (although they may not be 'good' in terms of our conventional writing system), overcome conflicts, searched for irregularities, and continually attached meaning to written texts. But the logical coherence they impose on themselves disappears when faced with what the teacher demands from them. They must worry about perception and motor control instead of the need to understand. They must acquire a series of skills instead of coming to know an object. They must set aside their own linguistic knowledge and capacity for thought until they discover, at a later point, that it is impossible to comprehend a written text without them. (Ferreiro and Teberosky, 1982: 279)

Discussing research from the 1970s and 1980s, which led to the growth of an 'emergent literacy' perspective, Hall (1985) wrote:

> While educationalists have always been aware that some children learn to read early in life most school activities related to beginning reading seem to presuppose that children, in general, do not know anything about literacy. Thus implicitly the judgement of teachers appears to be that children have to be taught from scratch all that they need to know about becoming literate. (1985: 7)

An emergent literacy perspective gives teachers and parents – and other education practitioners – a sense of what children already know about aspects of literacy before they begin formal education. Young children acquire some literacy knowledge and behaviour without any formal teaching. They are, however, immersed in literacy, they live in a literate environment, watch adults reading and writing, play with the 'tools' of literacy, pens, paper, books, digital technologies, and so on.

RESEARCH ON VARIOUS 'STRANDS' OF EARLY LITERACY DEVELOPMENT

The Raising Early Achievement in Literacy (REAL) Project (Nutbrown and Hannon, 1997) suggested that emergent literacy could be thought of as comprising four strands: environmental print, sharing books, early writing and key aspects of oral language (Figure 14.2).

If we consider these four elements we could say that *emergent literacy* is that which arises out of being involved in real life and realistic literacy activities, such as looking at books and sharing in the reading of stories; watching and imitating adults who write in everyday contexts such as letters, shopping lists, text messages and emails; and identifying some print in the environment such as street signs, door numbers, shop signs, advertisements, digital transport signs and food packages; sharing in storytelling and making jokes with sounds, words and rhymes.

Environmental print includes digital technology, advertisements, controls on household appliances, stickers, logos, labels, packaging, shop signs and graffiti (Baroody and Diamond, 2016). Young children often recognise familiar environmental symbols long before they can actually identify individual letters or spell words (Neumann et al., 2011). Environmental print can stimulate talk about literacy as children ask, 'What does that say?'

Books are essential for children to experience the pleasure of reading (Kotaman and Tekin, 2017). The cover, feel, size, shape, smell of a book are important parts of the experience for babies as well as young children (Egan and Murray, 2013). Sharing books creates interactions with babies using language and images. Rhythm, repetition, colour and language all come together when books are shared. Young children need many opportunities to enjoy books at home and in their group settings, and the range needs to be broad and not confined to stereotypical choices (Xeni, 2015; Ozturk et al., 2016).

Early writing begins with the first tentative marks children make. Often referred to (perhaps somewhat negatively) as 'scribble', these early marks eventually evolve into conventionally recognised writing. Research into emergent or developmental writing shows that as children get to know more about writing, and trying things out in the early years, they begin to develop their own rules about how writing works. This important foundation comes long before trying to form letters correctly, or copying words and later spellings (Niessen et al., 2011). When young children understand that speech can be written down, they can progress successfully in reading – because at that point in their development, words on a page mean something.

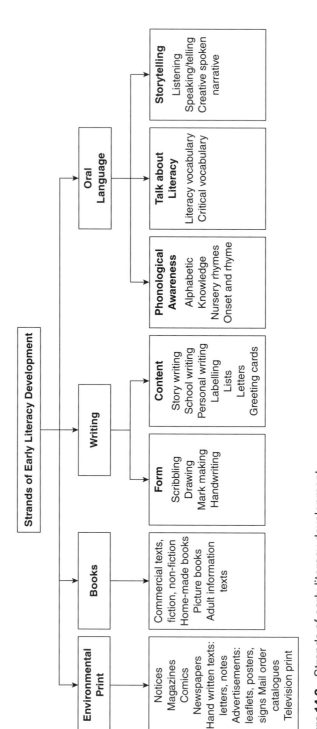

Figure 14.2 Strands of early literacy development

Oral language has an impact on children's literacy learning and development. Speaking is the foundation for written language and research shows that certain aspects of oral language are important for early literacy development. *Phonological awareness* is crucial in children's literacy development. Young children's awareness of beginning (onset) and end (rime) sounds in words is an important stage which makes learning to read easier, and singing nursery rhymes can help with this. *Storytelling* enhances developing understanding of how stories work and increasing children's vocabulary. *Talk about literacy* helps satisfy curiosity about words, and prompts asking questions, much as they might about anything that interests them.

Table 14.1 Some home experiences which foster early literacy development

ENVIRONMENTAL PRINT

Encounters with print in the environment – looking, watching adults use print

Experiences using print – selecting breakfast cereal

Noticing logos, at the shops, on packaging

Digital texts

INFORMATION AND HELP

Parents:

    answering children's questions

    providing 'incidental' information about literacy

    building on and extending children's interests in literacy

    help with use of digital technologies

EXPERIENCES

Wide range of experiences from being a baby – outings, walks, books, stories

Being part of literacy events in the family (Hall, 1987)

Always observant of their environment

BOOKS

Visiting library weekly from a baby – later choosing own library books

Being read to and told stories – daytime and bedtime

Having own books – interesting content – books which 'do' something, e.g. 'pop-up'

Enjoying and caring for books from the beginning

E-books and audio-visual stories

(Continued)

Table 14.1 (Continued)

MODELS OF LITERACY IN ACTION

Seeing adults in the family using:

    books

    knitting patterns

    magazines

    Do-It-Yourself books

    text messages

    emails

    search engines

    instruction sheets

    newspapers

Involvement in everyday literacy:

    shopping lists – shopping

    using Facebook and other social media

    Watching adults writing:

    form-filling

    letter-writing

    drawing plans – for example wiring diagrams or architect's drawings

    using computers for literacy

Parents making a point of sharing adult literacy experiences:

    looking something up in a book

    reading instructions

    using a car manual to repair the car

LANGUAGE AND TALK

Being given correct 'technical' language if it is part of an answer to a question

Being involved in 'adult' jobs, hearing correct terminology

Adults holding conversations with children – giving language models

Holding a video chat with friends or family

Interest in words – encouraged

IMAGINATIVE PLAY

Involving literacy – writing and reading

RESOURCES

Literacy materials and toys with literacy elements available

STUDIES WHICH ENHANCE OUR UNDERSTANDING OF DIGITAL TECHNOLOGIES AND MULTI-MODAL LITERACIES

The studies that gave rise to our current understanding of early literacy development were, of course, conducted in a non-digital world, so a considerable change in the focus of research has taken place in these last two decades, with researchers occupied with how digital literacies have changed and impacted on early literacy development.

Literacy arises and is developed in the social contexts in which people need to communicate, and this is particularly important for children and a new dimension is added when digital technologies and 'digi-literacies' are brought into the frame. As Bearne et al. (2007: 11) remark, 'very young children show expertise in on-screen reading, even where homes may not have computers'; they become 'digitally literate' (Glister, 1997) from being very young – toddlers are seen moving their finger across a screen to change the images on a tablet, for example – and they take these new technologies in their stride. However, Merchant (2007) has called for some clarity on the topic arguing that the term 'digital literacy' has been badly conceptualised in some instances, and that the study of digital literacy practices should focus on the 'study of written or symbolic representation that is mediated by new technology' (2007: 121).

One of the things that studies of literacy in the digital world have contributed to our understanding is an insight into the subtleties and sophistication of the process of becoming digitally literate, and Flewitt (2011) has called for more ethnographic studies to give us insights into early literacy in a digital age. Bearne (2004: 16) points out that texts for young readers have become multi-modal 'so that "text" has come to include not only words-plus-images but moving images, with their associated sound tracks too'. The bringing together of 'stationary' words and moving images, the spoken word, music and sound effects, stimulated researchers to think about how literacy is constructed and enacted in the 21st century, and to question whether constructions and definitions we once had have the same validity in the digital age. Reading and writing considered in the context of digital technologies are different now, prompting Marsh's observation that 'schools have been rather slow to recognise that changing landscape of communication. The school still hangs on to the printed text as the primary form of communication' (Hall, 2003: 173). However, the effect of new digital technologies on the school literacy curriculum is, Turbill (2001) argues, much more complex now. Considering that many young children experience immersion in digital technologies from being very young, Marsh et al. (2005) stress the:

 need for educators to respond to the challenge this presents by developing curricula and pedagogy which enable children to build on their digital 'funds of knowledge' (Moll et al., 1992) and provide them with opportunities to engage fully with the technological, social and cultural demands of the knowledge economy. (2005: 5)

In a small-scale study, Flewitt et al. (2009) have focused on inclusive practices around multimodal literacies with children with identified special educational needs and conclude that:

> Detailed multimodal analysis of a selected literacy event highlights the salience of embodied action and the shapes of inclusive learning spaces, and points to the importance of valuing individuals' idiosyncratic and multimodal meaning-making. (2009: 211)

Similarly, examining the 'techno-practices' of 26 families in interviews with parents of 13 boys and 13 girls in northern England, Marsh (2004) found that:

> young children's engagement with a range of contemporary texts and artefacts contributes to our understanding of 'emergent techno-literacy'. These practices should be valued and the place they play in the development of children as competent users and producers of media texts and artefacts acknowledged in curriculum frameworks for the early years. (2004: 62)

This is in line with the findings of a later, Australian study (Neumann, 2014; Neumann and Neumann, 2017) involving parents of 109 preschool children aged between three and five years who reported that tablets were easy for their children to operate, and some used them at home to support their children's early literacy development. Tablet use in preschool mark-making development has been similarly investigated (Price et al., 2015) with the conclusion that:

> while the tablet computer limited the number of fingers used for interaction, its material affordances supported speed and continuity, which led to more mark making, and different 'scales' of mark making extending the range of mark making practices. At the same time it limited the sensory experience of physical paint and resulted in more uniform final compositions. (2015: 131)

This is a strong indication that new technologies offer a new dimension to the development of literacy but do not necessarily replace existing 'traditional' literacy tools. Several researchers conclude their studies of emerging digi-literacies with calls for more curriculum embeddedness:

> Understanding the role of digital technologies in the processes of young children's literacy development is crucial to ensure that all children have equal access to opportunities to learn in schools today. (Wolfe and Flewitt, 2010: 397)

Reflecting on a five-year study of literacy play involving popular media and film making, Wohlwend (2017) concludes that:

> Throughout the projects, when children had opportunities to use their media knowledge, they transformed their participation, their play narratives and themselves, if only for moments. Timely teacher mediation can fan these promising sparks, providing time and materials that allow children to replay favorite themes and develop patterns of participation through repetition. (2017: 73)

This is an example of how the bringing together of new technologies with children's popular culture can enrich their curriculum experience and extend pedagogy.

SOME STUDIES OF THE ROLES OF PARENTS IN CHILDREN'S EARLY LITERACY DEVELOPMENT

Traditionally it has been mothers who have engaged in their children's early literacy practices, yet more recently (as we saw in Chapter 7) there have been more studies about fathers' involvement in their children's learning – and that includes early literacy development. Staying with mothers for a moment, Edwards (2014) studied the way that 15 American (significantly, 'upper class and white') mothers of 18–36 month old toddlers engaged in emergent literacy, and concluded that the mothers were importantly involved in supporting phonological awareness through rhyming games and songs, and aspects of written language development. Weigel et al. (2006) also focused on mothers, examining their beliefs about literacy and exploring home–preschool connections in terms of the literacy environment. Seventy-nine mothers participated and Weigel et al. (2006) identified two perspectives:

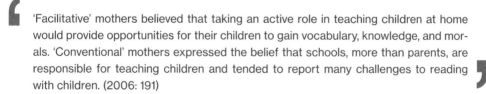

> 'Facilitative' mothers believed that taking an active role in teaching children at home would provide opportunities for their children to gain vocabulary, knowledge, and morals. 'Conventional' mothers expressed the belief that schools, more than parents, are responsible for teaching children and tended to report many challenges to reading with children. (2006: 191)

Unsurprisingly, in 'facilitative' homes the literacy environment and interactions were richer than those in the 'conventional' home, with 'facilitative' mothers showing more awareness of environmental print and reading with their children. This study, amongst many, points to the importance of working with parents to share theories of emergent literacy development and suggest practices for interacting with children around literacy at home. Further, this group of studies from different countries and contexts shows that there is an enduring interest in, and a need to research further, how literacies are practised in homes by families, and how home and school might collaborate to ensure continuities and maximise benefits to children.

The situation is similar in terms of the need for development in the Pacific Island of Vanuatu, where Hughes (2004) shows parents were keen for their children to develop their literacy in a context where literacy levels were low. Hughes plots the educational provision and parental ambition, concluding that:

> Overall, children who succeed in literacy will be those who come from families who value literacy development and encourage it from an early age; can afford to send their children to school; have access to or can afford printed material; and are intelligent enough to develop literacy, often in spite of teaching and school programs.
>
> High levels of literacy will not be achieved in Vanuatu until all children have access to schools and have well-trained teachers who understand literacy processes and literacy acquisition. Families may need community education to help them to understand their role in their children's literacy development. Preschool education can also play a role when the community understands the importance of an early education. Governments could improve literacy processes by assisting with the training of early childhood teachers and qualified primary school teachers and are in fact beginning to do this. (2004: 358–359)

Focusing on the need for partnership between home and school and the importance of sharing theory and practice with parents, the Sheffield REAL Project was the largest preschool literacy intervention study in the UK to date. Central to the REAL Project programme was the ORIM framework, designed to think about ways in which families can help children's early literacy development (Nutbrown and Hannon, 2003; Hannon et al., 2006).

Families are powerful influences on children's early literacy. The ORIM framework is based around parents providing four things for their children: Opportunities, Recognition, Interaction and Models of Literacy and also focuses attention on four key strands of literacy: environmental print, books, early writing and aspects of oral language (Hannon, 1995; Nutbrown et al., 2005).

The ORIM framework, developed by Hannon and Nutbrown (1997) can be used to describe how particular families support children's literacy (or other aspects of their development) and to plan work with parents. One can ask of each cell in the matrix (see Figure 14.3): 'How can we support the parents' role here?' Or 'What can we do to help parents improve children's experiences here?'

The ORIM framework was first used in the Sheffield REAL Project, a large preschool randomised control trial which used the ORIM framework to plan and evaluate work with families (Nutbrown et al. 2005). Since then ORIM has been used in many projects, forming the basis of Peeple's *Learning Together* (www.peeple.org.uk/orim), the National Children's Bureau's *Making it REAL* (Rix et al., 2016) and the Prison Advice and Care Trust (Pact's) *Family Literacy in Prisons* (Nutbrown et al., 2017).

There are now many projects that use the ORIM framework and details are on the REAL website (www.real-online.group.shef.ac.uk/index.html).

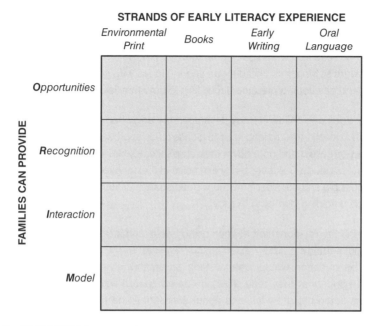

Figure 14.3 THE ORIM framework

RESEARCH QUESTIONS ON EARLY LITERACY DEVELOPMENT AND LEARNING

Early literacy research may be seen to have had two important 'moments' in the last four decades. In the 1980s and 1990s researchers uncovered the emergent literacy practices of young children and highlighted the importance of the home and family in young children's early literacy development, and in the last two decades, technologies have broadened and redefined our concept of literacy and what it means to be literate. The exponential burgeoning of digital technologies has moved the study of young children's literacy and emergent practices on to include the use of digital technologies to support early literacy development with new approaches to text, new ideas of what text is, and new possibilities for early literacy learning. Studies of children in their own homes, learning with their parents in ways that are very different from planned school practices, have informed new literacy pedagogies and extended our view of what the youngest children can do in terms of literacy. This, in turn, leads to new research questions to be explored.

Some suggested research questions for early years practitioners and students include:

○ How might the ORIM framework be used by practitioners in an early years setting to develop early literacy work with parents?

(Continued)

(Continued)

Some action research would be needed here to put the ORIM framework into practice in an early years setting; this would mean sharing ideas with parents and monitoring their responses, and developing practice according to how families responded.

⟲ How does one child's literacy develop in the preschool years?

This question would lend itself to a case study approach. A child whose parents are happy to collect and note down their child's literacy development would be the focus for such a study. Collect as many examples of their engagement with everyday literacy as possible and consider how the various strands of literacy are represented on one child's unfolding journey to literacy.

⟲ What is the relationship between using books and stories at home and in a pre-school setting?

This question would mean asking parents whether children share books at home and what they read. This can be compared with books shared in an early years setting to draw lessons about similarities and differences. There may well be a wide variety of differences between home and school reading cultures, and it is important not to make assumptions.

⟲ What are children's digital literacy practices at home?

This question would need the support of families to note down, and perhaps film or photograph, what their children do at home in relation to digital texts. Learning about children's digital encounters at home will demonstrate their versatility and identify a range of experiences.

A NOTE ON RESEARCH ETHICS AND INTEGRITY

One of the important things about working with families around literacy is that attention must be paid to any potential sensitivities around parents' own literacy. If parents themselves struggle with literacy, they may be reluctant to expose this to educators. All parents, whatever their own literacy levels, can engage with early literacy development and support their children, and educators need to find ways to do this which avoid embarrassment or experiences that lead to parents disengaging with family literacy opportunities or other means to learn more about how to support their children.

RECOMMENDED READING

Hannon, P., Morgan, A. and Nutbrown, C. (2006) Parents' experiences of a family literacy programme. *Journal of Early Childhood Research*, 4 (1): 19–44.

This paper reports on a family literacy programme from the perspectives of the parents involved in it. There was evidence, according to parent reports, of programme impact on family literacy practices. Implications for family literacy programmes are discussed.

Levy, R. (2009) 'You have to understand words … but not read them': Young children becoming readers in a digital age. *Journal of Research in Reading*, 32 (1): 75–91.

This paper examines how young children's home experiences of digital technology influence their perceptions of reading. Drawing from research conducted with 12 young children (aged three to six) this paper reports on the ways in which they were interacting with screen texts and using them to develop strategies to make sense of a whole variety of symbolic representations, including print.

Marsh, J., Hannon, P., Lewis, M. and Ritchie, L. (2017) Young children's initiation into family literacy practices in the digital age. *Journal of Early Childhood Research*, 15 (1): 47–60. DOI: i1.o0r.g1/107.171/1747/7164761781X8X151558822095.

This paper reports on a study that explored young children's digital literacy in the home. The aim of the study was to identify the range of digital literacy practices in which children are engaged in the home and to explore how these are embedded into family life and involve family members. Four children, two girls and two boys aged between two and four years, were the focus for study. Findings suggest that children were immersed in a range of multimedia, multi-modal practices which involved extensive engagement with other family members who scaffolded their learning and delighted in the children's technological capabilities.

Nutbrown, C. and Hannon, P. (2003) Children's perspectives on family literacy: Methodological issues, findings and implications for practice. *Journal of Early Childhood Literacy*, 3 (2): 115–145.

This paper reports on a study of family literacy practices from the perspectives of five-year-old children drawn from areas of social and economic deprivation in an English city. The comparison showed a modest, but consistent, increase in child-reported family literacy activity in the programme group, and concluded that the impact of a family literacy programme is discernible through children's perspectives.

REFERENCES

Bagdahn, M. (1984) *Our Daughter Learns to Read and Write*. Newark, DE: International Reading Association.

Baroody, A.E. and Diamond, K.E. (2016) Associations among preschool children's classroom literacy environment, interest and engagement in literacy activities, and early reading skills. *Journal of Early Childhood Research, 14* (2): 146–162. DOI: 10. 1177/1476718X14529280.

Bearne, E. (2004) Multimodal texts: What they are and how children use them. In J. Evans (ed.), *New Ways of Reading, New Ways of Writing: Using Popular Culture, NewTechnologies and Critical Literacy in the Primary Classroom*. New York: Heinemann, pp. 27–34.

Bearne, E., Clark, C., Johnson, A., Manford, P., Mottram, M. and Wolstencroft, H. (2007) *Reading on Screen*. Leicester: UKLA.

Bissex, G. (1985) *GNYS AT WRK: A Child Learns to Write and Read*. Cambridge, MA: Harvard University Press.

Edwards, C.M. (2014) Maternal literacy practices and toddlers' emergent literacy skills. *Journal of Early Childhood Literacy, 14* (1): 53–79. DOI:10.1177/1468798412451590.

Egan, S.M. and Murray, A. (2013) Does reading to infants benefit their cognitive development at 9-months-old? An investigation using a large birth cohort survey. *Child Language Teaching and Therapy, 30* (3): 303–315. DOI: 10.1177/0265659013513813.

Ferreiro, E. and Teberosky, A. (1982) *Literacy Before Schooling*. Oxford: Heinemann.

Flewitt, R. (2011) Bringing ethnography to a multimodal investigation of early literacy in a digital age. *Qualitative Research, 11* (3): 293–310. DOI: 10.1177/1468794111399838.

Flewitt, R., Nind, M. and Payler, J. (2009) 'If she's left with books she'll just eat them': Considering inclusive multimodal literacy practices. *Journal of Early Childhood Literacy, 9* (2): 211–233. DOI: 10.1177/1468798409105587.

Glister, P. (1997) *Digital Literacy*. New York: John Wiley and Sons.

Goodman, Y. (1980) The roots of literacy. *Claremont Reading Conference Yearbook, 44*: 1–32.

Goodman, Y. (1986) Children coming to know literacy. In W.H. Teale and E. Sulzby (eds), *Emergent Literacy: Writing and Reading*. Norwood, NJ: Ablex, pp. 1–14.

Hall, K. (2003) *Listening to Stephen Read: Multiple Perspectives on Literacy*. Buckingham: Open University Press.

Hall, N. (1985) When do children learn to read? *Reading, 19* (2): 117–128.

Hall, N. (1987) *The Emergence of Literacy*. London: Heinemann.

Hannon, P. (1995) *Literacy, Home and School*. London: Routledge.

Hannon, P. and Nutbrown, C. (1997) Teachers' use of a conceptual framework for early literacy education with parents. *Teacher Development, 1* (3): 405–420.

Hannon, P., Morgan, A. and Nutbrown, C. (2006) Parents' experiences of a family literacy programme. *Journal of Early Childhood Research, 4* (1): 19–44.

Hassett, D.D. (2006) Signs of the times: The governance of alphabetic print over 'appropriate' and 'natural' reading development. *Journal of Early Childhood Literacy, 6* (1): 77–103.

Hughes, D. (2004) Reflecting on early literacy development in the context of Vanuatu. *Contemporary Issues in Early Childhood, 5* (3): 349–360.

Kotaman, H. and Tekin, A.K. (2017) Informational and fictional books: Young children's book preferences and teachers' perspectives. *Early Child Development and Care, 187* (3–4): 600–614. DOI: 10.1080/03004430.2016.1236092.

Marsh, J. (2004) The techno-literacy practices of young children. *Journal of Early Childhood Research, 2* (1): 51–66

Marsh, J., Brooks, G., Hughes, J., Ritchie, L., Roberts, S. and Wright, K. (2005) *Digital Beginnings: Young Children's Use of Popular Culture, Media and New Technologies*. Report of the 'Young Children's Use of Popular Culture, Media and New Technologies' Study, funded by BBC Worldwide and the Esmée Fairbairn Foundation. Sheffield: Literacy Research Centre University of Sheffield. www.digitalbeginnings.shef.ac.uk/DigitalBeginningsReport.pdf (accessed 1 March 2018).

Merchant, G. (2007) 'Writing in the future in the digital age', *Literacy, 41* (3): 118–128.

Moll, L.C., Amanti, C., Neff, D. and Gonzalez, N. (1992) Funds of knowledge for teaching: Using qualitative approach to connect homes and classrooms. *Theory into Practice, 31* (2): 132–141.

Neumann, M.M. (2014) An examination of touch screen tablets and emergent literacy in Australian pre-school children. *Australian Journal of Education, 58* (2): 109–122. DOI: 10.1177/0004944114523368.

Neumann, M.M., Hood, M., Ford, R.M. and Neumann, D.L. (2011) The role of environmental print in emergent literacy. *Journal of Early Childhood Literacy, 12* (3): 231–258. DOI: 10.1177/1468798411417080.

Neumann, M.M. and Neumann, D.L. (2017) The use of touch-screen tablets at home and pre-school to foster emergent literacy. *Journal of Early Childhood Literacy, 17* (2): 203–220. DOI: 10.1177/1468798415619773.

Niessen, N.L., Strattman, K. and Scudder, R. (2011) The influence of three emergent literacy skills on the invented spellings of 4-year-olds. *Communication Disorders Quarterly, 32* (2): 93–102. DOI: 10.1177/1525740110363624.

Nutbrown, C., Clough, P., Stammers, L., Emblin, N. and Aston-Smith, S. (2017) Family literacy in prisons: Fathers' engagement with their young children. *Research Papers in Education.* DOI: 10.1080/02671522.2017.1402085.

Nutbrown, C. and Hannon, P. (eds) (1997) *Preparing for Early Literacy Education with Parents: A Professional Development Manual.* Nottingham: NES Arnold/REAL Project.

Nutbrown, C. and Hannon, P. (2003) Children's perspectives on family literacy: Methodological issues, findings and implications for practice. *Journal of Early Childhood Literacy, 3* (2): 115–145.

Nutbrown, C., Hannon, P. and Morgan, A. (2005) *Early Literacy Work with Families: Policy, Practice and Research.* London: Sage.

Ozturk, G., Hill, S. and Yates, G.C.R. (2016) Girls, boys and early reading: Parents' gendered views about literacy and children's attitudes towards reading. *Early Child Development and Care, 186* (5): 703–715. DOI: 10.1080/03004430.2015.1053477.

Payton, S. (1984) *Developing Awareness of Print: A Child's First Steps Towards Literacy.* Birmingham: Educational Review.

Price, S., Jewitt, C. and Crescenzi, L. (2015) The role of iPads in pre-school children's mark making development. *Computers and Education, 87*: 131–141. DOI: 10.1016/j. compedu.2015.04.003.

Rix, K., Lea, J. and Graham, B. (2016) *Year 3 Evaluation of Making it REAL (Raising Early Achievement in Literacy)*. London: National Children's Bureau Research Centre. www. ncb.org.uk/sites/default/files/field/attachment/project/Making%20it%20REAL%20 Year%20Three%20Evaluation%20Report.pdf (accessed 28 February 2018).

Schickedanz, J. (1994) *More than the ABCs: The Early Stages of Reading and Writing*. Washington, DC: National Association for Education of Young Children.

Turbill, J. (2001) A researcher goes to school: Using technology in the kindergarten literacy curriculum. *Journal of Early Childhood Literacy, 1* (3): 255–279.

Weigel, D.J., Martin, S.S. and Bennett, K.K. (2006) Mothers' literacy beliefs: Connections with the home literacy environment and pre-school children's literacy development. *Journal of Early Childhood Literacy, 6* (2): 191–211. DOI: 10.1177/1468798406066444.

Whitmore, K.F., Martens, P., Goodman, Y. and Owocki, G. (2004) Critical lessons from the transactional perspective on early literacy research. *Journal of Early Childhood Literacy, 4* (3): 291–325. DOI: 10.1177/1468798404047291.

Wohlwend, K.E. (2017) Who gets to play? Access, popular media and participatory literacies. *Early Years, 37* (1): 62–76. DOI:10.1080/09575146.2016.1219699.

Wolfe, S. and Flewitt, R. (2010) New technologies, new multimodal literacy practices and young children's metacognitive development. *Cambridge Journal of Education, 40* (4): 387–399. DOI: 10.1080/0305764X.2010.526589.

Xeni, E. (2015) Developing children's critical thinking through picture books: A guide for primary and early years students and teachers. *Educational Media International, 52* (1): 64–65. DOI: 10.1080/09523987.2015.1008785.

15

LANGUAGES AND EARLY LEARNING

THIS CHAPTER WILL:

- describe the international context of linguistic diversity
- consider research which focuses on the importance of relationships to language learners
- examine research focusing on teaching bilingual children
- consider research into the professional development needs of teachers in multilingual settings
- suggest some research questions on the topic of bilingual and plurilingual children and their communities
- provide some recommended reading to follow up the issues discussed.

T his chapter focuses on the contribution of research to understanding and practices in the development of languages and learning in early childhood education and care. Around half the world's population speak more than one language, some countries have more than one official language, and as the extent of languages increases in many parts of the world, many early childhood settings include plurilingual children who are growing up in multilingual communities. With the richness of languages brought about through migration it is now common for young children to live and learn in communities and settings where many languages are spoken. This chapter will describe the international context of linguistic diversity; consider research which focuses on the importance of relationships to language learners; and examine research focusing on teaching bilingual children. It will conclude with a consideration of research into the professional development needs of teachers in multilingual settings.

AN INTERNATIONAL CONTEXTUALISATION OF LANGUAGE AND HERITAGE

For half of the world's people it is quite usual to speak two or more languages (U.S. Census Bureau, 2013). According to the UK Office for National Statistics (2013), in 2011 there were 8.5 million residents aged 3 to 15 in England and Wales, between them speaking 89 languages. Eight million (94 per cent) of these had English as their main language and 0.4 million (5 per cent) spoke a language other than English and were considered 'proficient' in English. Those classified as 'non-proficient' amounted to 1 per cent (78,500). Less than 5 per cent of the population aged 3 to 15 in all local authorities in England and Wales had a main language other than English and were considered 'non-proficient' in English. In the US, 381 languages were identified as being spoken in the home in the 2011 census (including 169 distinct native North American languages). With the majority language in the US population of 291.5 million people aged over 5 years being English, 60.6 million people (21 per cent of this population) spoke a language other than English at home (U.S. Census Bureau, 2013).

In language rich Australia, the top five languages spoken at home were: English only – 72.7 per cent (17,020,417); Mandarin – 2.5 per cent (596,711); Arabic – 1.4 per cent (321,728); Cantonese – 1.2 per cent (280,943); Vietnamese – 1.2 per cent (277,400). The situation was, according to the Australian Bureau of Statistics (2017):

> In 2016, there were over 300 separately identified languages spoken in Australian homes. More than one-fifth (21 per cent) of Australians spoke a language other than English at home. After English, the next most common languages spoken at home were Mandarin, Arabic, Cantonese, and Vietnamese. Tasmania had the highest rate of people speaking only English at home with 88 per cent, while the Northern Territory had the lowest rate at 58 per cent.

Children who grow up learning and speaking more than one language are developing the potential to be able to communicate with more people and to have a broader outlook on life. Contrary to earlier concerns that learning more than one language in early childhood might be detrimental to a child's general learning and development, more contemporary studies have shown this not to be the case. More specifically, young children who acquire more than one language have no more or less difficulty in learning speech or developing language than their monolingual peers (Goldstein and Bunta, 2012; Hambly et al., 2013). When young children are exposed to listening and engaging in all the languages they speak in equal measure, their language learning in each of their languages develops well over the course of time (Hammer et al., 2011) and of course, as with all learning, as a longitudinal Australian study showed, relationships – with parents and other family members, and early years practitioners and peers – are crucial to language learning (Verdon et al., 2014). McLeod et al. (2015) argue for more sustained longitudinal studies in order to obtain a more comprehensive picture. They suggest that 'Longer-term monolingual-multilingual comparisons may give a different, more positive picture than do short-term comparisons at school entry' (2015: 269).

Considering the census data from Australia, the UK and the US alone, we can see that linguistic diversity means that languages flow around the world, and patterns of language use change over time, as the make-up of communities changes with migration as people, their cultures, heritages and languages come and go.

Our languages are an intrinsic part of our identity, and children's home languages are vital to their developing identities and self-esteem and confidence. It's clear that, if young children's home languages are different from the majority language of the country, the preservation of their heritage languages is essential to their holistic development.

STUDIES OF THE IMPORTANCE OF RELATIONSHIPS TO LANGUAGE LEARNERS

A qualitative case study showed that children's responses to picture books were strongly influenced by their relationships and interactions with their peers in bilingual settings (Kim, 2016). We know that positive social relationships between young children are crucial to their holistic development (Williford et al., 2013) and, though still an under-researched topic, this is no less the case for young children who are growing up in bilingual families. Though small in scale, Kim's (2016) study – conducted in a pre-kindergarten class of a Saturday, Korean Heritage Language School in the US, and involving five 4-year-old children – uses detailed observations to show how children's literary responses to stories are fluid and often peer dependent, i.e. children frequently endorse the view of their friend. The crucial role of the teachers in mediating the text for bilingual learners was apparent in the case study material, and especially so in keeping the exchanges of views about text fluid and open. A further important point that was well illustrated in the detail of the case study was the use of trans-languaging – where children reached to their (often) home language for a word when it was not easily available to them in their second language. Some studies have shown how young children use code-switching as necessary (Garcia and Wei, 2013) and this, researchers suggest, should be seen as a positive use of both (or more) of their developing languages (Hornberger and Link, 2012).

A survey of 86 parents whose children attended a Chinese-English preschool in San Francisco (Lao, 2004), found that partnership with parents was essential in order to understand and appreciate the expectations of parents and of teachers around the children's learning of both Chinese and English. However, the study showed that expectations and involvement of parents varied between parents and between parents and teachers. Again, positive relationships between home and school are essential to understand expectations and possibilities. Similarly, Oades-Sese and Li (2011), in a study of attachment, teacher– child relationships and parental acculturation involving 468 Hispanic-American three- to five-year-olds, found that:

> children's relationships with parents and teachers significantly contribute to their bilingual language skills. Higher quality teacher–child relationships were associated with higher levels of language skills over and above quality parental attachments. (2011: 707)

Oades-Sese and Li (2011) conclude that professional development for teachers of bilingual children should include positive relationship development, and they further point out that:

> These relationships become even more important for children from impoverished environments, which have been associated with more conflicting attachment relationships and lower language skills. However, the finding that teacher–child relationships influence language skills over and above those of parent attachment relationships highlights the importance of creating close relationships in schools. (2011: 720)

Studies of bilingual preschool education are much more scarce than studies focusing on older children; the wealth of research on school aged pupils in relation to languages and language learning and bilingual or plurilingual identities is not matched in the field of ECEC. In a study of the language practices of five bilingual preschool teachers in Finland (Finnish-Swedish and Russian-Finnish contexts) and Israel (an Arabic-Hebrew context), teachers reported that they changed their teaching approach over time beginning with 'strict separation of languages' and moving to more 'flexible bilingual practices' (Palviainen et al., 2016). Key themes from the study were flexibility in speaking both languages, code-switching, contextual and linguistic support, adjustments for individual children, and role-modelling. This small-scale study cannot be open to generalisation but the authors do point to the importance of considering:

 The shared experience of the bilingual preschool teachers [which] opens up the way to mutual learning and to viewing bilingual teachers not as separate and unrelated individuals each limited to their own context, but as a community of practice. Such a development could encourage early childhood practitioners from other educational contexts and countries to critically examine their current language practices and models and perhaps renegotiate and modify them. (Palviainen et al., 2016: 627)

As with other studies, the importance of relationship building – in this case, between teachers – is key in developing pedagogical understanding and development in bilingual learning. A year-long study in an Arabic-Hebrew preschool in Israel (Schwartz and Gorbatt, 2016), with 19 children whose first language was Arabic and 10 with Hebrew as their first language, found that actively talking about their languages supported children's ethnic identity development. This study showed that encouraging young children's meta-linguistic talk in the bilingual classroom gave and promoted children's agency in shaping the languages space and policy in their schools. The children in this study were languages aware, and showed interest and curiosity about languages. It might be concluded here that for young children to talk *about languages* is as important as *language learning* itself.

A larger Tunisian study of 127 five- to seven-year-olds focused on how language learning contributed to children's developing sense of identity (Ben Maad, 2016). A four-month programme fostered openness and awareness of other languages and of cultural differences. This, and other examples, demonstrate how young children have a curiosity about difference, are open to exploring new things, new words and new ways, and are not set against languages they don't know but rather seek to learn, try them out and embrace them. Sharing between people and the development of relationships seem to lie at the heart of such programmes.

RESEARCH FOCUSING ON TEACHING BILINGUAL CHILDREN

The emphasis in Singapore on developing bilingualism and promoting the use of mother tongues in favour of English, brought the focus to preschool children. Curdt-Christiansen and Sun (2016)suggest that:

 any successful implementation of bilingual programmes requires a cohesive policy, clear goals, shared visions, and interactions among policy-makers, parents, and teachers as well as consistency and continuity in curriculum provision. (2016: 692)

The authors report that English is on the rise to the detriment of 'mother tongues' with an increase in Chinese children using dominantly English when they enter school at seven years old, from 28 per cent in 1991 to 59 per cent in 2010 (MOE, 2011). Curdt-Christiansen and Sun (2016) suggest that this is due to parental attitudes towards their Chinese mother tongues as a 'functioning language' in Singapore. They point to a need for 'cohesive policy positions to promote MTs which involves both attitudinal changes and language behavioural changes' (2016: 702).An in-depth study of five Australian Chinese families focusing on their preschool children's bilingualism showed that parents were positive about their children's developing bilingualism because they felt it would help them in their futures to be able to speak English for work and Chinese with their families, though they worried that speaking Chinese at home might inhibit their progress in learning English, so they also used English at home (Hu et al., 2014).The study found that resources used at home to support Chinese were often 'rooted in English culture' and so parents might benefit from further understanding the relationship between first and second languages and from the involvement of Chinese community organisations.

When young children first use language they try out their own theories of how language works, and sometimes say things that display a logical reasoning of how words and language work, but which do not conform to grammatical or syntactical conventions and rules. For example – it is not uncommon for young children to say 'I wented' instead of 'I went' following a convention that they know is acceptable and have heard when using other words – for example 'I wanted' – but not knowing that this rule does not also apply to 'went'. Learning language is complicated, especially when not all words behave in the same way, and seem to play a sort of trick on the new language learner. But fortunately children are born curious and they are mostly willing to play and take risks with words (innocent of the burden of rules and conventions) and so they experiment – say things as they think they should be, building from what they know. And so, when learning more than one language it is to be expected that young children transfer what they know from one language to another, and they may not always get it right – because languages have their own rules – but in their borrowing and their transference from one language to another, preschool children are demonstrating their competence as users of languages and their capacity to use what they know. Young children have been found to cope well with learning more than one language at a time (Genesee, 2001) and bilingual children have been shown to draw on one language system to help them out in another if they need to (Meisel, 2006). Nicoladis et al. (2010) studied English-French cross-linguistic transfer in preschool children, finding that:

> Bilingual children seem to conceptualize a scene in a language-specific way in order to label some part of it in that language. For this reason, cross-linguistic transfer cannot be simply word-for-word translation of a linguistic structure from one language to another. Instead, cross-linguistic transfer may occur only when there is some structural ambiguity and when both the available linguistic structures and the conceptualization in the target languages are similar. (2010: 366)

This indicates a quite incredible capacity in young children to move between languages making decisions based on what they know as emergent bilinguals. Similar findings about the capacity of young bilingual children were found by Riojas-Cortez (2011) with a focus on socio-dramatic play in 12 Mexican American preschool children in a rural community in South Texas. Taking a 'funds of knowledge' approach (Moll et al., 1992) the study, based on observations of children's play, was filled with 'education' events – homework, going to school, being the teacher, and so on. Their home and community cultures were woven with that of the school during their socio-dramatic play, and they displayed considerable cultural knowledge, which had the potential to be an important tool for learning. Studies such as this show that, far from maximising children's funds of knowledge, some early years settings take a negative view of what children bring. Safford and Drury (2013) observe that many bilingual children:

> come into early years settings and primary schools with considerable language and cultural knowledge which is viewed as a disadvantage in policy, is not well understood by the education system and is not – with some notable exceptions – deeply explored by educational enquirers. (2013: 78)

Yet, the richness of emergent bilingual children has been illustrated through in-depth case studies which show the extent of children's linguistic and cultural knowledge. Drury (2007) focused on three- and four-year-old bilingual children learning in their home and group settings – concluding that a child can confidently use their languages in one context but the same child may well not display that confidence in another context.

PROFESSIONAL DEVELOPMENT FOR SUPPORTING BILINGUAL LEARNERS

Whilst paying attention to pedagogy is essential for all learning in the early years, there is an additional set of considerations to be borne in mind when young learners are also learning in two or more languages. This may well have implications for monolingual teachers who are teaching young bilingual learners. Recent research into the professional development of early years teachers around the linguistic and cultural diversities young learners bring to their settings is seemingly sparse. However, what exists indicates that there is a need in many international contexts for professional development for teachers who have a rich diversity of languages in their settings, where learners' needs are diverse and where there are many different contextual and cultural issues to take account of.

In a study of how preschool teachers supported the language and literacy learning of Spanish speaking bilingual learners, Sawyer et al. (2016) observed the practices of 72 teachers and drew on self-reports to explore language and culture beliefs, Spanish speaking ability and classroom composition. In a context where it is known that young bi- or dual- language learners benefit from high quality learning experiences around language, the study found little use of linguistically responsive practices by teachers. The authors suggest that specific professional development is needed for monolingual English speaking teachers working with young Spanish bilingual children so that they can facilitate emergent writing in both the children's languages and forge important home–school links for young dual-language learners. With the domination of English in contexts where it is the common language, though not the first language, of children, there is (as we saw earlier) a danger that the home language of young children can be marginalised.

In a different linguistic context, Ritchie (2003) raised the issue of practices to ensure the protection of Māori, the indigenous people of Aotearoa/New Zealand who, through British colonisation, have become marginalised in their homeland leading to a threat to the Māori language as well as culture. Ritchie's study involved interviews with Māori and non-Māori (Pacific Islanders, Asian heritage of New Zealanders of European descent) lecturers and questionnaire responses from their early childhood programme students. There was a strong feeling that it is crucial that early childhood teachers are 'culturally safe' – that is, that they were sufficiently prepared for work in a bicultural community where indigenous culture was understood, valued and respected, and the likelihood of racist practices (including unintended racist behaviours) were reduced by greater awareness of how racism towards indigenous people could be manifest. The extensive and thoughtfully developed professional development programme for New Zealand early childhood teachers was found to confront non–indigenous students to be aware of their own values and beliefs, and to develop their commitment to bicultural issues and skills. Ritchie concludes that early childhood settings could be 'responsive and affirming of their language and cultural identity' for Māori children and their families if teachers are sufficiently prepared and have a sensitive and respectful grounding in what it means to live and work 'biculturally' and how learning about a parallel culture can be fostered. Ritchie concludes that:

> Culture is recognised as a central feature of any educational interaction. Developing cultural awareness becomes a matter of respectful critique, whereby students are offered frameworks which enable them to recognise that their worldview is only one of many, despite the tendency for Western perspectives to assume the status of 'normal' with the consequent 'othering' of non-Western cultural perspectives. (2003: 55)

RESEARCH QUESTIONS ON BILINGUAL AND PLURILINGUAL CHILDREN AND THEIR COMMUNITIES

Language diversity offers a rich seam for research. The considerable changes in populations in various communities in many countries have brought about a shift in the languages of early years settings. Thus practitioners have been developing – or need to develop – specific approaches to support young children's learning in a context of linguistic diversity.

Some suggested research questions for early years practitioners and students include:

- What do young children know about the language they speak? Do they use different languages for different purposes and contexts?
  This study would require an approach that either talked with children about their languages, asked their parents or observed the children. It could well involve a combination of these approaches.

- How do parents whose language is different from English view the importance of their home language in children's lives and learning?
  This is the kind of study that would involve talking with parents – perhaps in their own homes –about their languages and the experiences they offer their children across the languages they speak. Open, informal interviews are probably best for such a study.

- What strategies do monolingual English speaking practitioners use to support the linguistic diversity of children in their settings?
  This is a question that would likely involve talking with practitioners to find out what they do to support young children who are learning English to both develop their English and continue to speak and value their home language. For detail, it would be useful to focus on a small number of practitioners. For a more generalisable 'broad sweep' study, an online questionnaire could be used.

- How do bilingual texts support linguistic awareness of monolingual children?
  A case study of a small number of children using dual language texts, using video recordings to collect the data, could be a good way of gaining insights into young monolingual children's language awareness.

A NOTE ON RESEARCH ETHICS

It will be important to develop in any study of linguistic diversity a set of protocols which emanate from a value position where all languages are valued and where there is no implied sense of superiority of language. There will be some elements of research integrity to address, such as how recordings are transcribed, especially when monolingual researchers encounter aspects of code-switching or trans-languaging. Maintaining the integrity of all languages in any study is important in the conduct of the research and its reporting.

RECOMMENDED READING

Hornberger, N.H. and Link, H. (2012) Translanguaging in today's classrooms: A biliteracy lens. *Theory into Practice*, 51: 239–247.

This paper focuses on how using more than one language in ECEC can support the development of languages across the languages used.

Lao, C. (2004) Parents' attitudes toward Chinese-English bilingual education and Chinese-language use. *Bilingual Research Journal*, 28 (1): 99–121.

This paper illustrates how the views of parents are important influences on how languages are used in ECEC settings.

Nicoladis, E., Rose, A. and Foursha-Stevenson, C. (2010) Thinking for speaking and cross-linguistic transfer in preschool bilingual children. *International Journal of Bilingual Education and Bilingualism*, 13 (3): 345–370. DOI: 10.1080/13670050903243043.

This paper discusses how using and supporting all languages in a child's linguistic repertoire is important to their thinking and learning.

Verdon, S., McLeod, S. and Winsler, A. (2014). Language maintenance and loss in a population study of young Australian children. *Early Childhood Research Quarterly*, 29 (2): 168–181. DOI: 10.1016/j.ecresq.2013.12.003.

This paper highlights the threats to heritage languages and the important role of preschool provision in language preservation.

REFERENCES

Australian Bureau of Statistics (2017) *Census of Population and Housing: Australia Revealed 2016*. www.abs.gov.au/ausstats/abs@.nsf/Latestproducts/2024.0Main%20 Features22016 (accessed 1 December 2017).

Ben Maad, M.R. (2016) Awakening young children to foreign languages: Openness to diversity highlighted. *Language, Culture and Curriculum, 29* (3): 319–336. DOI: 10. 1080/07908318.2016.1184679.

Curdt-Christiansen, X.L. and Sun, B. (2016) Nurturing bilingual learners: Challenges and concerns in Singapore. *International Journal of Bilingual Education and Bilingualism, 19* (6): 689–705. DOI: 10.1080/13670050.2016.1181606.

Drury, R. (2007) *Young Bilingual Learners at Home and School.* Stoke-on-Trent: Trentham Books.

Garcia, O. and Wei, L. (2013) *Translanguaging Language, Bilingualism and Education.* New York: Palgrave Macmillan.

Genesee, F. (2001) Bilingual first language acquisition: Exploring the limits of the language faculty. *Annual Review of Applied Linguistics, 21*: 153–168.

Goldstein, B.A. and Bunta, F. (2012) Positive and negative transfer in the phonological systems of bilingual speakers. *International Journal of Bilingualism, 16* (4): 388–401. DOI: 10.1177/1367006911425817.

Hambly, H., Wren, Y., McLeod, S. and Roulstone, S. (2013) The influence of bilingualism on speech production: A systematic review. *International Journal of Language and Communication Disorders, 48* (1): 1–24. DOI: 10.1111/j.1460-6984.2012.00178.x.

Hammer, C.S., Lawrence, F., Rodriguez, B., Davison, M.D. and Miccio, A.W. (2011) Changes in language usage of Puerto Rican mothers and their children: Do gender and timing of exposure to English matter? *Applied Psycholinguistics, 32* (2): 275–297. DOI: 10.1017/S014271641000041X.

Hornberger, N.H. and Link, H. (2012) Translanguaging in today's classrooms: A biliteracy lens. *Theory into Practice, 51*: 239–247.

Hu, J., Torr, J. and Whiteman, P. (2014) Australian Chinese parents' language attitudes and practices relating to their children's bilingual development prior to school. *Journal of Early Childhood Research, 12* (2): 139–153. DOI: 10.1177/1476718X13515429.

Kim, S.J. (2016) The role of peer relationships and interactions in preschool bilingual children's responses to picture books. *Journal of Early Childhood Literacy,* 16 (3): 311–337. DOI: 10.1177/1468798415577874.

Lao, C. (2004) Parents' attitudes toward Chinese-English bilingual education and Chinese-language use. *Bilingual Research Journal, 28* (1): 99–121.

McLeod, S. Harrison, L.J., Whiteford, C. and Walker, S. (2015) Multilingualism and speech-language competence in early childhood: Impact on academic and social-emotional outcomes at school. *Early Childhood Research Quarterly, 34* (1): 53–66. DOI: 10.1016/j.ecresq.2015.08.005.

Meisel, J. (2006) The bilingual child. In T.K. Bhatia and W.C. Ritchie (eds), *The Handbook of Bilingualism.* Malden, MA: Blackwell, pp. 91–113.

MOE (Ministry of Education) (2011) *Preschool Portal,* 2011. www.moe.gov.sg/initiatives/compularoty-education (accessed 15 August 2016).

Moll, L.C., Amanti, C., Neff, D. and Gonzalez, N. (1992) Funds of knowledge for teaching: Using qualitative approach to connect homes and classrooms. *Theory into Practice, 31* (2): 132–141.

Nicoladis, E., Rose, A. and Foursha-Stevenson, C. (2010) Thinking for speaking and cross-linguistic transfer in preschool bilingual children. *International Journal of Bilingual Education and Bilingualism, 13* (3): 345–370. DOI: 10.1080/13670050903243043.

Oades-Sese, G.V. and Li, Y. (2011) Attachment predictors as predictors of language skills for at-risk bilingual preschool children. *Psychology in the Schools, 48* (7): 707–722. DOI: 10. 1002/pits.20583.

Office for National Statistics (2013) *2011 Census: Detailed analysis – English Language Proficiency in England and Wales, Main Language and General Health Characteristics.* www.ons.gov.uk/peoplepopulationandcommunity/culturalidentity/language/articles/detailedanalysisenglishlanguageproficiencyinenglandandwales/2013-08-30#local-authority-analysis-for-english-language-proficiency-in-3-to-15-year-olds (accessed 20 February 2018).

Palviainen, A., Protassova, E., Mård-Miettinen, K. and Schwartz, M. (2016) Two languages in the air: A cross-cultural comparison of preschool teachers' reflections on their flexible bilingual practices. *International Journal of Bilingual Education and Bilingualism, 19* (6): 614–630. DOI: 10.1080/13670050.2016.1184615.

Riojas-Cortez, M. (2001) Preschoolers' funds of knowledge displayed through socio-dramatic play episodes in a bilingual classroom. *Early Childhood Education Journal, 29* (1): 35–40.

Ritchie, J. (2003) Bicultural development within an early childhood teacher education programme. *International Journal of Early Years Education, 11* (1): 43–56. DOI: 10. 1080/0966976032000066082.

Safford, K. and Drury, R. (2013) The 'problem' of bilingual children in educational settings: Policy and research in England. *Language and Education, 27* (1): 70–81. DOI: 10. 1080/09500782.2012.685177.

Sawyer, B.E., Hammer, C.S., Cycyk, M.L., López, L., Blair, C., Sandilos, L. and Komaroff, E. (2016) Preschool teachers' language and literacy practices with dual language learners. *Bilingual Research Journal, 39* (1): 35–49. DOI: 10.1080/15235882.2016.1138904.

Schwartz, M. and Gorbatt, N. (2016) 'Why do we know Hebrew and they do not know Arabic?' Children's meta-linguistic talk in bilingual preschool. *International Journal of Bilingual Education and Bilingualism, 19* (6): 668–688. DOI: 10.1080/13670050.2016.1181604.

U.S. Census Bureau (2013) *The 2011 Statistical Abstract. Languages Spoken at Home by Language: 2008*, Table 53. www.census.gov/prod/2013pubs/acs-22.pdf (accessed 20 February 2018).

Verdon, S., McLeod, S. and Winsler, A. (2014) Language maintenance and loss in a population study of young Australian children. *Early Childhood Research Quarterly, 29,* 168–181. DOI: 10.1016/j.ecresq.2013.12.003.

Williford, A.P., Whittaker, J.E. and Vitiello, V.E. (2013) Children's engagement within the preschool classroom and their development of self-regulation. *Early Education and Development, 24*: 162–187.

16

DIGITAL TECHNOLOGIES AND EARLY CHILDHOOD EDUCATION AND CARE

THIS CHAPTER WILL:

- briefly consider the dilemmas that digital technologies present to pre-school teachers
- discuss studies of digital technologies in children's lives and learning.
- consider some of the ethical issues in researching digital technologies
- suggest some research questions on the topic of digital technologies and ECEC
- provide some recommended reading to follow up the issues discussed.

C hapter 14 has already addressed some aspects of digital literacy, and other chapters have also considered digital impacts and paying attention to other fields of enquiry. This chapter focuses on the contribution of research to understanding the rapidly developing use of digital technologies in early childhood education and care. The 21st century has seen rapid developments in technology, which have in turn attracted researchers to ask new questions about curriculum and pedagogy, and to research previously researched themes (such as play) through a technological lens. Questions about if, how and when young children can, or should, use newly developed digital technologies in their play and learning have emerged, leading to new studies of children's engagement with technologies that previous generations could not have conceived of. This chapter begins with a brief consideration of the dilemmas that digital technologies seem to have brought to the preschool educator, it then acknowledges the research that is emerging both in children's use of the digital devices available to them at home and in preschool settings and how such devices are used to support a variety of learning. Finally some of the ethical tensions that arise with the affordances that researching with digital technologies offer are considered.

DIGITAL TECHNOLOGIES AND CHILDREN'S LEARNING: FROM 'SHOULD WE?' TO 'HOW CAN WE?'

It is commonly assumed that the development of digital technologies in the last two decades has changed the nature of play, though Arnott (2017) presents a clear analysis which challenges our beliefs about how technologies change play. Several researchers have highlighted emerging issues and developments around play which the incorporation of digital tools has given rise to (Herr-Stephenson et al., 2013; Marsh and Bishop, 2014; Stephen and Plowman, 2014; Bird and Edwards, 2015). Some studies have given a specific focus on storytelling and making (Skantz Åberg et al., 2014; Kocaman-Karoglu, 2015), on music (Lagerlöf et al., 2013), and on literacy (Marsh, 2010), as well as children's understandings of new technologies for play (Aubrey and Dahl, 2013; Nuttall et al., 2013). How we think about and observe play in digital contexts has changed how research is conducted and how we understand the outcomes of such studies such that new approaches are needed and analysis of play needs new perspectives (Marsh et al., 2016; Arnott, 2017).

A US survey data of 1,234 early childhood educators (Blackwell et al., 2014) showed, perhaps unsurprisingly, that teachers' attitudes to technology and their confidence and available support were pivotal in how such technologies were incorporated into children's learning. And, along with many other more qualitative studies, this highlights that the role of the teacher, or early childhood professional, and parents is key to children's use of technologies. As Lindahl and Folkesson (2012) report from a Swedish study, 31 preschool teacher students showed a lack of certainty around use of computers with children, with some embracing new technologies and others rejecting them as inappropriate for the preschool age range. Arguments around children's citizenship, competence and activity were put forward along with concerns about the importance of teachers maintaining 'control' and children needing to be independent but guided learners. As Lindahl and Folkesson (2012) conclude:

> Preschool practice, which develops in accordance with societal changes, needs to take children's participation into account. When this is done by sustaining the norms valuing independent, competent and active children, development of practice is facilitated since the ontological security is preserved. Ontological security can also be preserved by tuning in to the child's perspective with an open mind, since this reduces the risk of losing control in the activity. In such joint explorative activities, new tools, e.g. computers, with the potential to change the practice can be allowed. Thus, both children and educators can create new meaning and possibilities of learning and development. (2012: 434)

Of course, we need to bear in mind that this study focused on student teachers' thinking and so they had limited engagement with children around digital technologies and we have no way of knowing how their views might change with experience. In an earlier Swedish study (Ljung-Djärf et al., 2005), qualitative approaches were used in three preschool settings to analyse how teachers considered the computer as a tool in their preschools. They identified three uses and practices around single computer use in a setting: as a threat to other activities, as an available option, and as an essential activity, in learning environments categorised respectively as 'protective, supporting and guiding'. The authors suggest that:

> teachers' presumptions, qualifications, and attitudes to a great extent constitute the basis for decisions about how the technology is made available in a pre-school educational setting. In addition, the teachers' ways of organizing and relating to computer use, which the present study deals with, is one important aspect constituting the learning environment afforded in the practice. (Ljung-Djärf et al., 2005: 30)

And this shows the crucial role that preschool educators play in integrating technologies into preschool curricula and their pedagogical practices. However, digital technologies and ECE is one area where the pace of research and the relevance of findings is moving at a very fast rate. Nuttall et al. (2013), taking an international perspective on digital play, argue that it is necessary now to 'think differently' about why digital technologies have not been embraced in early childhood curricula internationally. They offer a counterpoint to the Swedish studies, arguing that:

> by focusing on children's play instead of teacher knowledge about using technologies with young children, the 'problem' of teacher uptake of technologies in the early years may be re-phrased as a field-specific problem concerned with defining and understanding young children's digital play. (2013: 222)

Shifting the focus to children's play rather than teacher attitude and knowledge brings fresh possibilities to young children's learning in preschool settings and to this field of research.

DIGITAL TECHNOLOGIES IN CHILDREN'S LIVES AND LEARNING

Whilst television was probably the first important technological tool for entertainment and learning, it brought (and still brings) controversy with some educators and parents believing television for the under-fives is bad for their well-being and health and a poor substitute for play and play outdoors, and others believing that good television is, as for adults, an important part of their learning and entertainment. Famously, Bolton (2016) reported that Steve Jobs, founder of Apple, never allowed his children to use Apple's iPad because he thought there were more important things that they should be doing – such as talking together. Parents adopt different approaches to their children's use of digital devices – some ban them, some limit screen time and others have no set limits. What is clear is that views about what is useful and what is harmful are many and varied and strongly held.

This was the case for television when it first became available, and will continue to be so with all new technologies. In a review of US research on children's television, Moses (2008) identified that television is an important activity for young children and her summary of US studies indicates that moderate viewing is beneficial to reading, content is an important factor, TV programmes seeking to promote literacy had a positive impact, and further studies were needed which would 'focus on methodological, theoretical, and measurement issues in this area, in addition to exploring a wider variety of programs watched by young viewers' (2008: 67).

That television can support young children's learning is well established, though questions about the quality and appropriateness of children's television remain (Calverta and Kotlerb, 2003). As new technologies develop and emerge at a rate of change never seen before, earlier fears about children's television seem be being transferred to other digital technologies used by children for entertainment and for learning. Scepticism in terms of the 'dangers' of digital technologies to children's learning and well-being formed an argument that emerged as soon as computers began to be common in children's homes and settings. There will never be agreement on this because, for some, concern about the digital in children's lives is born out of a value position or of health concerns, which are fuelled by different fields of research and personal belief. Whilst acknowledging that those concerns exist, this chapter does not focus on them, rather it focuses on educators' perspectives and children's engagement.

In an Australian-based study Edwards et al. (2017) highlight the importance of understanding the different priorities in homes and preschools around use of digital technology. It is argued that rather than seeing the two as disconnected, it is preferable to understand the different uses and access to technologies in homes and preschools and 'to explore the influence of setting, in particular the elements of activity, time, place and role on young children's use of digital technologies'. Edwards et al. (2017: 1) suggest that technology use is 'characterised by different imperatives' and that is it important to understand these differences.

Focusing on the different uses of digital technologies in six young children's homes and in their early years settings leads Edwards et al. (2017) to conclude that home was seen as a place where technologies were part of children's leisure activity whereas in early years settings they were seen as part of learning:

> thinking about digital differences may be more productive than thinking about digital disconnect because it enables a focus on the use of technologies relative to each setting. Difference does not need to imply deficit or 'separation' in the way suggested by disconnect. Instead, 'digital difference' can foster understanding about the uses of technologies in the home and early childhood education setting, and, in doing so, promote understandings about how technologies may be most feasibly employed in each to support young children's learning and development. (2017: 14)

Differences between home and school in terms of the use of digital devices are also of interest when it comes to digital play. Arnott (2013) describes how the social interactions of three- to five-year-old children evolved around different technologies in their preschool settings. Arnott comments on issues of agency and control as derived from knowledge and experience, where children show that 'a complex social dynamic, in addition to technological artefacts, shape children's social interactions in contemporary technology-rich preschools' (2013: 97). In a later study, focused on 90 children in two Scottish preschool settings, Arnott (2016) further explored children's social experiences during their digital play in early childhood settings. The study found that experiences were mostly child-led – with children making the choice about when and whether to use technologies in their play. Further, Arnott suggests that:

> Technologies are not omnipotent, deterministic artefacts that direct, scaffold or 'teach' children ... digital play is complex but not entirely unique to other forms of play; particularly when technologies are integrated into children's experiences as part of well-established playful pedagogies and are utilised as tools within the play rather than the central play experience ... Technologies form one element of a multifaceted and interconnected ecological preschool system. (2016: 285)

This finding attuned to the study by Howard et al. (2012) carried out in 12 early years settings in Wales, which found that some adults in early years settings tended to inhibit children's computer play, yet where teachers sought to integrate computer use into classroom practice, children rated these activities as 'play' and exhibited 'moderate to high levels of engagement' (2012: 175). Teachers faced challenges of outdated equipment which inhibited their work, and the children's, but where good resources existed, teachers felt positive and engaged.

The research literature internationally seems to be indicating that larger-scale studies are needed, as in general, relatively small-scale studies are being published focusing on small numbers of children, parents, educators and settings. Better investment is needed to study the place of digital technologies in young children's learning, and of what happens in young children's digital play – at home and in preschool settings.

ETHICAL ISSUES IN RESEARCHING ON/WITH DIGITAL TECHNOLOGIES

Without doubt, the new possibilities that digital technologies offer preschool teachers and young children give rise to new ethical considerations. As Eckhoff (2015) argues, when children use digital technologies to create images, and other art, researchers must consider how to represent children's work 'in ways that are ethical, respectful, and adhere to the child's artistic, creative, and aesthetic intent' (2015: 1617). Using a participatory approach to research with young children, Eckhoff suggests that the use of visual images requires particular consideration. She argues that young children can only agree to participate in image-based research in 'the moment only' because they do not necessarily understand the permanent nature of photos or film, noting:

> While parental/guardian consent is necessary for research with young children, researchers must consider whether a parent's consent is sufficient given the dissemination plans for the research. Visual imagery presented for consumption remains in the public sphere in perpetuity. Thus, our responsibilities to both the protection of our participants and our adherence to the responsibility of ensuring rigour in the data and findings we present are paramount. Practices involving blurring or editing photos to protect anonymity inevitably alter the work of the child and, in fact, may distort the child's original intent. On the other hand, the choice to not alter or blur images may necessitate that images or video stay hidden from public consumption and only appear through the words and writings of the researcher ... This trade-off protects the children ... but, without question, impacts the viewing context of their work and this research. The presentation of children's photographs and video is a tenuous decision-making process where aims to protect confidentiality and respect for children's rights must be balanced with the aim of representing children's voice, perspective, and artistic intent. (Eckhoff, 2015: 1627)

This was a concern raised by Nutbrown (2011) who argued that the pixilation of images by and of children should not necessarily be a problem-free default solution and that distortion of images distorts 'voice' and obscures meaning. This is an unresolved problem, and one that needs researchers' constant attention.

RESEARCH QUESTIONS ON DIGITAL TECHNOLOGIES AND ECEC

Digital technologies and digital play offer many opportunities for research. There is much more we need to learn about parental and educators' perspectives of children's use of digital devices and their digital play. The field is open for enquiry and this new territory for research needs wider international contributions which range from the small-scale and intensive individual case studies of a single child over time, to larger-scale studies that take account of diverse practices and possibilities.

Some suggested research questions for early years practitioners and students include:

- How do children use digital technologies in their home and group settings?
  Any study involving children's play at home needs parental understanding and support. To gather naturalistic data at home, parents need to be able and willing to keep records, film or otherwise report what their children do and how they engage with them (see Marsh et al., 2015).

- What are parents' views of their children's use of digital technologies in pre-school settings?
  When working with young children and incorporating digital technologies and devices into the early years setting it is important to understand how parents view these developments. Interviews with individual parents – perhaps in their own homes – can shed light on how young children use such tools at home and what parents' views are of their use by young children at home and in early years settings.

- How is play with traditional toys different from or similar to play with digital devices?
  A small number of children – or larger groups of children – could be included as research participants to learn more about how they play and how digital devices are used by them in their free play.

- What do digital devices contribute to children's learning and practices?
  Many technological devices and apps claim to support young children's learning. A study of how children use one or more apps to support their learning – and what the children think of such tools – would offer important insights onto this field which needs much more of a research focus.

A NOTE ON RESEARCH ETHICS AND INTEGRITY

Because digital technologies offer new possibilities, the use of digital devices in research with young children requires some new thinking. This chapter has already discussed the use of devices to make film or still images and the benefits and drawbacks of using those images in research. Children's engagement in all research needs particularly careful planning and their right to understand what is happening and to be able to withdraw must be respected. Research with children that takes them into new territories such as happens with digital technologies needs particularly careful guardianship (Nutbrown, 2011) to ensure the research protects their interests and does not waste their time.

RECOMMENDED READING

Eckhoff, A. (2015) Ethical considerations of children's digital image-making and image-audiancing in early childhood environments. *Early Child Development and Care*, 185 (10): 1617–1628. DOI: 10.1080/03004430.2015.1013539.

This paper draws attention to the ethical issues that arise in using digital image facilities in research with young children.

Edwards, S., Henderson, M., Gronn, D., Scott, A. and Mirkhil, M. (2017) Digital disconnect or digital difference? A socio-ecological perspective on young children's technology use in the home and the early childhood centre. *Technology, Pedagogy and Education*, 26 (1): 1–17. DOI: 10.1080/1475939X.2016.1152291.

This paper explores differences between home and early childhood education settings in the uses of digital technologies.

Marsh, J., Hannon, P. and Lewis, M. and Ritchie, L. (2017) Young children's initiation into family literacy practices in the digital age. *Journal of Early Childhood Research*, 15 (1): 47–60. DOI: 10.1177/1476718X15582095.

This paper offers insights into how parents can contribute significantly to the study of family literacy practices using digital technologies and devices.

Skantz Åberg, E., Lantz-Andersson, A. and Pramling, N. (2014) 'Once upon a time there was a mouse': Children's technology-mediated storytelling in preschool class. *Early Child Development and Care*, 184 (11): 1583–1598. DOI: 10.1080/03004430.2013.867342.

This paper reports on a Swedish study into children's use of technology to create and tell stories in their preschool setting.

REFERENCES

Arnott, L. (2013) Are we allowed to blink? Young children's leadership and ownership while mediating interactions around technologies. *International Journal of Early Years Education, 21* (1): 97–115. DOI: 10.1080/09669760.2013.772049.

Arnott, L. (2016) An ecological exploration of young children's digital play: Framing children's social experiences with technologies in early childhood. *Early Years, 36* (3): 271–288. DOI: 10.1080/09575146.2016.1181049.

Arnott, L. (ed.) (2017) *Digital Technologies and Learning in the Early Years*. London: Sage.

Aubrey, C. and Dahl, S. (2013) The confidence and competence in information and communication technologies of practitioners, parents and young children in the Early Years Foundation Stage. *Early Years, 34*: 94–108.

Bird, J. and Edwards, S. (2015) Children learning to use technologies through play: A Digital Play Framework. *British Journal of Educational Technology*, 46 (6): 1149–1160.

Blackwell, C.K., Lauricella, A.R. and Wartella, E. (2014) Factors influencing digital technology use in early childhood education. *Computers and Education, 77*: 82–90. DOI: 10.1016/j.compedu.2014.04.013.

Bolton, D. (2016) The reason Steve Jobs didn't let his children use an ipad. *Independent*, 24 February. www.independent.co.uk/life-style/gadgets-and-tech/news/steve-jobs-apple-ipad-children-technology-birthday-a6893216.html (accessed 20 February 2018).

Calverta, S.L. and Kotlerb J.A. (2003) Lessons from children's television: The impact of the Children's Television Act on children's learning. *Applied Developmental Psychology, 24*: 275–335.

Eckhoff, A. (2015) Ethical considerations of children's digital image-making and image-audiancing in early childhood environments. *Early Child Development and Care, 185* (10): 1617–1628. DOI: 10.1080/03004430.2015.1013539.

Edwards, S., Henderson, M., Gronn, D., Scott, A. and Mirkhil, M. (2017) Digital disconnect or digital difference? A socio-ecological perspective on young children's technology use in the home and the early childhood centre. *Technology, Pedagogy and Education, 26* (1): 1–17. DOI: 10.1080/1475939X.2016.1152291.

Herr-Stephenson, B., Alper, M., Reilly, E. and Jenkins, H. (2013) *T is For Transmedia: Learning through Transmedia Play*. Los Angeles, CA: USC Annenberg Innovation Lab and The Joan Ganz Cooney Center at Sesame Workshop.

Howard, J., Miles, G.E. and Rees-Davies, L. (2012) Computer use within a play-based early years curriculum. *International Journal of Early Years Education, 20* (2): 175–189. DOI: 10.1080/09669760.2012.715241.

Kocaman-Karoglu, A. (2015) Telling stories digitally: An experiment with pre-school children. *Educational Media International, 52* (4): 340–352. DOI: 10.1080/09523987.2015.1100391.

Lagerlöf, P., Wallerstedt, C. and Pramling, N. (2013) Engaging children's participation in and around a new music technology through playful framing. *International Journal of Early Years Education, 21* (4): 325–335. DOI: 10.1080/09669760.2013.867170.

Lindahl, M.G. and Folkesson, A. (2012) ICT in preschool: friend or foe? The significance of norms in a changing practice. *International Journal of Early Years Education, 20* (4): 422–436. DOI: 10.1080/09669760.2012.743876.

Ljung-Djärf, A., Åberg-Bengtsson, L. and Ottosson, T. (2005) Ways of relating to computer use in pre-school activity. *International Journal of Early Years Education, 13* (1): 29–41. DOI: 10.1080/09669760500048295.

Marsh, J. (2010) Young children's play in online virtual worlds. *Journal of Early Childhood Research,* 8: 23–39.

Marsh, J. and Bishop, J.C. (2014) *Changing Play: Play, Media and Commercial Culture from the 1950s to the Present Day.* Maidenhead: Open University Press/McGrawHill.

Marsh, J., Hannon, P. and Lewis, M. and Ritchie, L. (2017) Young children's initiation into family literacy practices in the digital age. *Journal of Early Childhood Research, 15* (1): 47–60. DOI: 10.1177/1476718X15582095.

Marsh, J., Plowman, L., Yamada-Rice, D., Bishop, J.C., Lahmar, J., Scott, F., Davenport, A., Davis, S., French, K., Piras, M., Thornhill, S., Robinson, P. and Winter, P. (2015) *Exploring Play and Creativity in Pre-schoolers' Use of Apps: Final Project Report.* www.techandplay.org/reports/TAP_Final_Report.pdf (accessed 1 March 2018).

Marsh, J., Plowman, L., Yamada-Rice, D., Bishop, D. and Scott, F. (2016) Digital play: A new classification. *Early Years, 36* (3): 242–253. DOI: 10.1080/09575146.2016.1167675.

Moses, A. (2008) Impacts of television viewing on young children's literacy development in the USA: A review of the literature. *Journal of Early Childhood Literacy, 8* (1): 67–102. DOI: 10.1177/1468798407087162.

Nutbrown, C. (2011) Naked by the pool? Blurring the image? Ethical issues in the portrayal of young children in arts-based educational research.*Qualitative Inquiry, 17* (3): 3–14. DOI: 10.1177/1077800410389437.

Nuttall, J., Edwards, S., Lee, S., Mantilla, A. and Wood, E. (2013) Kindergarten teachers' interpretations of young children's play in digital-consumerist contexts. *Journal of Cultural-Historical Psychology, 2013* (2): 54–62.

Skantz Åberg, E., Lantz-Andersson, A. and Pramling, N. (2014) 'Once upon a time there was a mouse': Children's technology-mediated storytelling in preschool class. *Early Child Development and Care, 184* (11): 1583–1598. DOI: 10.1080/03004430.2013.867342.

Stephen, C. and Plowman, L. (2014) Digital play. In L. Brooker, M. Blaise, and S. Edwards (eds), *The SAGE Handbook of Play and Learning in Early Childhood.* London: Sage, pp. 330–341.

17

ASSESSMENT IN EARLY CHILDHOOD EDUCATION AND CARE

THIS CHAPTER WILL:

- give an overview of the contribution of selected international research into the assessment of young children's learning
- consider what research has to say about the purposes of assessment
- highlight research on documenting and enhancing assessment practices
- suggest some research questions on the topic of assessment in ECEC
- consider research which challenges and offers a critique of countries' national policies on assessment in ECEC.

A ssessment of children's learning has always taken place in one form or another, usually informally through observation of and interaction with children, so there is nothing new about trying to identify, understand and record young children's learning and development. In recent decades the formalisation of such assessment has become popular in many parts of the world. This chapter examines some of the most recent research and critical responses of researchers to the assessment policies of a number of countries. It highlights the variety of purposes of assessment, and identifies key concerns around the assessment of young children and the need to pay special attention to the ways in which the learning and development of children under three are assessed. The chapter concludes with a summary of key points and a renewed call for more respectful assessment practices which identify and honour children's achievements and attuned pedagogy.

THE CONTRIBUTION OF INTERNATIONAL RESEARCH TO THE ASSESSMENT OF YOUNG CHILDREN'S LEARNING

Whilst research into aspects of assessment of young children's learning in early childhood education proliferated during the 1980s and 1990s there appear to have been surprisingly fewer empirical studies in the last two decades. The majority of 21st century studies emanate from the US, with relatively few in Europe. However, a general dissatisfaction with national policies of many countries seems to have resulted in a number of published policy critiques (Espinosa, 2005; Dunphy, 2010). Assessment of young children and the progress they make against predetermined (national and state) benchmarks is on the rise around the world, with assessment for accountability purposes becoming a key focus for many governments (Hatch and Grieshaber, 2002). In many countries this has prompted a number of authors to put forward alternative approaches to assessing young children's learning, which they consider more attuned to their learning styles and dispositions (Downs and Strand, 2006; Goldstein and Flake, 2016).

At the heart of the issue of assessing young children's learning is a tussle for priorities. On the one hand, the documentation of young children's learning in all its richness, and in ways which preserve the authenticity of children's learning, is promoted as the best way to appreciate their individuality and their strengths (Knauf, 2015). Making their learning visible through a Reggio Emilia styled 'pedagogy of listening' (Rinaldi, 2004) is preferred by many early educationists. On the other hand, it is sometimes argued that a more restrictive model of assessment is all that is necessary (Strand et al., 2007) and that some centres over-assess and over-measure young children's learning. However, this latter argument takes us into the realm of testing – and favours the assessment or measurement of selected skills, usually literacy and mathematical abilities (Strand et al., 2007) in the age phase from three to five years. The latter seems more suited to use of assessment for accountability purposes, where the progress of cohorts of children is tracked, whilst the former is more focused on understanding individual children's learning.

With the rise in demand for provision for children under three years of age, assessment of their learning and developmental needs has also come to the fore. Yet, it seems that research has been slow to respond to the need for authentic assessment to support the planning of learning opportunities for babies and toddlers:

> Despite the recognition that individualized assessment of learning and appropriate curricular planning go hand in hand, reliable, valid, and authentic options for implementing this cyclical system are extremely limited, particularly at the infant–toddler level. (Moreno and Klute, 2011: 484)

These issues will be further examined in this chapter, which focuses on the contribution of research to:

- understanding and furthering the purposes of assessment
- documenting and enhancing assessment practices
- focusing on authenticity in assessment practices
- challenging and critiquing national policies on assessment in ECEC around the world

Finally, the chapter will also provide some recommended reading to follow up the issues discussed.

PURPOSES OF ASSESSMENT

Three main purpose of assessment were put forward by Nutbrown (1997) who argued that assessment was for 1) learning and teaching, 2) measurement and accountability, or 3) research (such as randomised control trials and quasi-experimental studies), and that rarely could (or should) an instrument developed for one of these purposes also serve adequately for a different purpose.

Of course, assessment can have many purposes, and different practices of assessment are needed to fit the various reasons for assessment. In a US study, Downs and Strand (2006) identified four main purposes for assessment: 1) to hold schools and school leaders to account for their programmes and interventions, 2) to identify children with particular learning needs, 3) to evaluate trends in ECEC service provision and quality, and 4) to provide information about children's learning. They concluded that:

> [a] critical component of an effective, individualized preschool education is assessing child learning in response to intervention efforts and modifying those efforts when learning does not follow. Considering the intended purpose of ECE/ECSE (facilitating child learning and development in both the short- and long-term), it makes sense that the primary role of assessment in such programs should be to provide information to educators that will help them maximize intervention effectiveness for each child they serve. (Downs and Strand, 2006: 672)

Because assessment in early childhood education is for a range of purposes, it is important to maintain clarity about why children are being assessed. Alongside the purposes of supporting learning and development, and of curriculum planning, there is sometimes the need for diagnostic assessment and some assessments need to be shared with others (parents or professional specialists). Ntuli et al. (2014) warn about the dangers of inadequate assessment, which can lead to a misidentification of children's additional need, which in turn can impact on appropriate planning for children with additional, or special, needs. Ntuli et al. include the children of immigrant families in America in this discussion, pointing out that 'Factors that continue to affect gathering effective assessment data from immigrant children include language barriers, cultural clashes, socio-economic factors, and culturally and linguistically biased assessment measures' (2014: 13). These and other issues of inclusion and exclusion are discussed in Chapters 4 and 9.

In South Korea, assessment is seen to have two main purposes: as a baseline of children's 'knowledge, understanding, skills, interests, and dispositions' for educators to use in planning, and to 'contribute to important decisions about issues such as placing special children in intervention programs and moving students between levels as well as to communication with other professionals, administrators, interested parties in the community, and legislators' (Nah, 2011: 66). According to Nah, assessment practices are not consistent:

> In Korea, child assessment has been implemented to varying degrees, ranging from poor to systematic, according to settings because this procedure has not been mandated or been perceived as important by educators ... In addition, Korean government does not emphasize the achievements of learning goals at ECEC level. (2011: 66)

This situation appears to be changing with the introduction of national procedures for kindergarten evaluation and childcare accreditation procedures (Seo and Hong, 2009). Interestingly, the primary declared purpose of making observations of children in ECEC settings was to share them with parents – in Nah's study less use was made of observations to support pedagogy. This runs counter to the findings of a US survey of 61 Florida counties (Allen, 2007) where educators reported that they did not involve parents in the assessment process. Similarly in New Zealand, Cooper et al. (2014) found that whilst families were mentioned in 'portfolio documentation about infants' and toddlers' developmental milestones or progress (e.g. birthdays and trying new foods) and centre events where families were physically present in the centre (e.g. children starting the centre, grandparents' afternoon tea or family picnics)' (2014: 741) this was not the case when it came to evidence recorded about children's learning dispositions. Families, here, it seems were regarded as receivers of assessment outcomes rather than contributors or key partners in the assessment process.

What unites the US and South Korean studies is: 1) the lack of synergy with the curriculum and planning and the need to use assessments to promote good practice in learning and teaching in ECEC settings, and 2) the call for more uniformity (state or national) in assessment practices.

Of course, uniformity is not always seen as popular or desirable, and we shall consider this later in the chapter when focusing on what has come to be called 'authentic' assessment practices.

DOCUMENTING AND ENHANCING ASSESSMENT PRACTICES

Knauf (2015) suggests that, in Germany, the purpose of pedagogical documentation is 'to make learning visible and to stimulate discussion between educators and parents' (2015: 232) and summarises two different purposes for pedagogical documentation: 1) 'as a strategy for interacting with children and parents', and 2) as a tool for 'the evaluation and assessment of children's achievements' (2015: 233). For the most part, however, it is the former purpose that takes precedent, with educators using documentation as a means of celebrating and sharing children's learning actions, encounters and achievements.

In New Zealand, as a form of assessment to parallel the Te Whāriki curriculum (NZ Ministry of Education, 2017), the creation of 'learning stories' foregrounds a socio-cultural perspective on interactive pedagogy within a learning community (Carr, 2001; Carr and Lee, 2012) where assessment takes the form of narrative accounts of children's learning encounters. Mitchell's (2008: viii) survey of early childhood centres in New Zealand found 'more qualitative and interpretive methods of documentation', which uncovered the importance of relationships and environments to learning. Some 94 per cent of settings were found to be using learning stories as a means of understanding and documenting learning dispositions within the Te Whāriki curriculum, which itself stresses a socio-cultural approach to ECEC (NZ Ministry of Education, 2017).

Learning stories open up, rather than limit, opportunities for learning in home and group settings. In their discussion of narrative assessment of children's mathematical learning, Anthony et al. (2015) stress the importance of making learning visible and suggest that:

 learning stories can serve multiple purposes. More than just describing learning, they can facilitate discussions about the child's learning with other staff and parents, document learning over time and support planning decisions about 'where to next' for the child. (2015: 389)

However, learning stories are not without criticism. Blaiklock (2010) argues that short and frequent observations and accounts do not promote strong consideration of young children's learning over an extended time span. In Australia, Fleer and Quiñones (2013: 239) argue that the focus on the present and on retrospective consideration of learning can inhibit thinking about future learning.

Central to most of the arguments from assessment research during the 21st century is an underpinning value that young children's approach to learning and their particular needs from birth to six years should inform all meaningful assessment practices. Dunphy calls for 'rich pictures' of children's learning, which include 'critical issues of context, interactions and relationships', which she argues are crucial if educators are to understand 'the perspective or intent of particular children in the assessment situation' (2010: 48). Dunphy warns that shortcuts to assessment can inhibit importantly meaningful assessment processes:

> A further tension exists between the use of what educators might consider the more manageable tools for observation of learning such as checklists and the use of more time-consuming tools such as learning stories. The danger is that educators may, in the course of a busy day, find it more manageable to use the less demanding tool (checklists) rather than compiling rich and potentially more useful narrative accounts of children's learning (learning stories). (2010: 52)

Pressures of time for ECEC teachers and other practitioners to carry out assessments are a very real issue and many of the policy critiques discussed in this chapter argue for rich and authentic descriptions rather than brief, uniform and decontextualised lists of learning outcomes.

AUTHENTICITY IN ASSESSMENT PRACTICES

The notion and practices of what is commonly termed 'authentic' assessment were born out of early intervention programmes and studies where the deeper details of children's learning needs were needed (Linder and Linas, 2009; Bagnato et al., 2010). We can situate Carr's (2001) 'Learning Stories' within this approach, because it shares motive and values with other forms of authenticity in assessment. 'Authentic' assessment practices are now increasingly advocated in ECEC settings more generally (Dunphy, 2008; Kline, 2008; Meisels et al., 2010) and no longer restricted to specialist programmes. For Bagnato (2007) authentic assessment is conducted by 'familiar and knowledgeable caregivers about the naturally occurring competencies of young children in daily routines' (2007: 27).

According to Moreno and Klute (2011), despite widespread agreement that authentic assessments are preferred over testing of the youngest children, few systems have a strong evidence base of reliability. They put forward evidence of reliability and validity of authentic assessments specifically designed for use with babies and toddlers under three years of age. They conclude that the main purpose of such assessment practices is the enhancement of the quality of the youngest children's experiences in their group settings:

> As researchers in partnership with community early childhood programs, we are mutually interested in authentic assessment only insofar as it serves as a tool in the arsenal for improving the quality of early learning experiences. (2011: 494)

Fleer and Quiñones extend the notion of authenticity to include 'dynamism' whereby adults mediate the assessment so that:

> rather than measuring what a child can do on her/his own, dynamic assessment seeks to assess the child and the adult working together at a higher cognitive level, where the extent of the mediation is measured alongside what is achieved. (2013: 238)

This places assessment at the heart of pedagogy, rather than positioning what is assessed as an end outcome.

Some research critiques highlight the importance of accounting for and celebrating cultural and linguistic diversity in assessment practices; authenticity in these respects is, argues Espinosa (2005), likely to be effective for children from indigenous communities (including Native American and Native Hawaiian), where:

> with sensitive and responsive teaching, careful assessment, and collaborative partnerships with families, young children from highly diverse backgrounds can achieve to high standards. In addition, the cultural and linguistic strengths they bring to the classroom, when viewed as assets, can be transformed to lifelong skills. (2005: 850)

Similarly, in relation to Maori children, there are calls for culturally relevant assessment and an argument that:

> Assessment by and for Māori must support the development of a strong Māori identity in children, through reflecting Māori perspectives of the child, his/her world, and her/his place in the world. Māori narratives such as Māui Tikitiki a Taranga can provide the basis for assessment tools that are grounded in Māori world-views. (Rameka, 2011: 254)

These approaches to culturally relevant assessment practices which take a socio-cultural perspective on learning – and assessment of that learning – are important for all children. Taking the examples of the cruciality of cultural respect for indigenous children in the US and New Zealand we can see how the cultural capital of all children can be central to understanding their learning through authentic assessment practices which respect who they are and what they bring to the learning process.

CHALLENGING AND CRITIQUING NATIONAL POLICIES ON ASSESSMENT IN ECEC

Since 2000 researchers in several countries have published critiques of their own countries' national assessment policies – see for example, New Zealand (Rameka, 2011; Alcock, 2013; Cooper et al., 2014; Anthony et al., 2015; Zhang, 2017), the US (Espinosa, 2005; Allen, 2007; Strand et al., 2007; Ntuli et al., 2014; Goldstein and Flake, 2016), England (Basford and Bath, 2014; Bradbury, 2014a), Australia (Fleer, 2002; Hatch and Grieshaber, 2002), Japan (Kitano, 2011), South Korea (Nah, 2011), Zambia (Serpell and Jere-Folotiya, 2008), and Romania (Sporea and Sporea, 2014). It is the job of researchers to hold policy-makers to account and the proliferation of papers which question national policy developments demonstrates how assessment policy is often at odds with the ways in which children's learning is understood and with perspectives on what constitutes high quality engagement in learning opportunities in ECEC settings.

One example of national policy critique was the introduction of testing of four-year-olds during their first few weeks of schooling in England. A national Baseline Assessment of children as they start primary school was first introduced in 1997, to be abandoned in 2002 because it did not do what was intended. It sought both to assess individual children's learning and to identify the 'value added' by the school to achievement by cohort. The is because 'baseline' assessment would, it was argued, be used both to identify the progress made on predetermined national curriculum targets over the early primary school years, and to calculate the role of the school in children's learning achievements. Arguments against this form of testing included concern that children lost out on teaching time in their early weeks in school and that learning and other developmental needs could be better identified through observation (Nutbrown, 2015).

To the dismay of many researchers, educationalists, teachers and parents, in January 2015, Baseline Assessment for four-year-olds was reintroduced by the Department for Education which said:

> We will collect a score for each child following the assessment, but we will not use it to track individual pupil progress. The purpose of the reception baseline is to provide a score for each pupil at the start of reception. When pupils reach the end of Key Stage 2 [the end of primary school], we will use the reception baseline score to calculate how much progress they have made compared to others with the same starting point. (DfE, 2015)

This led to considerable campaigning against the reintroduction of what many considered a flawed assessment regime, and in April 2016, the government's own technical study concluded that three commercial tests that were developed for teachers to use were not 'sufficiently comparable' (Standards and Testing Agency, 2016: 5) to create a fair starting point from which to measure pupils' progress, and so the results cannot be used as the baseline for progress measures.

There was once again policy confusion and conflicting beliefs about the value and justification of the assessment instruments, with a government intent on early assessment for the purposes of both accountability and enhancing learning. Many researchers and educators were critical of the policy. Many called for a halt in the use of such instruments and argued for renewed trust in teachers' own observation informed judgements (Nutbrown, 2016) rather than investment in commercially produced measures. In February 2018, a dossier of evidence was published, furthering the campaign to lobby government to retract its estimated £10 million policy on Baseline Assessment (Bradbury et al., 2018). The dossier draws on recent research to demonstrate that:

- baseline assessment cannot provide a valid account of the learning of four-year-olds
- it cannot therefore provide a trustworthy basis on which to measure progress
- it will damage the early years curriculum and hold back the learning of many children
- it will adversely affect primary education as a whole
- its costs are not justified. (2018: 3)

In a critique of the English assessment policy Basford and Bath argue that assessment is 'framed within a regime of accountability, measurement and readiness' (2014: 121) and that assessment practices position parents 'apart from their children, as both subjects and objects of policy' (2014: 128). Critiquing English assessment practices and observing that ECEC practitioners are in a sense positioned to play an assessment 'game' by balancing policy requirements with a different set of practice and value imperatives, Basford and Bath argue that:

> if practitioners are sufficiently knowledgeable, they will potentially have greater power and confidence in playing the assessment game: a game that allows them to perform the technical duties to satisfy the gatekeepers of regulation whilst also satisfying their own moral and ethical duties to encourage children and their families to participate in learning which is representative of their social, cultural and historical heritage. (2014: 129)

Similarly, Bradbury (2014a; 2014b) reported professional criticism of 'increased formalisation and the bureaucracy involved in the assessment regime' (2014a: 324), which put England's assessment practices at odds with those in the other three countries of the UK, where less formal assessment practices were favoured. Bradbury suggests that:

> The unique and continued use of statutory assessment in the early years in England resonates with a wider policy context that relates funding to accountability, and which can be broadly characterised as neoliberal in nature. (2014a: 326)

RESPECTING CHILDREN'S ACHIEVEMENTS

This chapter has discussed the contribution of selected international research into the assessment of young children's learning. Drawing on research representing assessment issues in eleven countries, it has focused on the purposes of assessment, and the practices of assessing through authentic documentation of children's learning, and considered the ways in which some research stands as a challenge to many different national policies on assessment in ECEC.

What is clear from this consideration of recent international research on assessment of young children's learning and development is that policies in many countries seem out of step with what research has contributed to our understanding of that learning. Policies also seem, in many cases, to be out of kilter with a view of children as capable learners who are part of a family who also contribute to their learning, development and well-being.

It is difficult to see how these binary positions of governments and of educators can be shifted without a repositioning of perspectives on young children who deserve respectful assessment processes which identify, help communicate and celebrate their learning. There seems to have been less of a focus on assessment since 2000 in comparison with a proliferation in the 1980s and 1990s, when issues of accountability in education came to the fore and were also applied to children in the three to five age range. Perhaps the task for researchers in the next decade is to help highlight ways in which respectful assessment practices can be further developed and embedded so that assessment policies in ECEC further identify and honour children's achievements and are attuned to similarly respectful pedagogies.

RESEARCH QUESTIONS ON ASSESSMENT IN ECEC

We have always been interested in what young children have learned and tried to understand their needs and wants. The close adults of young children always 'assess' how children are developing – when they take their first steps, utter their first word, and so on. And assessment through observation, in close and informal proximity with children as they engage in their world, is a natural and important part of supporting their learning and development. It is essential to identify, understand, record and act on what we learn about young children's learning and development. The move in many countries towards imposed, formal, universal assessment has, as this chapter has shown, attracted much critique. There is still much to learn about assessment of young children and it is a vital topic for settings continually to examine in order to ensure respectful assessment practices which are true to children's achievements.

Some suggested research questions for early years practitioners and students include:

- ○ How do practitioners make decisions about which assessment instruments best suit their assessment needs?

This will require the examination of practitioners' beliefs and practices around the purposes of assessment, of why we assess young children's learning, and this leads to decisions about the type of assessment approach and instruments. This question is best researched by interviewing individual practitioners about their beliefs and practices and by analysing the assessment instruments used.

○ If the purpose of pedagogical documentation is 'to make learning visible and to stimulate discussion between educators and parents' (Knauf, 2015) how can practitioners and parents collaborate around the assessment of young children's learning?

This question centres around the contribution that parents and practitioners can make to the assessment of young children's learning and development. A study of this topic would include seeking the views of parents and practitioners and coming to shared understandings of what it is important to include in the assessments of young children. Mixed focus groups where priorities are discussed are a good starting point for reaching shared understandings of what is important to both parents and practitioners.

○ What factors influence the practice of 'culturally relevant' assessment?

This question focuses attention on what children bring to the learning and assessment process. It stresses their home and heritage cultures as central to their identities and learning processes. A starting point for understanding what is 'culturally relevant' in assessment can begin with an examination of the assessment instruments used and how this fits with children's lives and understanding.

○ What is the purpose of Baseline Assessment?

Recent attempts to introduce Baseline Assessment in England and Wales have conflated assessment purposes. An exploration of the understanding of the purposes of Baseline Assessment as understood by leaders, parents and practitioners can help to clarify the usefulness of this form of assessment and decide if or how it supports learning. A series of focus groups or individual interviews would help open up understandings, in a setting or settings, of what Baseline Assessment is for.

A NOTE ON ETHICS AND INTEGRITY

Studies focusing on how and why we assess young children's learning and development touch on a subject which has attracted political attention in many countries. Any study will need to make clear how children as learners are constructed and how researchers position themselves within their studies. Because assessment of young children has become a controversial issue with arguments for the documentation of their *learning* presented in opposition to government-imposed universal testing of *outcomes*, inevitable tensions arise.

As the questions suggested here are researched, it will be important to pay close attention to the terminology used, to clarify what is meant by those terms and to draw clear and careful understandings as data are analysed in order to avoid confusion about purpose and practice.

RECOMMENDED READING

Basford, J. and Bath, C. (2014) Playing the assessment game: An English early childhood education perspective. *Early Years*, 34 (2): 119–132. DOI: 10.1080/09575146. 2014.903386.

A critique of recent English ECEC assessment policy.

Nutbrown, C. (2016) After government U-turn on tests for four-year-olds, it's time to trust teachers. *The Conversation*, 11 April. https://theconversation.com/after-government-u-turn-on-tests-for-four-year-olds-its-time-to-trust-teachers-57498 (accessed 29 January 2018).

A short argument piece about the confusion over the purposes of Baseline Assessment and the need for a policy rethink.

Rinaldi, C. (2004) The relationship between documentation and assessment. *Innovations in Early Childhood: the International Reggio Exchange*, 11 (1): 1–4.

A brief but important overview arguing for the understanding of children's thinking and how documenting learning informs assessment.

Zhang, Q. (2017) Do learning stories tell the whole story of children's learning? A phenomenographic enquiry. *Early Years*, 37 (3): 255–267. DOI: 10.1080/09575146.2016.1151403.

A critique of 'learning stories' approaches.

REFERENCES

Alcock, S. (2013) Searching for play in early childhood care and education policy. *New Zealand Journal of Educational Studies*, *48* (1): 19–33.

Allen, S.F. (2007) Assessing the development of young children in child care: A survey of formal assessment practices in one state. *Early Childhood Education Journal*, *34* (6): 455–465. DOI: 10.1007/s10643-007-0153-z.

Anthony, G., McLachlan, C., Lim, R. and Poh, F. (2015) Narrative assessment: Making mathematics learning visible in early childhood settings. *Mathematics Education Research Journal*, *27* (3): 385–400. DOI 10.1007/s13394-015-0142-2.

Bagnato, S.J. (2007) *Authentic Assessment for Early Childhood Intervention*. New York: Guilford Press.

Bagnato, S.J., Neisworth, J.T. and Pretti-Frontczak, K. (2010) *LINKing Authentic Assessment & Early Childhood Intervention: Best Measures for Best Practices* (2nd edn). Baltimore, MD: Brookes.

Basford, J. and Bath, C. (2014) Playing the assessment game: An English early childhood education perspective. *Early Years*, *34* (2): 119–132. DOI: 10.1080/09575146.2014.903386.

Blaiklock, K. (2010) Assessment in New Zealand early childhood settings: A proposal to change from learning stories to learning notes. *Early Education*, 48: 5–10.

Bradbury, A. (2014a) Early childhood assessment: Observation, teacher 'knowledge' and the production of attainment data in early years settings. *Comparative Education*, *50* (3): 322–339. DOI: 10.1080/03050068.2014.921371.

Bradbury, A. (2014b) Learning, assessment and equality in Early Childhood Education (ECE) settings in England. *European Early Childhood Education Research Journal*, *22* (3): 347–354. DOI: 10.1080/1350293X.2014.912897.

Bradbury, A., Jarvis, P., Nutbrown, C., Roberts-Holmes, G., Stewart, N. and Whitebread, D. (2018) *Baseline Assessment: Why It Doesn't Add Up*. London: More than a Score. https://morethanascorecampaign.files.wordpress.com/2018/02/neu352-baseline-a4-16pp-crop.pdf (accessed 28 February 2018).

Carr, M. (2001) *Assessment in Early Childhood Settings: Learning Stories*. London: Sage.

Carr, M. and Lee, W. (2012) *Learning Stories: Constructing Learner Identities in Early Education*. London: Sage.

Cooper, M., Hedges, H. and Dixon, H. (2014) Weaving RIE with Te Whāriki: Re-thinking family involvement in assessment of learning dispositions. *Early Child Development and Care*, *184* (5): 733–748. DOI: 10.1080/03004430.2013.818987.

DfE (Department for Education) (2015) *Policy paper: 2010 to 2015 government policy: School and college funding and accountability*. www.gov.uk/government/publications/2010-to-2015-government-policy-school-and-college-funding-and-accountability/2010-to-2015-government-policy-school-and-college-funding-and-accountability#appendix-2-reception-baseline-assessment (accessed 28 February 2018).

Downs, A. and Strand, P.S. (2006) Using assessment to improve the effectiveness of early childhood education. *Journal of Child and Family Studies*, *15* (6): 671–680. DOI: 10.1007/s10826-006-9080-7.

Dunphy, E. (2010) Assessing early learning through formative assessment: Key issues and considerations. *Irish Educational Studies*, *29* (1): 41–56. DOI: 10.1080/03323310903522685.

Dunphy, L. (2008) Developing pedagogy in infant classes in primary schools in Ireland: Learning from research. *Irish Educational Studies*, *27* (1): 55–70. DOI: 10.1080/03323310701837871.

Espinosa, L.M. (2005) Curriculum and assessment considerations for young children from culturally, linguistically and economically diverse backgrounds. *Psychology in the Schools*, *42* (8): 837–853.

Fleer, M. (2002) Sociocultural assessment in early years education: Myth or reality? *International Journal of Early Years Education, 10* (2): 105–120. DOI: 10.1080/09669760220141999.

Fleer, M. and Quiñones, G. (2013) An assessment perezhivanie: Building an assessment pedagogy for, with and of early childhood science learning. In D. Corrigan, R. Gunstone and A. Jones (eds), *Valuing Assessment in Science Education: Pedagogy, Curriculum, Policy.* Dordrecht: Springer, pp. 231–247.

Goldstein, J. and Flake, J.K. (2016) Towards a framework for the validation of early childhood assessment systems. *Educational Assessment Evaluation and Accountability, 28* (3): 273–293. DOI: 10.1007/s11092-015-9231-8.

Hatch, J.A. and Grieshaber, S. (2002) Child observation and accountability in early childhood education: Perspectives from Australia and the United States. *Early Childhood Education Journal, 29* (4): 227–231.

Kitano, S. (2011) Current issues in assessment in early childhood care and education in Japan. *Early Child Development and Care, 181* (2): 181–187. DOI: 10.1080/03004430.2011.536639.

Kline, L.S. (2008) Documentation panel: The 'Making Learning Visible' project. *Journal of Early Childhood Teacher Education, 29* (1): 70–80.

Knauf, H. (2015) Styles of documentation in German early childhood education. *Early Years 35* (3): 232–248. DOI: 10.1080/09575146.2015.1011066.

Linder, T. and Linas, K. (2009) A functional, holistic approach to developmental assessment through play: The transdisciplinary play-based assessment, second edition. *Zero Three, 30* (1): 28–33.

Meisels, S.J., Wen, X. and Beachy-Quick, K. (2010) Authentic assessment for infants and toddlers: Exploring the reliability and validity of the Ounce Scale. *Applied Developmental Science, 14* (2): 55–71.

Mitchell, L.M. (2008) *Assessment Practices and Aspects of Curriculum in Early Childhood Education: Results of the 2007 NZCER National Survey for ECE Services.* Wellington, NZ: New Zealand Council for Educational Research. www.nzcer.org.nz/pdfs/16544.pdf (accessed 23 April 2012).

Moreno, A.J. and Klute, M.M. (2011) Infant–toddler teachers can successfully employ authentic assessment: The learning through relating system. *Early Childhood Research Quarterly, 26*: 484–496

Nah, K.-O.(2011) Child assessment in early childhood education and care settings in South Korea. *Asian Social Science, 7* (6): 66–78.

Ntuli, E., Nyarambi, A. and Traore, M. (2014) Assessment in early childhood education: Threats and challenges to effective assessment of immigrant children. *Journal of Research in Special Educational Needs, 14* (4): 2221–2228. DOI: 10.1111/j.1471-3802.2012.01256.x.

Nutbrown, C. (1997) *Recognising Early Literacy Development: Assessing Children's Achievements*. London: Sage

Nutbrown, C. (2015) We must scrap new baseline tests for primary school children. *The Conversation*, 21 January. https://theconversation.com/we-must-scrap-new-baseline-tests-for-primary-school-children-36558 (accessed 29 January 2018).

Nutbrown, C. (2016) After government U-turn on tests for four-year-olds, it's time to trust teachers. *The Conversation*, 11 April. https://theconversation.com/after-government-u-turn-on-tests-for-four-year-olds-its-time-to-trust-teachers-57498 (accessed 29 January 2018).

NZ Ministry of Education (2017) *Te Whāriki: He Whāriki Mātauranga mōngā Mokopuna o Aotearoa. Early Childhood Curriculum*. Wellington, NZ: Learning Media Limited.

Rameka, L.K. (2011) Being Māori: Culturally relevant assessment in early childhood education, *Early Years*, *31* (3): 245–256. DOI: 10.1080/09575146.2011.614222.

Rinaldi, C. (2004) The relationship between documentation and assessment. *Innovations in Early Childhood: the International Reggio Exchange*, *11* (1): 1–4.

Seo, E. and Hong, S. (2009) The teacher's recognition and actual conditions of early childhood assessment administered in the early childhood educational organizations. *The Korean Journal of Child Education*, *18* (3): 37–54.

Serpell, R. and Jere-Folotiya, J. (2008) Developmental assessment, cultural context, gender, and schooling in Zambia. *International Journal of Psychology*, *43* (2): 88–96.

Sporea, D. and Sporea, A. (2014) Results of Romanian teachers survey on assessment in early education. *International Journal of Information and Education Technology*, *4* (6): 495–501.

Standards and Testing Agency (2016) *Reception Baseline Comparability Study: Results of the 2015 Study*. London: DfE. www.gov.uk/government/uploads/system/uploads/attachment_data/file/514581/Reception_baseline_comparability_study.pdf (accessed 20 February 2018).

Strand, P.S., Cerna, S. and Skucy, J. (2007) Assessment and decision-making in early childhood education and intervention. *Journal of Child and Family Studies*, *16* (2): 209–218. DOI: 10.1007/s10826-006-9079-0.

Zhang, Q. (2017) Do learning stories tell the whole story of children's learning? A phenomenographic enquiry. *Early Years*, *37* (3): 255–267. DOI: 10.1080/09575146.2016.1151403.

REFLECTION ON PART III

RESEARCH FOCUSING ON LEARNING AND TEACHING

This part (of five chapters) has reviewed ECE research since 2000 organised around the broad theme of *Learning and Teaching*. In this reflection I have identified what stands out for me, and what I think needs to happen next.

ON CURRICULAR APPROACHES

Curriculum seems still to dominate policy – and there is far more control over *what* is taught than *how* it is taught. This, at least, allows knowledgeable practitioners to influence practice and also allows for a more fluid and open response to children's learning.

NEXT STEPS

Given the fascinating theories that children come up with in order to explain the questions they set themselves, or answer some of the questions that they meet as they explore and enquire over their world, research now needs to focus on 'thinking children' in ways that provide rich accounts. This would, in turn, give practitioners important starting points from which to understand more about how children think about their world and the funds of knowledge they draw on to answer their questions.

ON EARLY LITERACY DEVELOPMENT

The bringing together of 'stationary' words and moving images, the spoken word, music and sound effects, stimulated researchers to think about how literacy is constructed and enacted in the 21st century, and to question whether constructions and definitions we once had have the same validity in the digital age.

NEXT STEPS

The richness and widening definitions of 'text' that have come about with the development of digital technologies, and the widening access of such technologies in homes and families, mean that for many children, their home and ECEC-setting lives and experiences are poles apart. Of course, we must remember the inequities around digital technologies and research cannot make assumptions about children's access. So future studies need to focus more on how digital technologies support early literacy learning in ECEC settings to ensure equity of access and opportunity. These will build on existing studies of practice and continue to address possibilities as technologies that continue to change our definitions of literacy are further developed.

ON LANGUAGES AND LEARNING

Children who grow up learning and speaking more than one language are developing the potential to be able to communicate with more people and to have a broader outlook on life. Contrary to earlier concerns that learning more than one language in early childhood might be detrimental to a child's general learning and development, more contemporary studies have shown this not to be the case.

NEXT STEPS

There is much more to learn about how positively to use linguistic diversity in early years settings. As the majority of people in the world speak two or more languages, and as increasing numbers of children whose home language is not English attend early years settings with English speaking practitioners, so this particular perspective on the world needs to permeate learning. More research is needed on the richness of linguistic diversity in the early years and how 'learning' does not necessarily mean 'learning in English' at all times.

ON DIGITAL TECHNOLOGIES

As new technologies develop and emerge at a rate of change never seen before, earlier fears about children's television seem be being transferred to other digital technologies used by children for entertainment and for learning. Scepticism in terms of the 'dangers' of digital technologies to children's learning and well-being is an argument that emerged as soon as computers began to be common in children's homes and settings. There will never be agreement on this because, for some, concern about the digital in children's lives is born of a value position or of health concerns which are fuelled by different fields of research and personal belief.

NEXT STEPS

Researchers who have embraced the arrival of new digital technologies have begun to offer us new ways of seeing and defining learning and in particular to the reconceptualisation of literacy learning. As yet, there is a lack of parity between settings and homes, between some families and others, in the extent to which early years practitioners embrace the digital in early years settings and in how this is resourced. Recent work on digital play and digital literacies has shown the potential for development and this will surely be a growth area for early childhood education research in the next decade.

ON ASSESSMENT

It is the job of researchers to hold policy-makers to account and the proliferation of papers which question national policy developments demonstrates how assessment policy is often at odds with the ways in which children's learning is understood and with perspectives on what constitutes high quality engagement in learning opportunities in ECEC settings.

NEXT STEPS

It seems that the main issue of concern for research which focuses on assessment is the policy-practice-research mismatch. Many studies have pointed to the inappropriateness of Baseline Assessment in England and Wales, yet successive governments have persisted with this policy. Research in the future will still have to battle with the policy ambiguity around what assessment is for, and what specific purposes certain types of assessment are intended to serve. What is clear, is that research that supports respectful and positive ways of assessing young children's learning will continue to be needed, with good accounts of rich and deep learning – alongside those studies that measure achievements cohort upon cohort to evaluate curricular interventions.

── PERSONAL REFLECTION AND PLANNING ──

I have, above, identified some of the striking features from the third part of the book. But these are personal identifications, and you may well have found other things in these chapters that are more pertinent for you in terms of research focusing on *pedagogies* in early childhood education. I have included the questions below to suggest a way of thinking about these issues, and you may wish to make some notes and/or discuss in groups.

- What stands out for you? Which piece of research would you award a prize to? What gave you the biggest surprise? And what may be particularly useful to you as a practitioner? Did anything made you feel, 'Yes, but ... so what?'
- Are there any research findings here that you suspect, or doubt? Or that you strongly disagree with? Is this 'just a hunch' or do you have evidence – from your own life- and practice-experience, or from other reading – to support that view?
- Is there something (that you've come across) missing from this account?
- Which of the researchers reported would you like most to meet, and what would you want to ask them?

In the next five years ...

- What do *you* think are the most important topics for future research around learning and teaching and early childhood education research?
- What does your experience and reading of the literature suggest are likely to be the barriers to the development of work with and for young children's ECE in these early years?

18

RESEARCH IN EARLY CHILDHOOD EDUCATION IN THE 21ST CENTURY: SALIENCE, SIGNIFICANCE AND CHALLENGE

This final chapter reflects on recent international research to summarise what has been achieved and to consider what appears to be urgently needed in early childhood education research.

The Research Excellence Framework (REF) 2014 concluded, of early childhood education research carried out in the UK, that:

> Outputs of world-leading quality were reported in this REF from large scale, longitudinal research investments. Such work provided strong examples of research impact. Other early childhood work focused on the workforce, with particular attention to professionalism, identities, qualifications and leadership. The use of digital technologies in early education appeared to be a growing field. There were some studies of pedagogies for early education practitioners, but more theorised and sustained studies of curriculum, pedagogy, play, assessment and work with parents in early education appear to be needed. (Research Excellence Framework, 2015: 104–105)

Building on this, the BERA/TACTYC review of UK research in early childhood education and care carried out in the period 2003–2017 (Payler and Wood, 2017: 113) concluded that much UK research was 'small scale and interpretivist, using qualitative methods'.

The review concludes that:

> Concerns with children's rights, agency, self-determination and voices are strongly represented, and reflect difference and diversities in children's lives. These concerns also align with ethical commitments to conducting research that is relational, participatory and co-produced. These trends simultaneously mirror and counter contemporary political ideologies. (Payler and Wood, 2017: 113)

'Significant gaps' in ECEC research are also identified:

> There is less focus in the UK on issues of race and ethnicity. Secondly, there is little research on the impact on practice of regulatory bodies, such as Ofsted, and relatively little policy research ... Thirdly, there are few large-scale and longitudinal studies, probably because these are costly to fund, but also because they are most likely to come from international or at least EU studies ... Finally, there is a need for interdisciplinary research to shed light on multi-faceted and complex issues, and for co-produced research that draws on a wide range of methods to engage children, families, communities and professionals. (Payler and Wood, 2017: 119).

The REF (2014) report and BERA/TACTYC review both highlight trends, issues and gaps in UK research which this book shows also pervade internationally. I posit six themes that recur, in differing forms and with differing emphases, throughout the studies discussed in this book: children's rights, play, literacy, home learning opportunities and parents, inclusion, and professional development and training.

Many of these themes raise concerns about child poverty and deprivation, which are often addressed by what is now termed 'early intervention', and this too receives some consideration later in this chapter. Conspicuous for its absence is research into children's engagement in the arts, and arts-based research in ECEC.

This chapter first discusses the six overarching themes, in terms of their historical roots and present research concerns. It then considers research and policy engagement with 'early intervention' before addressing the lack of research in the arts. The chapter and the book end with a set of priorities for researchers as a form of agenda for action.

CHILDREN'S RIGHTS IN ECEC

Children's rights are an overarching theme to much ECEC research – whether implicit or explicit – and as such reach into many of the other themes identified in this book and in this final discussion. As we saw in Chapter 2, the UN Convention on the Rights of the Child (UNCRC) and issues of children's rights have gained currency in research over the last two or three decades. The Convention states children's rights to:

- prevention (of illness and neglect)
- provision (of education with specific references to children who are disabled)
- protection (from abuse and exploitation)
- participation (in decisions which affect them) (United Nations, 1989)

Children whose families are refugees or asylum seekers also have these rights when in a country which is a signatory to the Convention, and thus controversy arises when children in such circumstances are not treated according to their rights, as has been seen in what became known as 'the Jungle' in Calais (Harker, 2016), and with the recent arrival in Europe of many life-risking, and often violently opposed, refugees and asylum seekers.

In many countries, rights abuses take a multitude of forms, and as Chapters 2 and 6 in particular demonstrate, it is not exclusively in the poorer countries of the world where children struggle for their rights. As the studies considered of Chapter 2 have illustrated, issues of 'rights' have been variously embraced and disputed, and different countries take a range of views through their institutions and individuals.

The right to health care is, of course, fundamental, and issues of child mental health have now come to the fore, doubtless linked to poor housing, a lack of safe places to play and the many stresses families face. In response, the UK government in 2017 made several policy announcements designed to address the mental health of children and young people, including a promised injection of funding for support, treatment and for training staff in schools to be more aware of the signs of mental ill-health. The Care Quality Commission (2017) found that children and young people felt they were not listened to and many expressed concern that they could not get the help they needed, with only 25 per cent of children and young people who needed it able to access mental health support (Public Health England, 2016).

There are, however, some examples of practice where children's rights are a fundamental and guiding principle of curriculum and pedagogy. As discussed in Chapter 13, examples can be found in the infant-toddler centres and preschools in Reggio Emilia in northern Italy. Central concerns expressed by its founder Malaguzzi include:

The rights of children: the fact that the rights of children are recognised as the rights of all children is the sign of a more accomplished humanity;

The rights of teachers: for the teachers, each and every one of them, it is a condition that enhances communication and the comparison of ideas and experiences, all of which enrich the tools of professional evaluation;

The rights of parents: participation and research are, in fact, two terms that summarise much of the overall conception of our educational theory. These two terms

> might also be seen as the best prerequisites for initiating and maintaining a coopera-
> tive understanding between parents and teachers, with all the value that is added to
> the educational prospects of the children. (Malaguzzi, 1996: 2)

The theme of children's rights is all pervasive and we shall return to rights issues research throughout this chapter.

PLAY IN ECEC

We saw in Chapter 4 how play spaces are being restricted, are dangerous, or the opportunity to play freely outdoors is restricted for one reason or another. Children's rights to play are being eroded in many circumstances.

In terms of play in ECEC settings, as Chapter 4 showed, many teachers continue to struggle to 'fit' play into their pedagogic repertoire and, though it is recognised that play has a place in the early years, some practitioners still lack the necessary skills, support and confidence to make children's play an integral part of learning and pedagogy. The most recent report from the English Office for Standards in Education further confines play to specific times and specific purposes (Ofsted, 2017), confirming limited understanding of play in early education and limited appreciation of children's need to play when they are four years old and in school. There is an insistence that the 'disadvantaged' children cannot be allowed to waste time playing because they must get to grips with the basics, however research into 'playful pedagogies' reviewed in this book demonstrates how children engage with deep questions and apply themselves to learn many things when they are free to play. There remains a need to understand play as something children do in and of their own right on the one hand, and the ways in which adults seek to manipulate children's play to encourage specific learning objectives on the other. As we saw in Chapter 4, research on children's play continues to thrive, with new issues coming to the fore, including 'risk', interference from adults, and digital play. Play is seen in relation to all aspects of a child's day, integral to and part of, an holistic approach to ECEC for very young children.

Research continues to focus on definitions of play, children's roles and interests in play and how play is supported in various forms of early years provision in a variety of international contexts. But questions about the efficacy of play as a pedagogical tool remain, and successive governments have shown varied commitment to play in the early years and schools curriculum, and as *Bold Beginnings* (Ofsted, 2017) demonstrates, there is a strong and naive tendency in English policy to separate play, as something that supports physical development, from teaching 'the basics'.

Whilst healthy, happy children will always play (as Chapter 4 illustrates), research in some countries often confronts outcomes-driven policies, which seem to seek to restrict or manipulate play as a means to children achieving predetermined and somewhat universal targets. Research still reports that children from disadvantaged families do less well, their right to education as well as their spaces for play being inhibited.

EARLY LITERACY

As we saw in Chapter 14, until the 1970s early literacy development was effectively overlooked and nursery education tended to focus simply on oral language and story-telling. Literacy only properly became part of the early years curriculum during the 1980s with the growth of research in emergent literacy, and a shift from a belief that literacy learning at too young an age could be harmful; this gave way to the development of practices which incorporated meaningful literacy activities – based on children's everyday lives – into the curriculum. New ways of teaching literacy were developed during the 1980s as researchers and teachers became more aware of how children learned about writing and reading. The *emergent literacy* perspective, which research brought to early years practice, led early years teachers to actively encourage children to use reading and writing in many aspects of their play. But during the last 20 years, the excitement that research into emergent literacy brought seems to have been lost in curriculum policy, with most recent policy containing little to indicate the importance of excitement and pleasure in the written word.

In most, if not all countries, print abounds on clothing, buildings, packaging, household equipment, mobile phones, iPads, laptops and so on. It may be temporary and ever-changing, as with digital billboards and screens in shopping centres, in cars and transport depots. Chapter 16 has highlighted the new contribution that research is making to our understanding of how children incorporate digital practices into their home literacy activities, although many settings and schools have yet to catch up with what children know and can do with digital devices, and have also yet to incorporate digital tools into literacy and learning resources. As we saw in Chapter 14, context-based print, such as that found on household packaging and shop signs, is meaningful to young children and has a place in their reading development as they draw meaning from familiar symbols in their environment (Goodman et al., 1978; Hiebert, 1981). It has been suggested that reading begins the moment young children become aware of environmental print (Smith, 1976) and many develop a sense of such print awareness long before going to school (Goodman, 1980; Burke, 1982). Environmental print can stimulate talk about literacy as children ask questions such as 'What does that say'? It also prompts children, at times, to pick out and identify from signs, some letters that are familiar to them, perhaps in their own name. Environmental print can stimulate some children to write, and children often imitating the writing, such as notices or notes left for others. Some of the studies in Chapter 16 show how new technologies can build on existing knowledge to create new possibilities in early childhood pedagogy.

In recent years there has been a growth of literature for children based on the popular culture of the time. Books related to children's television programmes and films abound and numerous related comics for children are available in most newsagents. Marsh (2005a; 2005b) has argued that literacy related to children's popular culture should be valued and children's use of texts in comics, film and TV-related story books, television and other multi-media literacies, and more recently digital texts (Marsh, 2016), should be a part of children's school literacy repertoires because many are already familiar with such texts at home. Because literacy is so important to learning it remains inseparable from any concerns of early learning and the focus of many research studies with parents.

HOME LEARNING OPPORTUNITIES AND PARENTAL INVOLVEMENT IN EARLY EDUCATION

Research in the past three decades has shed light on parents' roles in their own children's learning and prompted the development of programmes to involve parents more systematically in their own children's education. During the 1960s programmes to involve parents began to be developed largely as a way of addressing poor home experiences – what we now more routinely know as the *home learning environment*. However, a more recent understanding of parental involvement can be properly traced back to the Rumbold Report *Starting with Quality* (DES, 1990); this championed the idea that parents were their children's 'educators'. Government policy has for some time made it clear that involvement with parents is an expected part of early childhood education and care in all settings:

Parents are children's first and most enduring educators. When parents and practitioners work together in early years settings, the results have a positive impact on the child's development and learning. Therefore, each setting should seek to develop an effective partnership with parents. (QCA, 2000: 9)

There are many examples of parental involvement in children's learning, and the studies discussed in Chapters 7, 14 and 15 emphasise a more directly participative role for parents. Specific initiatives to involve parents in the early years have often focused on young children's learning or aspects of curriculum and helping parents learn more about their children's ways of learning. In the late 1980s the Froebel Early Learning Project (Athey, 2007) identified ways of helping parents to understand their children's learning interests so that they could better support them. This theme was further developed by Nutbrown (2011a), who also argued that the more parents know about how children's learning developed, the better position they were in to understand what their children were doing and how they might further enhance learning opportunities for them.

Key issues for research continue to be how to work with parents in ways that are inclusive, participative, respectful and meaningful. In some cases initiatives have been targeted specifically at minority groups, including families for whom English is not the language of the home, as seen in Chapter 15, where the richness of language diversity is regarded as a positive benefit to learning and not a hindrance.

INCLUSION

'Inclusion' is not a single movement; it is made up of many strong currents of belief, many different local struggles and a myriad of forms of practices (Clough, 2000: 6). At its heart, though – as I wrote in Chapter 8 – inclusion might be thought of as essentially a matter of *respect for all* and of *everyone belonging*.

In the UK of the 21st century there is increasing demand for inclusive practices and equality of opportunity and access to educational provision, but as the research reviewed in Chapter 8 has shown, the definition of inclusion is ever broadening, and the need for personal and political commitments to inclusion is as important as ever. The language and divisive policies of Donald Trump in the US, and the 2016 UK referendum on leaving the European Union, to name but two issues, have brought upheaval and divisions to communities that will begin to shape the research agenda. Already, researchers are beginning to investigate the impact of the outcome of the UK's EU referendum vote on children and communities of those European citizens who are not UK citizens and studies in the coming years will doubtless track changes in their lives. From a period in the late 1990s and early 2000s when there was great hope for inclusion, and research had contributed significantly to this state, there is a danger now that we may be returning to a *de facto* acceptance of divided communities.

Early education – at its best – is inclusive education because of the emphasis, in practice, of identifying and meeting the individual learning needs of all young children (Nutbrown, 1998). It is often the experience of those who work in early years settings that young children, whatever their learning needs, have a right to inclusion. Many such settings would argue that supporting children with physical and learning difficulties is as much about an attitude as it is about practical responses.

Reviewing a history of 'inclusion' Nutbrown and Clough (2013) suggest that:

> the current phase of the history (of inclusion) is a properly radical one: a broadly-understood inclusion movement which seeks to realise a sociology that insists that it is primarily in the environment where we will discover the root cause of, and the root solution to, exclusive practices. In contrast to integration, the inclusion ideology looks to change not the individual – so that s/he can be 'brought in from the cold' – but, quite simply, to change the environment, the school, society, the world ... It is no less radical a task. And in this sense it is about eradicating prejudice, injustice, and inequality. (2013: 3)

In the first decade of the 21st century, in the UK, there was considerable expansion of provision for children whose families lived in areas of deprivation and who were targeted to receive additional help through government initiatives such as Sure Start championed by the late Baroness Tessa Jowell. Thus, inclusive policies of provision were designed to offer additional support to families who needed it. However, despite policy-driven expansion in 'childcare' places, Sure Start centres and other provisions are closing around the country – with, all Sure Start Children's Centres in Oxfordshire reported to be closed by early 2018. And, further, the horrors of the Grenfell Tower fire (Davies and Bowcott, 2017) show the potential consequences of bad housing design and the naked clarity of the truth that disadvantage – still in 2017 – breeds disadvantage. Those excluded will remain excluded, until policies change with an imperative to save lives as well as to eliminate disadvantages and the consequences of social injustice.

PROFESSIONAL DEVELOPMENT, QUALIFICATIONS AND STATUS

An overarching theme that brings together the issues highlighted in this chapter is that of the professional development, qualifications and status of the early childhood education and care workforce. Those who currently work in ECEC have a need for collaboration and partnership and as Chapter 10 has demonstrated, there is an urgent need to address issues of remuneration, qualifications, status and with those, professionalism. There is a considerable job to do here – for many of the studies reviewed in Chapter 10 are small scale and offer short-term, qualitative perspectives of practitioners or students following particular initial training courses. Whilst this is useful, it is not sufficient, and we need a better understanding of how different qualifications are equipping people to work with young children to ensure they receive the best possible early years experiences.

The quality of early years provision (Rahilly and Johnston, 2002), and the need for a well-trained and appropriately qualified workforce (Nutbrown, 2012) were key issues for government in the early part of the 21st century. There has for some time been recognition that a 'highly skilled workforce' is central to increasing the number of education and care places and that 'working with children is a demanding, skilled profession' (DfEE, 1999: 1), and the many studies reviewed in Chapter 10 indicate what a critical area for policy and research this is, internationally. There have been several attempts to develop a single qualifications framework for the education and childcare profession in England, but in 2018, despite many proclamations that this is a clear priority, it remains a goal still to be achieved. Workforce reform builds on recent history in policy and the (then) innovative recommendations of the Rumbold Report (DES, 1990), which stressed the importance of highly qualified professionals who could provide what was needed for children and their families.

In July 2011, continuing the attempt to address the concern that has exercised several governments, the government commissioned an independent review of the qualification of the early education and childcare workforce. The Nutbrown Review made 19 recommendations on how to improve the quality of experiences for children from birth, in home and group care, and reported on 19 June 2012 (DfE, 2012). Despite widespread support, the government rejected or adapted most of these recommendations in its policy document, *More Great Childcare* (DfE, 2013), published in January 2013. Workforce issues continue to be unresolved and to cause widespread concern.

Whatever the policy commitment, until there is adequate funding for further and higher education programmes or a political will to address issues of pay for early childhood educators and carers, the policy of high quality early childhood provision will not be fully realised. Whilst inadequately rewarded women and men do their best to provide for young children in their settings, there is still a job for research to do here in highlighting the critical issues that will need to be addressed as a result of having an often under-qualified, inadequately equipped, stressed and under-valued workforce.

EARLY INTERVENTION AND RESEARCH

The belief that the early years are crucial to children's later educational achievement has prompted the widespread development of intervention programmes – many of which feature in this book – that target young children who are 'at risk' in some way (Allen, 2011; Field, 2010). Early intervention programmes are based on the premise that 'beginning early' means a greater chance of being successful and are often designed to prevent difficulties as well as to overcome or minimise any difficulties that young children already experience.

Of course, it is important that those working on early intervention programmes are well equipped and appropriately qualified (Jackson, 2012; Nutbrown, 2012). Making it possible to attend some form of preschool provision does not necessarily reach the most vulnerable groups, and can fail to provide the necessary support for children who are at risk of later school failure.

Educational disadvantage is clearly structurally linked to other factors such as housing, poverty, parents' educational qualifications and so on. The Sure Start programme in the UK can be seen as a large-scale early intervention programme which sought to address multiple factors threatening children's development. Such programmes seek to provide something specific and additional to the usual mainstream provision, and are often targeted at the groups likely to benefit most.

Learning which early intervention programmes and strategies will achieve their aims requires funded studies, strong research capacity, and can be complex and costly. As far back as the 1970s, Bronfenbrenner (1974) reviewed findings from 26 experimental early intervention studies and reported on findings from two types of programme: 'group' and 'parent-child'. Bronfenbrenner's review showed that programmes involving parents had longer lasting effects than those which only provided for or worked with the child. He concluded that future programmes which addressed all the factors contributing to educational failure should be developed. Such a strategy underpinned the Sure Start programmes to support children's learning and development alongside strategies to tackle difficulties for families and their communities which militate against healthy progress in childhood.

The Field Review (2010) of the effects of childhood poverty noted that:

 the early years (age zero to three in particular) are crucial and that interventions early in a child's life are most effective in improving outcomes and life chances. (Field, 2010: 90)

Further, the Allen *Review of Early Intervention* (2011) set out key recommendations after the observation that: 'All who care about realising the potential of our babies, children and young people need to work together and take the pathway to a long-term Early Intervention culture in the UK' (Allen, 2011: i). This review recommended that:

 the nation should be made aware of the enormous benefits to individuals, families and society of Early Intervention – a policy approach designed to build the essential social and emotional bedrock in children aged 0–3 and to ensure that children aged 0–18 can become the excellent parents of tomorrow. (2011: xvii)

It further recommended that:

 the nation should recognise that influencing social and emotional capability becomes harder and more expensive the later it is attempted, and more likely to fail. (2011: xvii)

And finally, it recommended:

 proper co-ordination of the machinery of government to put Early Intervention at the heart of departmental strategies, including those seeking to raise educational achieve-ment and employability, improve social mobility, reduce crime, support parents and improve mental and physical health. (2011: xviii)

Providing the best bespoke support, early in the lives of children, as many of the studies in this book describe, can enhance life chances, promote social mobility and reduce inequalities.

So, the collective advice to government from research is clear: high quality work with very young children and their families is a worthwhile and necessary investment. Many studies have demonstrated how effective work with families can be, for example, we know that graduate qualified professionals positively influence young children's outcomes, and we know that good programmes to involve parents in their children's literacy can bring lasting benefits. The problem is often that even though a study shows benefits, funding for 'roll-out' of that programme is difficult to obtain.

THE ARTS AND CREATIVITY IN THE EARLY YEARS: GAPS IN OUR KNOWLEDGE

As this book has shown, a wide range of issues has attracted research attention, but what is missing from this book tells a story too. The arts are largely neglected in ECE research. We have studies of literacy, of technology, and of language learning; indeed, the BERA/TACTYC review of UK research (Payler and Wood, 2017) identified some studies of STEM (specifically, science, technology and maths) subjects, whilst noting that 'Arts-based learning also merits further exploration' (2017: 117); the lack of research into young children's engagement in the arts was highlighted as a concern nationally and internationally, and though there are some important contributions to our understanding of the arts in early childhood education research, more are needed. Whilst in policy terms, outcome-driven curricula favour achievements in English and mathematics and science, we forget the importance of the arts and the innate need for human beings to enjoy and create art, at our peril.

It has long been recognised by many that inclusion of the arts in curricula helps young children to develop their vital aesthetic sense, which is so much part of their humanity (Dewey, 1902; Gardner, 1989; Dissanayake, 1995; Eisner, 2002). If we look to developments in Europe, we can see in Scandinavia and in northern Italy, for example, how a focus on the arts can enhance children's learning in all aspects of their development. The now familiar work of Reggio Emilia (Reggio Children, 1995) demonstrates how arts-based curricula and support from experienced artists can give rise to learning in all aspects of an early years curriculum. Such projects promote shared thinking and foster children's learning 'in community'.

Engaging in creative arts experiences is important for human development, for the sheer joy it can bring, part of which is the self- and shared-expression that is enabled through creative processes. But although creative arts experiences have been shown to impact on cognitive, social and emotional development, the arts are suffering. In England we have seen reductions in funding for the arts year on year, risking a narrowing of opportunity for children and their families to enjoy the arts in their leisure time. The arts are suffering in the early years (birth to five) and in primary schools too, often regarded as of a lesser value than the sciences and mathematics, and perhaps, something to be kept for leisure time.

However, from a widely shared view of the arts as co-foundational of our humanity (Dissanayake, 1990; 1995; 2000; Eisner, 2002), we see them as an inalienable feature of young children's learning and development, as Dissanayake wrote:

 Viewing the species *Homo sapiens* as it evolves and expresses a behaviour of art is a way of understanding ourselves and the modern *condition humaine*. (1990: xi)

Discussing the inseparability of the arts from notions of human being, Dissanayake (2000) suggests that infants are born with *aesthetic incunabula*, a sort of 'swaddling' which makes emotional effects of the arts discernible from the earliest months.

The human need to seek out and organise through the aesthetic is what Clough (2002) calls an 'aesthetic attending', the way in which, as a condition of being in the world, we attend – through the senses – to the 'objects' we encounter. So, the youngest of human beings engage with the world first through an innate aesthetic attending, through their senses – because babies are sensory beings (Trevarthen, 1984; Goldschmeid and Jackson, 1999) they seek experiences which smell or taste, or feel or sound or look pleasing, because sense craves satisfaction.

Early education must pay due regard to the human need, in all young children, for aesthetics in the design of inclusive curricula. And this argument is not simply an academic or historical one – it is also a matter of rights. For the UNCRC, Article 31 states:

> That every child has the right to rest and leisure, to engage in play and recreational activities appropriate to the age of the child and to participate freely in cultural life and the arts.
>
> That member governments shall respect and promote the right of the child to participate fully in cultural and artistic life and shall encourage the provision of appropriate and equal opportunities for cultural, artistic, recreational and leisure activity. (United Nations, 1989)

One explanation of the decimation of arts curricula in many schools (NACCCE, 1999; Chapman, 2004) is the redistribution of timetabling in response to concerns about under-achievement in English and Maths (the so-called 'basics'). However, developments in Scandinavia (Barratt, 2006; Hopperstad, 2008a; 2008b; Pramling Samuelsson et al., 2009), in northern Italy (Reggio Children, 1995) and in Melbourne, Australia (Deans, 2010) show how, far from inhibiting children's achievement in the 'basics', a focus on the arts positively and disproportionately enhances this and other aspects of their development. The work of Reggio Emilia (Filippini and Vecchi, 1996) has long-demonstrated how an arts-based curriculum and the involvement of experienced artists, as well as teachers, can give rise to many forms and foci of learning in the early years; and in the UK, a number of arts-based learning projects has shown how the involvement of artists can enhance the early years curriculum (Gillespie, 2006; Brown et al., 2010; Hallowes, 2013). Such claims rest ultimately on the considered and life-long observations of scholars such as Gardner (1990) and Eisner (2002) who have shown how young children need the arts to help them learn central lessons in life; how, for example, to communicate ideas, collaborate with others, persist with a problem, deal with disappointment, and enjoy the support of peers and adults (Nutbrown and Jones, 2006).

Internationally, research into aspects of arts-based learning often focuses more specifically on the practice of elements of particular skills in the arts, rather than the experience and more holistic development and understanding of music per se (Young, 2008), for which they are 'wired from birth' (Trehub, 2003: 3). We know little about the place of dance in early years curricula (Bannon and Sanderson, 2000) and the use of arts generally in the early years appears to be 'means to ends'. Art forms such as poetry, dance and graphic arts are sometimes used as vehicles through which other things are taught, rather than experiences of learning in their own right (Brown et al., 2010). There is a need to pursue and conceptualise arts-based learning in early childhood education, and to give it due status in curricula (Nutbrown, 2011b).

Projects in the UK have confirmed that the youngest children can respond to, and enjoy, involvement in the arts. Work at Tate Britain for children under three and their parents has shown how artist involvement can open up new avenues for parents to explore and enjoy the arts with their young children (Hancock and Cox, 2002). We know also of the importance of talk in early years settings and recent research demonstrates the centrality of oracy and storytelling in the early years curriculum (Harrett, 2002). Arts-based learning projects, including work once funded through the Creative Partnerships, have shown that even short-term involvement of artists can enhance the early years curriculum (Gillespie, 2006) and current policy acknowledges the place of the arts in young children's learning (DfE, 2012). However, many practitioners are ill equipped and under resourced to offer truly inspiring arts experiences for young children to enjoy and learn from.

EARLY CHILDHOOD EDUCATION RESEARCH: THE FUTURE

Any research act is personal and political, which should, I suggest, be aimed at changing some aspect of ECEC – *for the good* – and to make a positive difference to the lives of young children, their families and their educators. Research is about telling stories about the issues that matter, and the factors that can improve lives and learning. Educational researchers engage in critical enquiry because they believe in the power of education to make a difference – to policy, to people and to themselves. Though in this era of 'fake news' (Hunt, 2016) there is always the danger of research findings being misinterpreted or manipulated to achieve different ends from those intended by the researcher, so it is the duty of researchers to report their approach, their methodology and findings faithfully.

As researchers we rely on those who create and use ECEC provision, and who are parents, educators, policy-makers and children, to tell us about the things we focus our research lenses on. We take their words, and their thoughts and their images and their test results, and we craft them into meaningful accounts of how things are.

But there are some things that are lessons well learned, which require political action on research findings. For, when all is said and done, whatever researchers tell us, whatever educators tell us, whatever parents tell us, whatever children tell us … the fact that in the richest economies on earth children live in poverty is an atrocity. That the basic needs of food, shelter and safety are not met for so many children in the world – and that so many families struggle to provide for their children's basic needs – is disgraceful and inhumane. That so-called 'food poverty' is now in UK parlance is a matter of shame. Research tells us that hungry children don't learn well, or that poor housing damages relationships and threatens mental health. We know this, the studies have been done and the life experiences are only too real; for these matters it is a question of *acting on* research findings.

Governments choose how to spend the budget, and whilst there seems to be the funding for wars, somehow there is rarely a willingness to fund adequately what is needed for young children. And there are several key lessons emerging from the research featured in this book, which I have highlighted in the reflection sections at the end of each part of the book.

In one sense this book is a celebration of international ECEC research, but in another it is a call for action. Researchers have raised many issues specific to their research foci as highlighted throughout the book, but there are some issues that appertain to almost all of the studies featured and these relate to funding, and to methodology. I offer four points about ECEC research in general before concluding with five points about substantive lessons from research.

Research capacity is growing, with more ECEC professionals having Master's degrees and doctorates than ever before, there is growing research capacity in increasing numbers of energised and passionate ECEC researchers. But they are mostly limited in their capacity to carry out research, and to publish, not because they do not have the skills but because their professional lives, in early years settings and services and large teaching commitments in universities, give them little time for research.

Funding for ECEC research is limited, and until this is addressed we shall likely continue to see numerous small-scale and pilot studies that cannot be generalised and, whilst providing valuable insights, are shot through with apologia for their shortcomings. In spite of this, researchers continue to generate some research income and as this book shows, the range of studies and topics is considerable. We do, however, need to scale up research, as well as maintain the momentum for carrying out those studies which shine an intense light on the fine detail otherwise not seen.

The methodological range of ECEC research is broad, but there is a tendency towards small-scale qualitative studies. What is needed is a wider range of research methodologies that span the methodological continuum and push boundaries in qualitative design, better incorporate arts-based methodologies, and tell stories of living and learning in early childhood. Those should sit alongside robustly designed quantitative studies, including randomised control trials, which evaluate the effectiveness of interventions and challenge programmes where effects are over-claimed. We need longitudinal as well as short-term timescale studies; single life stories as well as large cohort studies.

There is a need for greater policy recognition of research, too much research is disregarded because it does not provide policy-makers with easy or convenient answers. Though the research impact agenda is placing greater emphasis on how research changes things and makes a difference to research participants, users and communities, it often requires a policy commitment to heed the lessons of research in order to bring about the important changes that are necessary to make a difference to the lives and learning of young children. Too often, research advice to avoid particular policy directions (such as the call to discard the policy on reintroducing Baseline Assessment, for example) are ignored, and policy wheels get reinvented – at a cost to the public purse and to those who live through the negative effects of flawed policies.

Finally, I want to bring the many issues discussed in this book together and highlight just five key points:

Poverty in the 21st century is threatening the lives and learning of many young children – we know that children living with disadvantage suffer educationally and in terms of health and well-being. Many studies reviewed in this book highlight the impact of poverty. Such studies need to be brought again to the attention of policy-makers. Child poverty is a national and international disgrace.

It is important to see young children as people – valued, important citizens – who are crucial to society – not 'just' as future citizens, but as 'now' citizens. Researchers raising these issues are focusing on three things: rights, voice and participation. Much of the research reviewed in this book indicates how these three aspects of citizenship are being enacted by children and better understood by teachers and ECEC researchers.

Well-educated and properly remunerated practitioners are crucial to the provision of early education worthy of the name. There are many different roles with different responsibilities in the early years workforce and clarity about these roles and due recognition for the work done, appropriate qualifications and professional recognition, are essential. And, I suggest, a matter of right for young children. A well-educated workforce would be the greatest and most effective form of early intervention, where work to combat disadvantage can be tailored to individual children and implemented in collaboration with parents.

We need studies of young children's engagement with the arts. Whilst we know that the arts are important for our humanity, early childhood education policy foregrounds STEM subjects, which might be considered more 'academic' subjects. But the arts support well-being and creative thinking, without which children will lose out on an holistic early education. ECEC has a responsibility to ensure that *all* young children have the opportunity to engage in the arts as a source of nourishment for learning and human development and this should not be dependent upon parental income, where those living in poverty lose out yet again.

Play is fundamental to children's lives, learning and well-being. The research studies featured in this book have shown how play is threatened by outcomes-driven policies, and why play must be given space in early childhood education. Play and play pedagogies must continue to be a key focus of ECEC research in the future to provide robust advice to policy-makers and depress the rise of outcomes dominated ECEC policies and practices. Young children need good learning spaces and facilities for play, collaboration, experimentation, noise, quiet and talk. We know the types of settings and practices that allow children to flourish and these need to be properly resourced.

Whilst I do not claim that my review of the recent research included in this book is comprehensive, my searches have led me to suggest some international trends in research. It seems that whilst many US studies perpetually mine national datasets to ask this question or that, there seems overall to be relatively few high quality quantitative studies, in comparison to the number of small-scale qualitative studies published. There is a clear lack of original randomised control trials, and relatively few systematic reviews of literature, or meta-analyses of research on particular themes. With a few exceptions, there seems to be a tendency towards small-scale, short-duration studies which cannot be generalised and, in many cases, do not seem to be replicable. This is probably due to the difficulties in obtaining funding, but it may also be related to the time available to carry out research. This is not to say that qualitative studies with a small number of participants are not meaningful and useful, they can be, if rigorously conducted and reported, but it does point to an issue that might be a cause for concern if the future of ECEC research is to be strong.

As the canvas of research methodologies is broadening, and as the need for fine-grain detail of the lives and learning of children in all their diversities is much needed, we need to look to a future for ECEC research which confidently spans the methodological continuum from large-scale, longitudinal quantitative studies that answer some of the vexing questions about 'effectiveness' and 'readiness', to the minute detail of sustained, interactive pedagogical exchanges with individual children. We need to sharpen our existing research tools, and continue to create new approaches which will help us answer pressing questions. Particular attention must be paid to the fitness of research approaches for the conduct of ethical research with young children. Researcher-enhanced understanding about ethical stances and practices in research with children has called for more refined approaches to methods, and we need to hone new tools that will help us to push the methodological boundaries of qualitative research, whilst continuing to evolve approaches to the use of visual and multi-modal methods and to innovative ways of reporting research, including social media, visual and narrative tools.

Finally, ECEC researchers have a duty of care to the children, parents and practitioners who participate in their research. We have a duty to conduct research with integrity and to report it honestly and in ways that will reach the widest audiences. We need to continue to carry out research which has due regard for young children, and ask research questions that will help us to find answers that will make a positive difference to their early education and care as well as enhance their learning and their lives.

REFERENCES

Allen, G. (2011) *Review of Early Intervention*. HMSO: London.

Athey, C. (2007) *Extending Thought in Young Children: A Parent–Teacher Partnership* (2nd edn). London: Paul Chapman Publishing.

Bannon, F. and Sanderson, P. (2000) Experience every moment: Aesthetically significant dance education. *Research in Dance Education*, *1* (1): 9–26.

Barratt, M.S. (2006) Inventing songs, inventing worlds: The 'genesis' of creative thought and activity in young children's lives. *International Journal of Early Years Education*, *14* (3): 201–220.

Bronfenbrenner, U. (1974) *A Report on Longitudinal Evaluations of Preschool Programs. Vol 2: Is Early Intervention Effective?* Washington, DC: DHEW.

Brown, E.D., Benedette, E. and Armistead, M.E. (2010) Arts enrichment and school readiness for children at risk. *Early Childhood Research Quarterly*, *25*: 112–124.

Burke, C. (1982) *Redefining written language growth: The child as informant*. Paper presented at the 8th Australian Reading Association Conference, Adelaide.

Care Quality Commission (2017) *Review of Children and Young People's Mental Health Services Phase One Report*. London: Care Quality Commission. www.cqc.org.uk/sites/default/files/20171103_cypmhphase1_report.pdf (accessed 20 February 2018).

Chapman, L.H. (2004) No child left behind in art? *Arts Education Policy Review*, *106*: 3–17.

Clough, P. (2000) Routes to inclusion. In P. Clough and J. Corbett (eds), *Theories of Inclusive Education*. London: PCP/SAGE, pp. 7–51.

Clough, P. (2002) *Narratives and Fictions in Educational Research*. Buckingham: Open University Press.

Davies, C. and Bowcott, O. (2017) Grenfell Tower fire: Death toll raised to 79 as minute's silence held. *The Guardian*, 19 June. www.theguardian.com/uk-news/2017/jun/19/grenfell-tower-fire-death-toll-rises-to-79-police-say (accessed 22 February 2018).

Deans, J. (2010) Young children and music: Adults constructing meaning through a performance for children. *Australian Journal of Music Education*, 2.

DES (Department for Education and Science) (1990) *Starting with Quality: Report of the Committee of Inquiry into the Quality of Educational Experience Offered to Three and Four Year Olds*. London: HMSO.

Dewey, J. (1902) *The Educational Situation*. Chicago, IL: University of Chicago Press.

DfE (Department for Education) (2012) *Statutory Framework for the Early Years Foundation Stage*. London: DfE. http://webarchive.nationalarchives.gov.uk/20130404110654/ https://www.education.gov.uk/publications/standard/AllPublications/Page1/DFE-00023-2012 (accessed 22 February 2018).

DfE (Department for Education) (2013) *More Great Childcare: Raising Quality and Giving Parents More Choice*. London: DfE. www.gov.uk/government/uploads/system/uploads/attach-ment_data/file/219660/More_20Great_20Childcare_20v2.pdf (accessed 1 March 2018).

DfEE (Department for Education and Employment) (1999) *Sure Start: Making a Difference for Children and Families*. London: Department for Education and Employment, Ref. SSMDCF.

Dissanayake, E. (1990) *What Is Art For?* Seattle, WA: University of Washington Press.

Dissanayake, E. (1995) *Homo Aestheticus*. Seattle, WA: University of Washington Press.

Dissanayake, E. (2000) *Art and Intimacy: How the Arts Began*. Seattle, WA: University of Washington Press.

Eisner, E.W. (2002) *The Arts and the Creation of the Mind*. New Haven, CT: Yale University Press.

Field, F. (2010) *The Foundation Years: Preventing Poor Children from Becoming Poor Adults: The Report of the Independent Review on Poverty and Life Chances*. London: HMSO. http://webarchive.nationalarchives.gov.uk/20110120090128/http:/povertyreview.independ ent.gov.uk/media/20254/poverty-report.pdf (accessed 29 January 2018).

Filippini, T. and Vecchi, V. (eds) (1996) *The Hundred Languages of Children: The Exhibit*. Reggio Emilia: Reggio Children.

Gardner, H. (1989) The key in the key slot. *Journal of Aesthetic Education*, *23* (1): 141–158.

Gardner, H. (1990) *Art Education and Human Development: An Essay Commissioned by the J. Paul Getty Center for Education in the Arts, Occasional Paper 3*. Los Angeles: The J. Paul Getty Museum.

Gillespie, A. (2006) Children, art and artists. *Early Education*, *24* (3): 5–7.

Goldschmeid, E. and Jackson, S. (1999) *People Under Three*. London: Routledge.

Goodman, K., Goodman, Y. and Burke, C. (1978) Reading for life: The psycholinguistic base. In E. Hunter-Grundin and H.U. Hunter-Grundin (eds), *Reading: Implementing the Bullock Report*. London: Ward Lock, pp. 47–59.

Goodman, Y. (1980) The roots of literacy. *Claremont Reading Conference Yearbook*, 44: 1–32.

Hallowes, A.A. (2013) Drawing on the potential of 'Once Upon a Time': An examination of the effect of a live and interactive storytelling process on subsequent drawings by children in a Reception Class. *EdD thesis, University of Sheffield*. http://etheses.whiterose. ac.uk/3764/1/AA_Hallowes_Drawing_on_the_Potential.pdf (accessed 22 February 2018).

Hancock, R. and Cox, A. (2002) 'I would have worried about her being a nuisance': Workshops for children under three and their parents at Tate Britain. *Early Years*, 22 (2): 118–123.

Harker, J. (2016) Stop calling the Calais refugee camp the 'Jungle'. *The Guardian*, 7 March. www.theguardian.com/commentisfree/2016/mar/07/stop-calling-calais-refugee-camp-jungle-migrants-dehumanising-scare-stories (accessed 20 February 2018).

Harrett, J. (2002) Young children talking: An investigation into the personal stories of key stage one infants. *Early Years, 22* (1): 19–26.

Hiebert, E.H. (1981) Developmental patterns and inter-relationships of preschool children's print awareness. *Reading Research Quarterly, 16*: 236–259.

Hopperstad, M.H. (2008a) Relationships between children's drawing and accompanying peer interaction in teacher-initiated drawing sessions. *International Journal of Early Years Education, 16* (2): 133–150.

Hopperstad, M. (2008b) How children make meaning through drawing and play. *Visual Communication, 7* (1): 77–96.

Hunt, E. (2016) What is fake news? How to spot it and what you can do to stop it. *The Guardian*, 17 December. www.theguardian.com/media/2016/dec/18/what-is-fake-news-pizzagate (accessed 20 February 2018).

Jackson, L. (2012) *Securing Standards, Sustaining Success: Report on Early Intervention.* London: National Education Trust. www.theministryofparenting.com/wp-content/uploads/2012/02/EarlyYearsReport.pdf (accessed 1 March 2018).

Malaguzzi, L. (1996) The right to environment. In T. Filippini and V. Vecchi (eds), *The Hundred Languages of Children: The Exhibit.* Reggio Emilia: Reggio Children, pp. 17–18.

Marsh, J. (ed.) (2005a) *Popular Culture, New Media and Digital Literacy in Early Childhood.* London: RoutledgeFalmer.

Marsh, J. (2005b) Digikids: Young children, popular culture and media. In N. Yelland (ed.), *Critical Issues in Early Childhood Education.* Buckingham: Open University Press, pp. 51–69.

Marsh, J.A. (2016) The digital literacy skills and competences of children of pre-school age. *Media Education: Studi, Ricerche, Buone Practice, 7* (2): 197–214.

NACCCE (National Advisory Committee on Creative, Cultural Education) (1999) All our futures: Creativity, culture and education. In *Report to the Secretary of State for Education and Employment and the Secretary of State for Culture, Media and Sport.* London: HMSO.

Nutbrown, C. (1998) Managing to include? Rights, responsibilities and respect. In P. Clough (ed.), *Managing Inclusive Education: From Policy to Experience.* London: Sage, pp. 167–176.

Nutbrown, C. (2011a) *Threads of Thinking: Schemas and Young Children Learning.* London: Sage.

Nutbrown, C. (2011b) Conceptualising arts based learning in the early years. *Research Papers in Education, 28* (2): 239–263. DOI:10.1080/02671522.2011.580365.

Nutbrown, C. (2012) *Foundations for Quality: The Independent Review of Early Education and Childcare Qualifications, Final Report.* Cheshire: Department for Education. www.gov.uk/government/uploads/system/uploads/attachment_data/file/175463/Nutbrown-Review.pdf (accessed 12 January 2018).

Nutbrown, C. and Clough, P. (2004) Inclusion in the early years: Conversations with European educators. *European Journal of Special Needs Education, 19* (3): 311–339.

Nutbrown, C. and Clough, P. (2013) *Inclusion in the Early Years* (2nd edn). London: Sage.

Nutbrown, C. and Jones, H. (2006) *Daring Discoveries: Arts Based Learning in the Early Years*. Doncaster: Creative Partnerships and the Arts Council.

Ofsted (2017) *Bold Beginnings: The Reception Curriculum in a Sample of Good and Outstanding Primary Schools*. Manchester: Ofsted

Payler, J. and Wood, E. (eds) (2017) *BERA-TACTYC Early Childhood Research Review 2003– 2017*. London: British Educational Research Association. www.bera.ac.uk/wp-content/ uploads/2017/05/BERA-TACTYC-Full-Report.pdf?noredirect=1 (accessed 29 January 2018).

Pramling Samuelsson, I., Carlsson, M.A., Olsson, B., Pramling, N. and Wallerstedt, C. (2009) The art of teaching children in the arts: Music, dance and poetry with children aged 2–8 years old. *International Journal of Early Years Education*, 17 (2): 119–136.

Public Health England (2016) *The Mental Health of Children and Young People in England*. London: Public Health England.

QCA (2000) *Curriculum Guidance for the Foundation Stage*. London: Qualifications and Curriculum Authority.

Rahilly, S. and Johnston, E. (2002) Opportunity for childcare: The impact of government initiatives in England upon childcare provision. *Social Policy and Administration*, 36 (5): 482–495.

Reggio Children (1995) *Le Fontane: Da un progetto per la construczione di u Luna Park degli uccellini* [The Fountains: From a project for the construction of an amusement park for birds]. Reggio Emilia: Reggio Children.

Research Excellence Framework (2015) *Research Excellence Framework 2014: Overview Report by Main Panel C and Sub-panels 16 to 26*. www.ref.ac.uk/2014/media/ref/con tent/expanel/member/Main%20Panel%20C%20overview%20report.pdf (accessed 20 February 2018).

Smith, F. (1976) Learning to read by reading. *Language Arts*, 53 (3): 297–299.

Trehub, S. (2003) Toward a developmental psychology of music. In G. Avanzini, C. Faienza, D. Minciacchi, L. Lopez and M. Majno (eds), *The Neurosciences and Music: Annals of the New York Academy of Sciences*, Vol. 999. New York: New York Academy of Sciences, pp. 402–413.

Trevarthen, C. (1984) Emotions in infancy: Regulators of contact and relationships with persons. In K. Scherer and P. Ekman (eds), *Approaches to Emotion*. Hillsdale, NJ: Erlbaum, 129–157.

United Nations (1989) *Convention on the Rights of the Child*. New York: United Nations.

Young, S. (2008) Collaboration between 3- and 4-year-olds in self-initiated play on instru- ments. *International Journal of Educational Research*, 47: 3–10.

AUTHOR INDEX

SUBJECT INDEX